Listening and Human Communication
in the 21st Century

Listening and Human Communication in the 21st Century

Edited by
Andrew D. Wolvin

WILEY-BLACKWELL

A John Wiley & Sons, Ltd., Publication

This edition first published 2010
© 2010 Blackwell Publishing Ltd

Blackwell Publishing was acquired by John Wiley & Sons in February 2007. Blackwell's publishing program has been merged with Wiley's global Scientific, Technical, and Medical business to form Wiley-Blackwell.

Registered Office
John Wiley & Sons Ltd, The Atrium, Southern Gate, Chichester, West Sussex, PO19 8SQ, United Kingdom

Editorial Offices
350 Main Street, Malden, MA 02148-5020, USA
9600 Garsington Road, Oxford, OX4 2DQ, UK
The Atrium, Southern Gate, Chichester, West Sussex, PO19 8SQ, UK

For details of our global editorial offices, for customer services, and for information about how to apply for permission to reuse the copyright material in this book please see our website at www.wiley.com/wiley-blackwell.

The right of Andrew D. Wolvin to be identified as the author of the editorial material in this work has been asserted in accordance with the Copyright, Designs and Patents Act 1988.

Wiley also publishes its books in a variety of electronic formats. Some content that appears in print may not be available in electronic books.

Designations used by companies to distinguish their products are often claimed as trademarks. All brand names and product names used in this book are trade names, service marks, trademarks or registered trademarks of their respective owners. The publisher is not associated with any product or vendor mentioned in this book. This publication is designed to provide accurate and authoritative information in regard to the subject matter covered. It is sold on the understanding that the publisher is not engaged in rendering professional services. If professional advice or other expert assistance is required, the services of a competent professional should be sought.

Library of Congress Cataloging-in-Publication Data

Listening and human communication in the 21st century/edited by Andrew D. Wolvin.
    p.   cm.
  Includes bibliographical references and index.
  ISBN 978-1-4051-8165-5 (hardcover : alk. paper) — ISBN 978-1-4051-8164-8 (pbk. : alk. paper)
  1. Listening—Textbooks. 2.   Communication—Textbooks. I.   Wolvin, Andrew D.
  P95.46.L55 2009
  302.2'44—dc22
                                                    2009015235

A catalogue record for this book is available from the British Library.

Set in 10/13pt Palatino by SPi Publisher Services, Pondicherry, India
Printed and bound in Malaysia by Vivar Printing Sdn Bhd

1   2010

Contents

Figures

Tables

Notes on Contributors

Melissa L. Beall is a professor of Communication Studies at the University of Northern Iowa, Cedar Falls, Iowa. Dr Beall teaches a variety of classes including: Listening, Oral Communication, Critical Thinking in Communication, Intercultural Communication, Introduction to Graduate Study and Research, Communication Theories, Message Design and Delivery, Senior Seminar, Instructional Communication, and Communication and Technology.

Sheila C. Bentley of Bentley Consulting resides outside of Memphis, TN, and has been a communication consultant for 24 years. With clients nationwide, she works with FedEx, Nike, Disney, the US Army, Hilton Hotels, and numerous education institutions. She has also served as adjunct faculty at the University of Memphis and Arizona State University. Her focus in listening has been in business applications – how to use listening skills to bring about a positive impact on the business, whether as a financial return or improved relations with employees and customers.

Graham Bodie is an Assistant Professor in the Department of Communication Studies at The Louisiana State University. He is devoted to the study of listening and information processing in context and has published in outlets such as *Communication Yearbook*, *Health Marketing Quarterly*, and *The International Journal of Listening*.

Judi Brownell is a Professor and Dean of Students in the School of Hotel Administration at Cornell University. She is also a past president of the International Listening Association. She has authored several listening textbooks, her most recent being *Listening: Attitudes, Principles, and Skills,* and over 30 articles on managerial listening behavior. She has applied her HURIER model of the listening process to a wide variety of hospitality contexts including the hotel, casino, club, and cruise industries.

Diana Corley Schnapp has taught Speech Communication courses, including Listening, in secondary school, community colleges, and universities for 35 years. A former Executive Director of the International Listening Association, she has published articles about listening in academic journals, popular magazines, and religious publications. Most recently a Communications Adjunct Professor at Rockhurst University in Kansas City, Missouri, she has been a consultant in communication for government organizations, private business, non-profit organizations, and faith communities. She has written and taught religious studies for over 40 years.

Margaret Fitch-Hauser is an Associate Professor and Chair of the Department of Communication and Journalism at Auburn University. She has engaged in listening research for 30 years and has presented to all but one ILA conference. Her current research focuses on listening fidelity and cross-cultural elements of listening.

John Flowerdew is a Professor of Applied Linguistics in the Department of English at City University of Hong Kong. He has published extensively in the areas of discourse analysis, pragmatics, listening, and corpus linguistics. He is co-author with Lindsay Miller of *Second Language Listening: Theory and Practice*.

James J. Floyd is a Professor of Communication at the University of Central Missouri. He is currently editor of *The International Journal of Listening*.

Margarete Imhof is Professor for Educational Psychology in the teacher education program at the Johannes Gutenberg University in Mainz, Germany. She has been working on the psychology of attention and listening for many years. Her area of interest is to investigate listening as a mental process and research on how listening skills can be learned and taught.

Laura A. Janusik is an Assistant Professor and the McGee Chair of Communication at Rockhurst University in Kansas City, Missouri. She considers herself a listening cognitivist, and has designed the

Conversational Listening Span, an instrument to measure one's conversational listening capacity. Her work can be found in *The International Journal of Listening*, *Communication Studies*, and the *Journal of Intercultural Communication Research*.

Pamela Leintz, former Staff Assesor at Alverno College, has taught, assessed, and worked on curriculum design. She is currently on staff at the Georgia State University School of Music.

Lindsay Miller is an Associate Professor of Applied Linguistics in the Department of English at City University of Hong Kong. He has published widely in the areas of teacher education, listening and learner autonomy. He is co-author with John Flowerdew of *Second Language Listening: Theory and Practice*.

Barbara Nevers, Assistant Professor in Liberal Studies at Alverno College, teaches the first semester communication seminar and Integrating Learning, a course developing students' proficiency in the eight Alverno abilities.

Michael W. Purdy is a Professor in the Communications Program at Governors State University (Illinois), University Park. His academic work has focused on the study and teaching of listening, as well as broader concerns of dialogic communication. With Deborah Borisoff, he has authored *Listening in Everyday Life: A Personal and Professional Approach*. He has also authored articles and book chapters on listening, research, and communication philosophy.

Kathleen Thompson is a Professor in the Professional Communication Department at Alverno College. She chairs the Listening Task Group, which coordinates the teaching and assessing of listening across Alverno's ability-based curriculum. A member and former Executive Director of the International Listening Association (ILA), she received ILA's Outstanding Teacher of the Year and the Hall of Fame Award for notable achievements involving listening in academic, business, and other settings.

Susan Witkowski is Assistant Director of Instructional Services at Alverno College, develops language programs and provides teacher training, in addition to teaching communication courses.

Andrew D. Wolvin is a Professor in the Department of Communication at the University of Maryland, College Park. His academic career has been devoted to the study and teaching of listening. With Carolyn G. Coakley, he has authored widely used books in listening including *Listening, Perspectives on Listening, Experiential Listening,* and *Listening in the Quality Organization.*

Introduction: Perspectives on Listening in the 21st Century

Andrew D. Wolvin

Listening and Human Communication in the 21st Century

The twenty-first century brings with it any number of challenges to the world order. Nation states are in disarray as rulers make life-ending decisions for thousands of followers. Natural resources are in limited supply, and the fury of nature has threatened to bring devastation to entire countries and regions throughout the world. The fragility of economic systems is revealed in major ways, impacting millions of people who find it increasingly difficult to afford their present lifestyle. Human medical advances cannot keep up with the mutations that continue to bring down, or threaten to bring down, vast numbers.

Against the doom and disaster of today's dysfunctional world, people are embracing new ways to connect with each other through modern-day technology, through religious organizations, and through renewed attention to personal and professional relationships alike.

Never has it been so apparent that the world needs listeners. Leaders need to listen to their followers to formulate policy and create programs that will be responsive to the needs of their constituents. And people need to listen to each other throughout the world to increase international understanding and bring a sense of order to world affairs.

Getting people to listen to each other, however, is not an easy objective. Unfortunately, listening has come to be viewed, at least in American society, as a passive, simple act that we just do. The word "just" is all too frequently used to describe listening in the admonition "Just listen." This reduces listening, then, to the non-active, receptor, part of human communication.

To establish the listener as a serious, active participant in the communication process, it is necessary to understand what is involved in this highly complex aspect. Indeed, listening may be one of the most, if not the most, complex of all human behaviors.

Listening scholars have made remarkable strides in attempting to understand the complexities of listening and, at the same time, encourage more engaged, purposeful behaviors on the part of listeners in both personal and professional settings. This collection of essays by some of the leading listening scholars in the field is designed to document some of those remarkable strides in what we know about listening in human communication. The essays review the theory and research paradigms used to study listening. And applications of our understanding of listening focus on pedagogy and practice. The chapters are structured so that the reader will first have a theoretical overview of what we know about listening and an introduction to research methods that guide listening scholars in the study of listening. Essays about listening as a cognitive and relational activity follow these introductory chapters. The final part of the book, then, situates listening in particular contexts.

In the first part of this book, *Theoretical Overview of Listening*, Wolvin begins with a framework for listening theory: applying theoretical perspectives of some disciplinary paradigms to understanding listening. We then turn to the research methods, *Listening Research Methods*, both qualitative and quantitative, used by researchers to study systematically this complex process. Purdy analyzes the state of qualitative research in listening, while Bodie and Fitch-Hauser examine the role of quantitative research in listening scholarship. Both chapters offer solid advice to readers interested in conducting listening research.

Part III, *Listening as a Cognitive and Relational Activity*, offers cognitive and relational perspectives on listening. The authors provide an expanded view of the complexities of listening from their various theoretical and research agenda. Imhof, a cognitive psychologist, takes us into the intricacies of listening cognition. Floyd develops a model of listening as dialogue, while Brownell looks at listening as a communication behavior. Flowerdew and Miller review the research on second language listening and draw implications for learning and teaching language skills.

Other listening scholars offer contemporary perspectives on listening in specific contexts in our final part, *Listening in Contexts*. Bentley looks at listening practices in the corporate setting, while Janusik reviews what we know about listening instruction. Beall provides a global view of listening in the intercultural context, while Corley Schnapp summarizes the role of listening in spirituality and religion. Thompson and colleagues provide an integrative model of listening that establishes an interesting foundation for educating today's listeners.

From this overview of perspectives on listening, the reader should gain an understanding of the state-of-the-art of our present knowledge on listening cognition and behavior as it is central to human communication. Hopefully, such an understanding can enhance decisions on how to make the world a better listening world where all of us, as global citizens, willingly engage in listening to each other.

— will I learn how to be a better listener?

— is this all theoretical?
○ could I teach any of it in a regular classroom?
○ if it is, what's the point?

Part I

Theoretical Overview of Listening

On the other hand, the study of listening has not proceeded from a totally atheoretical perspective. Admittedly, much of the listening instruction model has focused on a "quick fix" list of skills. But even that skill set has a solid empirical origin. In a pioneering study, Nichols (1948) subjected the incoming University of Minnesota freshmen to a battery of tests to determine what makes for good and poor listening in the classroom student context. His profile enabled him to describe some familiar characteristics of poor listening: (1) condemning a speaker's subject as uninteresting; (2) criticizing the speaker's delivery rather than focusing on the message; (3) preparing an answer to a point or question before comprehending it; (4) listening only for facts; (5) wasting the advantage of thought speed over speech speed; (6) tolerating or creating distractions; (7) faking attention; (8) permitting personal prejudices to interfere; (9) avoiding difficult material; and (10) attempting to take outline notes even when the message isn't structured to be outlined. To this day, these characteristics (essentially the Ten Commandments of listening) continue to be listed (see Gilbert, 1988) for students as the issues to overcome in order to be good listeners.

Missing from this instructional recipe is the foundation for understanding *why* these are listening issues. Overloaded with messages, a listener may find faking attention to be a workable strategy in today's work environment, for example, if the communication relationship and the outcome of the communication really are not all that important. Listening competency, like any communication competency, builds on a tripartite cognitive, affective, and behavioral foundation (Wolvin and Coakley, 1994). The listener needs to know what he or she is doing (and why), be willing to be engaged in the communication, and – finally – perform the necessary behaviors that counter some of what Nichols' popular magic list of poor listening habits suggests.

As a result, listening scholars have explored the listening competency model in an effort to develop listening theory that can inform/support our claims. A group of listening specialists participated in a summer conference sponsored by the International Listening Association to establish a definition of listening so that we may begin to work from a more unified perspective. That definition – "Listening is the process of receiving, constructing meaning from, and responding to spoken and/ or nonverbal messages" (An ILA Definition of Listening, 1995) – can frame theoretical perspectives underpinning listening instruction and listening research. The definition effectively organizes the elements of the listening process into the physiology, psychology, sociology, and communication perspectives of this complex communication pheno-menon. These theoretical perspectives intersect to provide for building a foundation of listening engagement.

The Physiology of Listening

Entering into the communication, the listener must receive the verbal/nonverbal message. The auditory reception of this (usually) vocal mes-sage is a detailed audio-logical process involving the intricate, delicate hearing mechanism. The sound enters the middle ear, setting into vibra-tion the tympanic membrane, and conducts through the inner ear to the brain (Newby and Popelka, 1992). Problems with the hearing mechanism compound this receptive process. Researchers at the National Institute on Deafness and Other Communication Disorders (1996) estimate that as many as 28 million Americans have some type of hearing impairment. For some listeners, this loss, which can block or distort sound reception, can be profound. Excessive exposure to noise pollution and to loud music on headsets is of particular concern to researchers in the field of audiology.

Frequently, the listener also receives visual stimuli – the speaker's non-verbal cues such as facial expressions, body language, eye contact, and appearance. The visual process occurs when light rays, reflected from an object, fall on the cornea in the front of the eye. The rays then pass through the liquid aqueous humor contained in the anterior chamber behind the cornea. The rays pass through the lens and the vitreous humor behind the lens to the retina, the innermost part of the eyeball. The back of the retina contains the optic nerve fibers which pass to the visual cortex where the nerve fibers are formed into images. Cataracts usually result from the aging process and macular degeneration, a deterioration of the retina that leads to progressive loss of central vision, is a leading cause of blindness in people between the ages of 45 and 74. The National Eye Institute (2002) estimates that as many as 2 million Americans suffer from glaucoma, a disorder which usually begins in middle age or later.

The physiology of listening extends to the neurology of the process (Goss, 1995). Once the auditory and/or visual receptors have received the message stimulus, that stimulus is recorded in the brain. The brain contains billions of neurons, the transmitters of the electrical-chemical information throughout the brain. The occipital lobe (the visual area) and the temporal lobe (the auditory area) in the cerebral cortex coordinate the association and storage functions. Specifically, the Wernicke's and Broca's regions of the brain are activated in response to auditory stimuli (Just, Carpenter, and Keller, 1996), and the prefrontal cortex is where comprehension is believed to occur (Kane and Engle, 2000). Brain damage can, of course, interrupt the processing of messages. Neurological research on the effects of aging on the brain (Salk Institute, 2002) most currently supports the view that the nerve cells – neurons – in the brain regenerate through mental use throughout one's lifetime.

Clearly, listening is a highly complex physiological process involving the human receptors and influenced by the human sensory capacity. The genetic structure of these receptors has a profound effect on the listener's sensory capacity. MRI brain research at the Indiana University School of Medicine (Phillips, Low, Lurito, Dzemidzic, and Mathews, 2001), for example, illustrates that male listeners process language through the left side of the temporal lobe. Female listeners were seen to process language in the temporal lobe through both sides of the brain. However, a larger scale MRI study (50 men and 50 women) concluded that men and women actually do not have substantive differences in lateralization of brain activity or brain activation patterns during a listening task (Frost, Binder, Springer, et al., 1999).

The physiology of listening has received some attention from listening researchers. Villaume, Brown, Darling, et al. (1997), for example, looked at the effects of presbycusis (age-related hearing loss) on conversation characteristics of elders. Beatty and McCroskey (Beatty, McCroskey, and Valensic, 2001; Heisel, McCroskey, and Richmond, 1999) argue that communication theory must account for the human biological system, that communication is a biological process. And nowhere does this have greater bearing than in our efforts to understand the complex process of listening behavior. The neurobiology and the psychobiology of the listener are at the core of his/her functioning as a listening communicator.

The Psychology of Listening

The operationalization of listening extends beyond the physiology of the process to the psychological functions as well. After the message has been received through the auditory and visual channels, it must be attended to through the short-term memory system. While researchers disagree as to how the short-term memory system receives and holds the information, they do agree that the attention span is quite limited, possibly as short as a few hundred milliseconds to a longer phase of up to about 30 seconds (Cowan, 1995). Cognitive psychologists (Lang and Basil, 1998) have come to understand attention as a limited resource of a fixed capacity of sensory systems and memory mechanisms. Janusik (2005) stresses that listening researchers need to apply the principle of working memory (in which information is both processed and stored synergistically) originally conceptualized by Baddeley and Hitch (1974) to explain the listener's attention limits. This theory of attention, which guides attention and memory research today, explains how the listener shifts stimuli from and into long-term storage while, at the same time, creating meaning.

Attention to the message is affected not only by the listener's working memory system but also by the listener's perceptual filter. The perceptual filter serves to screen the stimulus so that one's predispositions alter the message received. The listener's background, experience, roles, and mental and physical states make up this filter and shape the listener's expectations for the messages being presented. Studies suggest that "the louder, the more relevant, and the more novel the stimuli, and the more likely they are to be perceived by the listener" (Barker, 1971, p. 31; Driver, 1992).

Once the message has been received by the listener through the auditory, visual, and attention processors, the message must be interpreted. This stage of the process involves fitting the verbal and/or nonverbal messages into the proper linguistic categories stored in the brain and then interpreting the messages for their meanings. Van Dijk and Kintsch (1983) suggest that this interpretation results from three different mental representations: a verbatim representation; a semantic representation that describes the meaning; and a situational representation of the situation to which the message refers. Lundsteen (1979) describes this as the internal speech process during which the listener "may give to a word or message a meaning that probably includes an internal picture of the thing or event named by the word (p. 34)." Burleson (2007) depicts the interpretation process as multi-dimensional; listeners interpret others' meanings, intentions, and motives. This interpretation usually occurs at the surface level, though at times the listener may be required to engage in-depth processing through a systematic analysis of the speaker and/or the message. Decoding the verbal and nonverbal language varies according to each listener's perceptual filter and linguistic category system. Consequently, the original intent of the speaker's message may be interpreted, misinterpreted, or even changed as the listener assigns semantic meaning in this cognitive process.

Early theory and research in attitude change supports our understanding of this process. For example, Osgood's (Snider and Osgood, 1969) semantic space is descriptive of this function. The listener may interpret messages according to a sense of evaluation (good or bad), activity (active or inactive) and potency (strong or weak). Likewise, the interaction of the listener's values, attitudes, and beliefs (Rokeach, 1969) shapes the meaning that is constructed in the listener's cognition. "Selective attention is not so much the conscious 'tuning out' of inconsistent information as it is the unconscious 'tuning in' of consistent information" (McCroskey, 1971, p. 172).

The cognitive process of assigning meaning is understood by cognitivists as mental schema. Schema theorists (Edwards and McDonald, 1993) describe the decoding/interpreting process as a mental organizational task. Humans carry schemata, mental representations of knowledge, in the brain. These organized information structures consist of nodes (concepts, events, objects) and links (relationships of the nodes). New information is first run through these existing schemata – scripts – and then interpreted. Smith (1982) suggests that these generic scripts serve important listening purposes in telling us to what we should attend; serving as the framework for interpreting incoming information; and guiding the reconstruction of messages in memory. Those who are perceived to be more competent conversationalists have a better schema for processing conversation (Miller, deWinstanely, and Carey, 1996).

A listener's processing requirements vary as the length and the speed of the message varies. Beatty (1981) identifies "cognitive backlog" as a significant part of this process: the listener continually adds (backlogs) material to be remembered for later recall. Listeners who confront increased message length and/or speed may experience higher levels of listening anxiety and diminished listening ability (King and Behnke, 2004).

The reconstruction of messages in memory returns us to the listener's working memory capacity and how the listener is, then, able to recall and to use the information which has been communicated. Thomas and

Levine (1994) have argued that verbal recall and listening are related but separate constructs. They call for more research on how recall fits into the theoretical model of the listening process: "As each element of listening – hearing, attending, understanding, and remembering – is more fully explored, a more contemporary theory of listening becomes attainable" (p. 122).

The psychological functions that bear on listening behavior are profound. Halley (2001) characterizes how listeners make meaning of the messages they have received and attended: "Meaning is assigned based on what is organized, the listener's intent, the listener's value system, and the expectations of the listener or the probability that a particular pattern should occur based on the experience of the listener" (n.p.). As the listener creates meaning, the "degree of congruence between the cognitions of a listener and the cognitions of a source" (Mulanax and Powers, 2001, p. 70) yields listening fidelity (accuracy). Listening research demonstrates that many psychological variables – including listening styles (Johnson, Weaver, Watson, and Barker, 2000; Mullen and Narain, 2005; Worthington, 2004), apprehension (Schrodt and Wheeless, 2001), and perceptions (Ryan, Kwong See, Meneer, and Trovato, 1994) – influence the way listeners create their meaning from the listening experience. "Successful message reception ... requires an understanding of the goals and intentions of the communicator as well as the literal implications of the message being transmitted," note Wyer and Adaval (2003, p. 292), confounded by the listener's purpose and expectations of the complexities of the communication.

The Sociology of Listening

Once the listener receives and interprets the message through his/her cognitive psychological process, he/she then responds to the message. This response, the listener's feedback, takes listening beyond the internal, self-controlled cognitive processing and back into the communication relationship. Some listening scholars (Wolvin, 1989) argue that overt listener responses go beyond the act of listening, that listening is limited to the receiving/decoding process. Perry (1996), in his review of feedback, concludes that it is a separate function: "Knowledge effects, the reconstruction of memory, and the evocation of schemas before response all point toward a complex series of steps that make feedback distinct from the three stages of listening" (pp. 23–4). And indeed, the complexity of the listening stages does support this perspective. Others argue that listening within the context of communication must include an overt response in order to distinguish the act of listening from cognitive processing (Janusik, 2002).

However, the listener's feedback is an essential part of the *communication* function of the interaction. As Daly (1975) observes, "No matter how effective, skilled, or competent an individual is in listening, unless he or she is perceived as listening by the other interactants, little may be accomplished" (pp. 1–2). The perception of being listened to is important and difficult, for, as Beach and Lindstrom (1992) observe, "speakers also rely upon recipients to display whatever effect(s) speaker's utterance(s) might have in the course of their delivery" (p. 27). And Cooper and Husband (1993) demonstrate that these perceptions created by feedback behaviors that "show an *accurate* understanding of the message as well as demonstrate *support* for the relationship between the communication participants…" (p. 13) really define listening competency.

The listener's feedback puts listening into the relational context, providing a more complete picture of the listener/communicator. Rhodes (1993) has noted that the transactional perspective requires that we "look at a 'listener' in relation to a 'speaker' – to look at both parties simultaneously – to look at both parties together as a whole" (p. 224). Pecchioni and Halone (2000) have built a construct of relational listening in social and personal relationships. Others have looked at listening in family interactions (Coakley and Wolvin, 1997; Ross and Glenn, 1996) and in professional settings such as health care (Arnold and Shirreffs, 1998; Trahan and Rockwell, 1999). Imhof (2004) developed a profile of listeners across contexts made up of professional, instructional, family, and friends. Further, the concept of empathic listening requires that the listener must attempt to understand why the fellow communicator is responding as he/she responds (Walker, 1997). And I would argue that a meaningful interpretation of any message requires listening empathy, situating the competent listener front and center in any communication relationship.

Purdy (2003) emphasizes that "listening creates community" (p. 1). ← Historical roots of communication in Western society, he observes, center on the speaker. "With the advent of the late modern world, communication can no longer be speaker dominated. It is now critical that listening also be central to the shaping of community …" (Purdy, 2003, p. 1).

The sociology of listening, then, extends beyond the relationship to the culture of the listening community itself. As Purdy (2000) stresses, "Different cultures express their listening differently ..." (p. 65). Edward Hall's (Hall and Hall, 1989) model of low and high context cultures suggests that listeners in high context cultures rely on a common understanding of cultural values and rules whereas listeners in low context cultures must attend more explicitly to the verbal message. "In high context cultures, it is the responsibility of the listener to understand." Reisner (1993) explains, while "in low context, it is the speaker who is responsible for making sure the listener comprehends all" (p. 31). Thomlison (1997) identifies any of a number of cultural variables – values and beliefs, language, nonverbal codes, cognitive processing – that bear on listeners' attempts to reduce uncertainty and gain understanding across cultures. In their interesting contrast of American and Swedish conversation patterns, Beach and Lindstrom (1992) illustrate intercultural listening as "passive recipiency" in their research on Swedish conversational interactions that move toward fuller participative "speakership" (p. 34).

The notion of speakership suggests that listening theory does not necessarily have to center on the listener only. Admittedly, most of what we know about listening behavior has been applied to our understanding of listening competence (Wolvin and Coakley, 1994). Rubin (1993), however, argues that what we know about listening supports a model of "listenability," text that is oral-based and rhetorically considerate of the listener's perspective. Listenable prose, he (Rubin, Hafer, and Arata, 2000) has discovered, contains "less dense syntax, greater frequency of personal pronouns, more verb-based rather than nominal constructions, and less lexical diversity than literate-based style" (p. 130). Earlier, Weaver (1972) offered a listenable model couched in terms of "what the talker can do to help (p. 107)." Stressing the need for speakers to create and present listenable messages, Wolvin, Berko, and Wolvin (1999) center listenability on the clarity, conciseness, and color of the communicator's language.

The Communication of Listening

Effective listening and listenable speaking ultimately converge into the communication perspective of listening behavior. Adapting Johannesen's (1971) theory of dialogue as communication, Floyd (1985) describes this as dialogic listening. He characterizes the listener who truly engages in the dialogue with his/her fellow communicator: (1) genuineness; (2) accurate empathic understanding; (3) unconditional positive regard; (4) presentness; (5) spirit of mutual equality; and (6) supportive psychological climate. And it is the listener who assumes an active role in the interaction who can be characterized as a communicator. For he or she will consciously share the responsibility for the outcome of the communication and will engage in these behaviors that furthers/supports that outcome. Roberts and Vinson's work on willingness to listen (1998) offers further empirical support for listening attitudes and behaviors as positively correlated with communication skills. Their scale accounts for the level of acquaintance (friend, stranger, acquaintance), physical location (school, work, interperson), communication context (dyadic, small group, public speaking) and mediated/face-to-face interaction. Their research suggests that, while listeners are possibly predisposed to be willing listeners through personality trait, they can and do manipulate their level of listening willingness.

Interestingly, Cornwell and Orbe (1999) note that "throughout our research on building dialogic relationships, listening received very little explicit attention, if any at all, from scholars," leading them to conclude that "conceptualizing communication as dialogue ... requires a reconceptualization of listening" (p. 86). As we reconceptualize listening communication, Bentley (1997) argues that we need to pay more attention to speaker expectations in defining and describing effective listening, because effective listening behaviors in real-time listening are behaviors that are speaker-determined. "Listening as a linking function," explains Purdy (1997), "serves to build relationships. We build strong links with others by listening to why they are and what they mean" (p. 10).

Grounding Listening Theory

The construct of listening from physiological, psychological, sociological, and communication perspectives yields a description of how listeners (and listenable speakers) behave or ought to behave in communication transactions. Some researchers (Imhof, 1998; Stein, 1999) have expanded the methodological base to provide elaborated models of listening behavior before, during, and after the listener performs.

Goss (1995) stresses that the ability to gather, store, and retrieve information (human information processing) is at the center of our understanding of the intrapersonal, listening communicator. Beatty and Payne (1984) associate cognitive complexity with the listener's information processing ability.

This human information processing perspective of listening, however, is not without critics. Thomas (1992), for instance, argues that the information processing model is at best a metaphor, not a representation, for human developmental and communication processes. He notes that humans are not mechanical information processing devices. Humans are distinguished by continuously changing brain structures, ability to self-regulate, self-awareness, and internal processes. Emmert (1989) has emphasized that it is important that we abandon the notion of listening as "a" process and "begin to develop a multivariate/multiple process view of listening in our theories and definitions ..." (pp. 12–13). Janusik (2002) stresses that current models of listening neglect the more widely-accepted notion of working memory over the traditional short-term memory/long-term memory models, thereby limiting our conceptualization of the process.

Purdy (2000) also argues for an expanded model of listening. He believes that this cognitive, rational approach to understanding listening by focusing on stages in the listening process limits listening theory: "Listening (and actually most of communication) theory works to develop constructs that lump the characteristics/attributes of listening together into categorizations that fit some preconceived or data directed conception that can be perceived and interpreted in different ways (pp. 48–9)." Purdy (2000) suggests that listening research needs to expand beyond the more traditional qualitative and quantitative methodologies to a descriptive/phenomenological approach in order to reflect better the complexities of listening behavior. After all, Purdy (1991) notes, the resulting meaning that is constructed in a communication is more of a community event, something more than the results of the listener's assigned meanings alone.

While such an approach can indeed enrich our understanding of listening, it should be recognized that our (Halone, Cunconan, Coakley, and Wolvin, 1998) quantitative analysis of our qualitative exploration of the dimensions of listening does support a preliminary conceptualization of listening. The identifiable cognitive, affective, and behavioral dimensions of listening further the understanding of listening behavior as a multidimensional communication phenomenon. And this multidimensionality also has been demonstrated (Halone, Wolvin, and Chung, 2001) in how listeners symbolically conceptualize what listening is/is not in human interaction. Additional support for our theoretical framework of listening competency suggests that listeners recognize behaviors specific to the taxonomic level of listening – discriminative, comprehensive, therapeutic, critical, appreciative – in which they engage (Ford, Wolvin, and Chung, 2000).

An Engagement Theory of Listening

It is clear that the listening models which have been developed to date assume that the listener is engaged in the communication with the speaker. (Beyond the scope of this chapter, another exploration of listening could take us to a consideration of non-human listening: listening to animals; listening to music; listening to the environment.) As Roberts and Vinson's work on willingness to listen exemplifies, the listening models assume listener engagement in the communication.

An engagement theory of listening might borrow from Shneiderman's work on the concept in electronic and distance education environments. "The fundamental idea underlying engagement theory is that students must be meaningfully engaged in learning activities through interaction with others and worthwhile tasks," note Kearsley and Shneiderman (1999, p. 1). Applying the model to computer-based learning, they argue that engagement offers a more sophisticated perspective on how students engage, not just interact, in cyber-learning. Using engagement as a conceptual framework for technology-based learning and teaching, Miliszewska and Horwood (2006) suggest that engagement theory may serve as a valuable paradigm for understanding how learners behave.

Extending this educational model, it is possible that the concept of engagement can serve a useful framework for understanding how listeners (like learners) function. Given the multidimensionality of listening competency, it is recognized that listeners are guided by their communication goals.

The taxonomy of listening functions, expanding on previous work on the hierarchical nature of listening skills by Lundsteen (1979), correlates with five general purposes of listeners – purposes which should be aligned with the speaker's goals (Wolvin and Coakley, 1979).

There are specific listening skills unique to each of these listening purposes, skills which operate in a hierarchical sequence depending upon the listener's need or objective at any particular time. Discriminative listening enables the listeners to distinguish the auditory and/or visual stimuli at the sensory level. Comprehensive listening requires the listener to use the discriminative skills while functioning to understand and recall the speaker's information. At a higher order, listeners build on their discriminative and comprehensive listening skills to be therapeutic (providing a sounding board for a person to talk through a problem), critical (assessing the acceptability of the speaker's message), or appreciative (enjoying the stimulus) listeners.

This taxonomy of listening functions, which has shaped instruction in listening skills, knowledge, and attitudes (Wacker and Hawkins, 1995), is consistent with perspectives that have been developed in communication theory. In a series of studies, for example, Berger and colleagues have utilized a communication plans model for understanding how communicators organize knowledge and skills necessary for reaching communication goals (see Berger, 2007, for a summary of this work). Berger suggests that understanding the interaction of communicators' planning dialogues and verbal dialogues could be useful to communication scholars to explain what is communicated and how. And uncovering these dialogues also may help explain how we decode messages from others.

Indeed, Imhof's (1998) important work elaborates students' listening plans with a model of communication content-related activities that listeners strategize before ("Before going to class, I think about the subject matter that I might be expecting"), during ("When I take notes, I am trying to catch every detail"), and after ("After class, I go over my notes as soon as possible").

Likewise, Stein's (1999) research on student listening described a similar metacognitive planning model: processes before listening (constructs goals and prepares to listen); processes during listening (evaluates, expresses affective reactions, infers, interprets, monitors and activates comprehension, selectively attends, integrates, and takes notes); and processes after listening (evaluates retrospectively, notes relevance to goals, asks questions, interprets retrospectively). Similarly, Pecchioni and Halone (2000) model listening in a relational context as pre-interaction, during interaction, and post-interaction.

A related communication perspective that can inform listening engagement theory is communication scholars' work on communication goals. Kellerman (1992) notes that "communication is goal-directed ... We don't communicate (i.e., engage in symbolic exchange) randomly" (p. 289). Clark and Delia (1979) identified the need for interaction goals which must be negotiated for the desired outcome of the communication to be achieved. Communicators may have both primary and secondary goals that drive their interaction behaviors. Dillard, Segrin and Harden (1989) have looked at influence goals in communicating: "the primary goals serve to initiate and maintain social interaction, while the secondary goals act as a set of boundaries which delimit verbal choices available to sources" (p. 32). Building on a model of interpersonal support in which listeners were found to assess a speaker's goal as the basis for establishing a listening goal (Horowitz, Krasnoperova, Tatar, et al., 2000), Young and Cates (2004) looked at the listener's goals in providing social support in peer mentoring. They determined that emotional listening (expressing empathy, support, sensitivity) and directive listening (offering opinions and perspectives) were negotiable listening goals that furthered the communicators' relationship.

Another relevant perspective for understanding how listeners engage as communicators is Searle's (1969) speech acts theory. Searles notes that "speaking a language is engaging in a rule-governed form of behavior" (p. 16) which results in speakers uttering words, referring and predicating propositions, and/or performing illocutionary acts such as stating, questioning, commanding, and promising – all of which are designed to fulfill an intention. If the speech act is successful, the listener will understand the speaker's intention. It would follow, then, that listeners must engage in the process and negotiate their listening intentions with the speaker's intentions in order to accomplish their communication objectives. Much like speech acts, listening acts derive from negotiated communication goals that are subject to variables (see Wolvin and Coakley, 1996, ch. 4) that can be manipulated and modified in the process.

The level of listening engagement also is guided by the listener's level of involvement. Chaiken (1980) outlined a dual processing model of decoding messages. In her important work, recipients of persuasive messages were found to employ systematic information processing strategies (detailed processing of the persuasive content and strategies) when the messages triggered high involvement. Low involvement in the messages, however, led listeners to use heuristic processing strategies (utilizing simple rules from past experiences and observations). Petty and Cacioppo (1986) expand on this dual processing model with their Elaboration Likelihood Model of persuasion. When exposed to persuasive messages, this model describes, listeners may take a central route to cognitively process the information, thoughtfully examining content issues. Rather than engaging in full elaboration of the content, however, listeners frequently use a peripheral route for processing in the information. Using simple decision rules, they may be more influenced by such heuristic factors as the speaker's credibility, if they like the speaker, or if they perceive that others believe/support the speaker's claim. Not surprisingly, much of what we receive as listeners (and that increases significantly in today's information-overloaded society) is processed peripherally. Only that information which we perceive to be of high personal relevance usually makes it into our central processing. Expanding this dual-processing theory beyond critical listening, interpersonal communication scholars are making some interesting applications of the model to listening outcomes in supportive communication (Burleson, 2009).

A listener's level of engagement in processing messages requires self regulation. We can turn back to work in the field of education on self-regulated learning to study how listeners can manage their listening engagement. Self-regulated learning has been defined as "an active, constructive process whereby learners set goals for their learning and then attempt to monitor, regulate, and control their cognition, motivation, and behavior, guided and constrained by their goals and the contextual features of the environment" (Pintrich, 2000, p. 453). Pintrich's influential education model of self-regulated learning organizes the regulatory processes in four phases: planning; self-monitoring; control; and evaluation. Pintrich's model, much like the work on listening strategies by Imhof (1998), Stein (1999), and Pecchioni and Halone (2000), aptly describes self-regulated listening – as listeners set goals for their listening and then apply their knowledge, attitudes, and skills as communicators to their listening acts. The core of listening self-regulation is metacognitive self monitoring. Lundsteen (1993) has explained how listeners use their metacognitive capacity for "monitoring their comprehension processes, selecting and implementing specific strategies in pursuit of a goal" (p. 107). She observes that "younger and less able listeners tend not to apply productive metacognitive strategies" (p. 121) as they engage as listening communicators.

Thus, listeners bring different levels of engagement to the listening process. These levels of engagement will be modified depending upon the communication goals of the listeners (and their speakers) and the perceived degree of involvement the listeners bring to the process.

To expand the theoretical frame by which we study the complexities of listening behavior, then, we need to recognize from whence we come. The human information processing perspective has allowed us to build a theoretical base for explicating the definition of listening as receiving, constructing meaning from, and responding to spoken and/or nonverbal messages. The qualitative/quantitative approach to this model has enabled us to establish a theory by which we can, as Littlejohn (1999) stresses, functionally organize and summarize, focus, clarify, observe, predict, research, and communicate what we have come to know about listening communication. Indeed, we are at an important intersection whereby we can use the theoretical grounding of listening cognition, affect, and behavior to understand more fully how listening communicators function at various intrapersonal and interpersonal levels. At the same time, this theoretical grounding can help us shift our paradigm and lead us beyond describing how listeners function to understanding more fully what listening is – the complex construct of listening (see Halone, Wolvin and Chung, 2001, p. 15).

As we expand our study of listening in the 21st century, we can be informed by the physiological, psychological, sociological, and communication perspectives that ground our theoretical base. The intersection of these perspectives offers considerable opportunity for broadening our framework to listening cognition/behavior/affect in the broadest sense of listening engagement.

QUESTIONS FOR DISCUSSION

1 What is listening? How should listening be defined? What characteristics of listening should be included in a definition of listening?

2 Discuss the perspectives on listening that inform a theory of listening: physiological, psychological, sociological, communication. Which perspective seems to offer the best approach to understanding the complexities of listening.

3 The research on listening and related human behaviors and cognitions demonstrates that listening is very much a multidimensional construct. What variables appear to be most relevant to understanding the complex nature of listening? What variables ought to receive more research attention?

4   How do the different perspectives on listening (physiological, psychological, sociological, and communication) intersect to create a listening model that could be used as the basis for listening research and listening instruction?

5   What is listening engagement? How does this serve as a foundation for understanding the self-regulated listener?

References

An ILA Definition of Listening. (1995, April). *The Listening Post*, 53, 1, 4–5.

Arnold, W.E., and Shirreffs, J.H. (1998). Patient perceptions of patient-physician communication with allopathic and naturopathic physicians. *International Journal of Listening*, 12, 1–11.

Baddeley, A.D., and Hitch, G.J. (1974). Working memory. In G. Bower (Ed.). *The psychology of learning and motivation* Vol. 8, pp. 47–90. New York: Academic Press.

Barker, L.L. (1971). *Listening behavior*. Englewood Cliffs, NJ: Prentice-Hall.

Beach, W.A., and Lindstrom, A.K. (1992). Conversational universals and comparative theory: Turning to Swedish and American acknowledgment tokens in interaction. *Communication Theory*, 2, 24–49.

Beatty, M.J. (1981). Receiver apprehension as a function of cognitive backlog. *Western Journal of Speech Communication*, 45, 277–81.

Beatty, M.J., and Payne, S.K. (1984). Listening comprehension as a function of cognitive complexity: A research note. *Communication Monographs*, 51, 85–9.

Beatty, M.J., McCroskey, J.C., and Valensic, K.M. (2001). *The biology of communication: A communibiological perspective*. Cresskill, NJ: Hampton Press, Inc.

Bentley, S.C. (1997). Benchmarking listening behaviors: Is effective listening what the speaker says it is? *International Journal of Listening*, 11, 51–68.

Berger, C.R. (2007). Plans, planning, and communication effectiveness. In B.B. Whaley, and W. Samter (Eds.). *Explaining communication: Contemporary theories and exemplars*. Mahwah, NJ: Erlbaum.

Burleson, B.R. (2007). Constructivism: A general theory of communication skill. In B.B. Whaley, and W. Sampter (Eds.). *Explaining communication*, pp. 105–28. Mahwah, NJ: Erlbaum.

Burleson, B.R. (2009). Understanding the outcomes of supportive communication: A dual-process approach. *Journal of Social and Personal Relationships*, 26, 21–38.

Chaiken, S. (1980). Heuristic versus systematic information processing and the use of source versus message cues in persuasion. *Journal of Personality and Social Psychology*, 39, 752–66.

Clark, R.A., and Delia, J.G. (1979). Topoi and rhetorical competence. *Quarterly Journal of Speech*, 65, 187–206.

Coakley, C.G., and Wolvin, A.D. (1997). Listening in the parent – teen relationship. *International Journal of Listening*, 11, 88–126.

Cooper, L.O., and Husband, R.L. (1993). Developing a model of organizational listening competency. *Journal of the International Listening Association, 7*, 6–34.

Cornwell, N.C., and Orbe, M.P. (1999). Critical perspectives on hate speech: The centrality of "Dialogic Listening." *International Journal of Listening*, 13, 75–96.

Cowan, N. (1995). *Attention and memory: An integrated framework*. New York: Oxford.

Craig, R.T. (1993). Why are there so *many* communication theories? *Journal of Communication*, 43, 26–33.

Daly, J. (1975). *Listening and interpersonal evaluations*. Paper presented at the Central States Speech Convention, Kansas City, MO.

Dillard, J.P., Segrin, C., and Harden, J.M. (1989). Primary and secondary goals in the production of interpersonal influence messages. *Communication Monographs*, 56, 19–38.

Driver, J. (1992). A selective review of selective attention research from the past century. *British Journal of Psychology*, 92, 53–79.

Edwards, R., and McDonald, J.L. (1993). Schema theory and listening. In A.D. Wolvin, and C.G. Coakley, (Eds.), *Perspectives on listening*, pp. 60–77. Norwood, NJ: Ablex.

Emmert, P. (1989). *The reification of listening*. Paper presented at International Listening Association research conference, Atlanta, GA.

Floyd, J.J. (1985). *Listening: A practical approach*. Glenview, IL: Scott, Foresman.

Ford, W.S.Z., Wolvin, A.D., and Chung, S. (2000). Students' self-perceived listening competencies in the basic speech communication course. *International Journal of Listening*, 14, 1–13.

Frost, J.A., Binder, J.R., Springer, J.A., Hammeke, T.A., Bellgowan, P.S.F., Rao, S.M., and Cox, R.W. (1999, February). Language processing is strongly left lateralized in both sexes. *Brain: A Journal of Neurology*, 122, 199–208.

Gilbert, M.B. (1988). Listening in school: I know you can hear me – but are you listening? *Journal of the International Listening Association*, 2, 121–32.

Goss, B. (1995). Th*e Psychology of human communication*. Prospect Heights, IL: Waveland.

Hall, E.T., and Hall, M.R. (1989). *Understanding cultural differences*. Yarmouth, ME: Intercultural Press.

Halley, R. D. (2001). *Listening models and procedures*. Paper presented at Listening Summit, Washington, DC.

Halone, K.K., Cunconan, T.M., Coakley, C.G., and Wolvin, A.D. (1998). Toward the establishment of general dimensions underlying the listening process. *International Journal of Listening*, 12, 12–28.

Halone, K.K., Wolvin, A.D., and Chung, S. (2001). *The everyday language of (not) listening*. Paper presented at International Listening Association convention, Chicago, IL.

Heisel, A.D., McCroskey, J.C., and Richmond, V.P. (1999). Testing theoretical relationships and non-relationships of genetically-based predictors: Getting started with communibiology. *Communication Research Reports*, 16, 1–9.

Hewes, D.E., and Graham, M. (1989). Second-guessing theory: Review and extension *Communication Yearbook*, 12, 213–48.

Horowitz, L.M., Krasnoperova, E.N., Tatar D.O., Hansen, M.B., Person, E.A., Galvin, K.L., and Nelson, K.L. (2000). The way to console may depend on the goal: Experimental studies of social support. *Journal of Experimental Social Psychology*, 37, 49–61.

Imhof, M. (1998). What makes a good listener? Listening behavior in instructional settings. *International Journal of Listening*, 12, 81–105.

Imhof, M. (2004). Who are we as we listening? Individual listening profiles in varying contexts. *International Journal of Listening*, 19, 36–45.

Janusik, L.A. (2002, March). *The intent to communicate. What role does attention play on listening?* Paper presented at the International Listening Association annual convention, Scottsdale, AZ.

Janusik, L. (2005). Conversational listening span: A proposed measure of conversational listening. *International Journal of Listening*, 19, 12–30.

Johannesen, R.L. (1971). The emerging concept of communication as dialogue. *Quarterly Journal of Speech*, 57, 373–82.

Johnson, M.K., Weaver, J.B.III, Watson, K.W., and Barker, L.B. (2000). Listening styles: Biological or psychological differences? *International Journal of Listening*, 14, 32–46.

Just, M.A., Carpenter, P.A., and Keller, T.A. (1996). The capacity theory of comprehension: New frontiers of evidence and arguments. *Psychological Review*, 103, 773–80.

Kane, M.J., and Engle, R.W. (2000). Working-memory capacity, proactive interference, and divided attention: Limits on long-term memory retrieval. *Journal of Experimental Psychology: Learning, Memory, and Cognition*, 26, 336–58.

Kearsley, G., and Shneiderman, B. (1999). Engagement Theory: A framework for technology-based teaching and learning. Retrieved on July 28, 2007, from: http://home.sprynet-com/gkearsley/engage.htm.

Kellerman, K. (1992). Communication: Inherently strategic and primarily automatic. *Communication Monographs*, 59, 288–300.

King, P.I., and Behnke, R.R. (2004). Patterns of state anxiety in listening performance. *Southern Communication Journal*, 70, 72–80.

Kuhn, T.S. (1977). *The essential tension: Selected studies in scientific tradition and change*. Chicago: University of Chicago Press.

Kuhn, T.S. (1998). Objectivity, value judgment, and theory choice. In I. McCord, and J. Coven, (Eds.) *Philosophy of Science: The Central Issues*, pp. 102–18. New York: Norton.

Lang, A., and Basil, M.D. (1998). Attention, resource allocation, and communication research: What do secondary task reaction times measure, anyway? *Communication Yearbook*, 21, 443–73.

Littlejohn, S.W. (1999). *Theories of human communication*. Belmont, CA: Wadsworth.

Lundsteen, S.W. (1979). *Listening: Its impact on reading and the other language arts*. Urbana, IL: NCTE ERIC.

Lundsteen, S.W. (1993) Metacognitive listening. In A.D. Wolvin and C.G. Coakley (Eds.) *Perspectives on listening*, pp. 106–23. Norwood, NJ: Ablex.

McCroskey, J.C. (1971). Human information processing and diffusion. In L.L. Barker, and R.J. Kibler (Eds.), *Speech communication behaviors*, p. 172. Englewood Cliffs, NJ: Prentice Hall.

Miliszewska, I., and Horwood, J. (2006). Engagement Theory: A universal paradigm? *SGCSXE'06 Bulletin*, 38, 158–92.

Miller, J.B., deWinstanley, P.A., and Carey, P. (1996). Memory for conversation. *Memory*, 4, 16–31.

Mulanax, A., and Powers, W.G. (2001). Listening fidelity development and relationship to receiver apprehension and locus of control. *International Journal of Listening*, 15, 69–78.

Mullen, T.P., and Narain, M. (2005). I Understand All That … But What's the Strategy? Working Paper. New York: Park Li Group.

National Eye Institute (2002). National Eye Institute Report on Blindness and Visual Impairment in the USA. Hospital Management.Net. Retrieved on March 24, 2002, from: http://www.hospitalmanagement.net/informer/breakthroughs/break126/.

National Institute on Deafness and Other Communication Disorders (1996). National Strategic Research Plan: Hearing and Hearing Impairment. Bethesda, MD: HHS, NIH, 1996.

Newby, H.A., and Popelka, G.R. (1992). *Audiology*. Englewood Cliffs, NJ: Prentice-Hall.

Nichols, R.G. (1948). Factors accounting for differences in comprehension of materials presented orally in the classroom. PhD dissertation, University of Iowa.

Pecchioni, L.L., and Halone, K.K. (2000). Relational listening II: Form and variation across social and interpersonal relationships. *International Journal of Listening*, 14, 69–93.

Perry, R.L. (1996). *Toward a construct of feedback and its relationship to listening*. Paper presented at the International Listening Association convention, Sacramento, CA.

Petty, R.E., and Cacioppo, J.T. (1986). *Communication and persuasion: Central and peripheral routes to attitude change*. New York: Springer-Verlag.

Phillips, M.D., Lowe, M.J., Lurito, J.T., Dzemidzic, M., and Mathews, V.P. (2001). Temporal lobe activation demonstrates sex-based differences during passive listening. *Radiology*, 220, 202–7.

Pintrich, P.R. (2000). The role of goal orientation in self-regulated learning. In M. Boekaerts, P.R. Pintrich, and M. Zeidner (Eds.) *Handbook of self regulation*, pp. 451–502. San Diego: Academic Press.

Powers, J.H. (1995). On the intellectual structure of the human communication discipline. *Communication Education*, 44, 191–222.

Purdy, M. (1991). Listening and community: The role of listening in community formation. *Journal of the International Listening Association*, 5, 51–67.

Purdy, M. (1997). What is listening? In M. Purdy, and D. Borisoff, (Eds.). *Listening in everyday life*, pp. 1–20. Lanham, MD: University Press of America.

Purdy, M. (2000). Listening, culture, and structures of consciousness. *International Journal of Listening*, 14, 47–68.

Purdy, M. (2003). *Listening and community*. Paper presented at Eastern Communication Association convention, Washington, DC.

Purdy, M. (with N. Newman). (1999). Listening and gender: Characteristics of good and poor listeners. International Listening Association convention, Albuquerque, NM.

Reisner, R. (1993). How different cultures learn. *Meeting News*, 17.

Rhodes, S.C. (1993). Listening: A relational process. In A.D. Wolvin, and C.G. Coakley, (Eds.). *Perspectives on listening*, pp. 217–40. Norwood, NJ: Ablex.

Roberts, C.V., and Vinson, L. (1998). Relationship among willingness to listen, receiver apprehension, communication apprehension, communication competence, and dogmatism. *International Journal of Listening*, 12, 40–56.

Rokeach, M. (1969). *Beliefs, attitudes, and values: A theory of organization and change*. San Francisco: Jossey-Bass.

Ross, C.S., and Glenn, E. (1996). Listening between grown children and their parents. *International Journal of Listening*, 10, 49–64.

Rubin, D.C., Hafer, T., and Arata, K. (2000). Reading and listening to oral-based versus literate-based discourse. *Communication Education*, 49, 121–133.

Rubin, D.L. (1993). Listenability = oral-based discourse + considerateness. In A.D. Wolvin and C.G. Coakley (Eds.) *Perspectives on listening*, pp. 261–81, Norwood, NJ: Ablex.

Ryan, E.B., Kwong See, S.K., Meneer, W.B., and Trovato, D. (1994). Age-based perceptions of conversational skills among younger and older adults. In M.L. Hummert, J.M. Wiemann, and J.F. Nussbaum (Eds.). *Interpersonal communication in older adulthood*. Thousand Oaks, CA: Sage.

Salk Institute (2002) Salk scientists demonstrate for the first time that newly born brain cells are functional in the adult brain. La Jolla, CA: Salk Institute.

Retrieved on February 27, 2002, from: http://www.salk.edu/NEWS/gage.

Schrodt, P., and Wheeless, L.R. (2001). Aggressive communication and informational reception apprehension: The influence of listening anxiety and intellectual inflexibility on trait argumentativeness and verbal aggressiveness. *Communication Quarterly*, 49, 53–69.

Searle, J. (1969). *Speech acts: An essay in the philosophy of language*. Cambridge: Cambridge University Press.

Smith, M.J. (1982). Cognitive schemata and persuasive communication: Toward a contingency rules theory. In M. Burgoon (Ed.). *Communication Yearbook 6*, pp. 33–62. Beverly Hills, CA: Sage.

Snider, J., and Osgood, C. (Eds.) (1969). *The semantic differential technique*. Chicago: Aldine.

Stein, S.K. (1999). Uncovering listening strategies: Protocol analysis as a means to investigate student listening in the basic communication course. Unpublished PhD dissertation, University of Maryland, College Park, MD.

Thomas, L.T., and Levine, T.R. (1994). Disentangling listening and verbal recall: Related but separate constructs? *Human Communication Research*, 21, 103–27.

Thomas, R.M. (1992). *Comparing theories of child development*. Belmont, CA: Wadsworth.

Thomlison T.D. (1997). Intercultural listening. In M. Purdy, and D. Borisoff (Eds.). *Listening in everyday life*, pp. 79–120. Lanham, MD: University Press of America.

Trahan, B.C., and Rockwell, P. (1999). The effects of listening training on nursing home assistants. *International Journal of Listening*, 13, 62–74.

Van Dijk, T.A., and Kintsch, W. (1983). *Strategies of discourse comprehension*. New York: Academic Press.

Villaume, W.A., Brown, M.H., Darling, R., Richardson, D., Hawk, R., Henry, D.M., and Reid, T. (1997). Presbycusis and conversation: Elderly interactants adjusting to multiple hearing losses. *Research on Language and Social Interaction*, 30, 235–62.

Wacker, K.G. and Hawkins, K. (1995) Curricula comparison for classes in listening. *International Journal of listening*, 9, 14–28.

Walker, K. (1997). Do you ever listen?: Discovering the theoretical underpinnings of empathic listening. *International Journal of Listening*, 11, 127–37.

Weaver, C.H. (1972). *Human listening*. Indianapolis: Bobbs-Merrill.

Witkin, B.R. (1990). Listening theory and research: The state of the art. *Journal of the International Listening Association*, 4, 7–32.

Wolvin, A.D. (1989). Models of the listening process. In C.V. Roberts, and K.W. Watson, (Eds.). *Intrapersonal communication processes*, pp. 508–27, New Orleans: Spectra.

Wolvin, A.D., and Coakley, C.G. (1979). *Listening instruction*. Urbana, IL: ERIC.

Wolvin, A.D., and Coakley, C.G. (1994). Listening competency. *Journal of the International Listening Association*, 8, 148–60.

Wolvin, A.D., and Coakley, C.G. (1996). *Listening*. New York: McGraw-Hill.

Wolvin, A.D., Berko, R.M., and Wolvin, D.R. (1999). *The public speaker/the public listener*. Los Angeles, Roxbury.

Wolvin, A.D., Halone, K.K., and Coakley, C.G. (1999). An assessment of the "intellectual discussion" on listening theory and research. *International Journal of Listening*, 13, 111–29.

Worthington, D. (2004). Exploring the relationship between listening style preference and verbal aggressiveness. *International Journal of Listening*, 19, 3–11.

Wyer, R.S. Jr., and Adaval, R. (2003). Message reception skills in social communication. In J.O. Greene, and B.R. Burleson, (Eds.). *Handbook of communication skills*, pp. 291–355. Mahwah, NJ: Erlbaum.

Young, R.W., and Cates, C.M. (2004). Emotional and directive listening in peer mentoring. *International Journal of Listening*, 18, 21–33.

Part II

Listening Research Methods

2

Qualitative Research: Critical for Understanding Listening

Michael W. Purdy

This chapter uses an autobiographical history of qualitative research to discuss listening behavior as experiential and grounded. The first concern is the lack of qualitative listening research. Purdy reviews the research that has been carried out and evaluates its relevance for understanding listening. He offers concrete steps for doing qualitative research and he suggests directions for future work based on a philosophical approach. The chapter enables listening scholars, teachers, and practitioners to think and conceptualize listening differently, as well as to consider diverse research methods.

> At the very moment when Descartes introduces his analytic method – a method which is invariably quantitative – Pascal is drafting his philosophy of the heart, preeminently valuative and qualitative in character,
> (Guardini, cited in Gebser, 1985, p. 401)

The study of listening is approached from many perspectives. Each must be understood in its own manner. One way of understanding listening is to describe it as it is manifested in behavior. The first study of listening by Rankin in 1928 was a measurement of the time spent in a typical day listening, speaking, reading and writing. Many of the early important studies of listening were attempts to measure listening ability before and after listening instruction or training. There were other studies which attempted to measure perceptions of effective listening such as measures of how well managers were perceived to listen by their employees. These studies, which are designed to quantify listening outcomes, begin with concepts about listening; some attempt to further conceptualize our understanding of listening.

The qualitative approach to listening starts with the realization that the strength of quantitative research – attempts to measure and quantify in some way what listening is – must begin with an understanding of the experience of listening. The experience of listening is not just what an individual thinks or perceives listening to be, or how they behave when they listen. Listening is not only an ability we learn while growing up, but is also a practice reinforced by our family, social/ethnic group and culture. Any serious study of listening, then, must begin by understanding where and how we get our conceptualizations for research, what listening means, and how it is performed in our personal, social and professional lives. This chapter is a historical but also a personal journey to understand the role of qualitative research in the understanding of listening.

Qualitative Research: Critical for Understanding Listening

This chapter is central to the spirit and direction of this book. In particular, my intention is to demonstrate how qualitative research and even a particular version of qualitative research is necessary for the study of the full experience of listening.

Accomplishing that will take us through the following steps:

- my own growth through various understandings of qualitative research;
- the limited focus for conceptualizations of listening;
- how a broad sense of qualitative research is critical to understanding listening;
- a brief review of the qualitative research in the listening/communication field; and
- qualitative methods that could be useful for the study of listening.

My Research Education and the Nature of Qualitative Research

To understand my research growth, you should understand that I was a total positivist as an undergraduate in the 1960s with a major in mathematics, followed by a masters in rhetoric and public speaking and then a PhD minor in empirical research methods. My research philosophy began as similar to Pythagoras' thought – an ancient Greek philosopher who believed that mathematics accurately represented the structure and harmony of all that exists. In my graduate statistics classes in Psychology in the early 1970s, I was taught statistics as a pragmatic way to figure out the patterns of the social world. However, I also came to a fundamental awareness about the nature of statistical analysis. My studies covered the gamut from simple linear to non-linear and complex, multi-variate methods, including the latest Bayesian theory. From Bayesian statistics I began to appreciate that human judgment could be useful input for a statistical argument. A Bayesian approach allows for the use of subjective probabilities as part of the statistical inference process. One inputs personal, expert knowledge as a probabilistic statement at the start of building a statistical argument for a study.

Another significant learning along the way came from a graduate Psychology paper on the philosophy of statistics. I learned that all statistical methodology involves two interpretations critical to the argument being made: we interpret human experience as we reduce it to numbers, and then we must interpret again to understand the results in a social context after crunching the numbers. That is to say, when we decide to study something from a quantitative perspective, we take the fullness of a lived context and we identify and measure certain concepts indicated by behaviors in the context we are studying. That phase of the research leaves us with the bare numbers on which we can freely perform statistical operations according to the structure of the argument we have set up. When the tests are completed we end up with another set of numbers according to our statistics, (F's, t's, etc.), and these must be understood, but they can only be interpreted sensibly in a particular context.

My research education continued with a PhD minor in empirical research methods which fortunately included a solid dose of phenomenology. Phenomenology is a philosophy developed by Edmund Husserl (1859–1938) at the beginning of the 20th century, but it is also a very rigorous descriptive method which allows the experience of the facts to speak for itself. The method of description is much more than self introspection (an early misunderstanding of the method). My study of phenomenology brought a turn toward an awareness of the critical role of qualitative research. Phenomenology is initially descriptive and qualitative, but it doesn't reduce the contextual data to numbers; all experience, behavioral and otherwise, is allowed its richness and diversity. In the application of phenomenology to cultural and anthropological studies – such as ethnomethodology – the result is called thick description because it is rich with cultural detail. An excellent book for understanding the basics and conducting this type of research is *Experiential Phenomenology* by Don Ihde (1986).

My educational experience in the 1960s and early 1970s prepared me for my professional career. Since the 1970s each decade has brought a different understanding of qualitative research in the communication field. Whereas in the earlier decades, quantitative research was dominant, by the early 1980s quantitative and qualitative research were beginning to be perceived as complementary. Each had something to offer to the other. Qualitative provided the rich contextual study and quantitative research came up with pragmatic conclusions based on the hard data available.

By the late 1980s, I had begun a radical shift to agree with those who argued that all experience was essentially qualitative and that quantitative research was a subset of qualitative (Purdy, 1986, 1988, 1989). Some careful thought about the grounded role of contextual study shows that this clearly makes sense.

The way research was being redefined during the 1980s and 1990s led me to realize that qualitative research had been co-opted by the authority of the dominant quantitative milieu. That is, qualitative research had a respected place in research but there was a demand for clarity, certainty and rigor – the metaphysics of modern thought – before qualitative research could be accepted. This led me to develop a third research category – phenomenological (or descriptive) – a method which doesn't have to squeeze itself into a rigorous practice to be accepted. I realized qualitative research could not be free to do the work of rich, thick description if it had to meet the rigorous demands of the dominant research paradigm. Qualitative research had to adapt its methods to the demands of the contextual experience being studied, and not to some pre-given rigor like quantitative research.

Denzin and Lincoln (2005), who have edited *the* definitive handbook on qualitative research, say that qualitative methods are now more accepted in research. Perhaps that is true, but a look at other contemporary research texts indicates that perhaps the situation is otherwise. Babbie's *The Basics of Social Research* (1999), doesn't even define "qualitative research," but does recognize "qualitative analysis." Qualitative "analysis" is not good enough.

To understand the phenomenon of listening we require robust qualitative *research*, a wholistic and open project for the understanding of human experience in situations of receptivity or listening. Even Denzin and Lincoln's basic understanding of qualitative research is what they call a "narrative turn" (2000, p. x). To be fair, this handbook includes more than narrative approaches, calling in addition for a blurring of disciplinary boundaries. However, the authors' overall orientation is limited by the narrative framework. The narrative approach to communication is one of the latest ways to study human experience, but the approach does not begin to exhaust human interaction. For example, in listening we may focus on interpretive aspects of perception, or cognitive elements of memory. Narrative is one level of analysis – that of human interactive episodes or stories – and misses some experiences of both micro and macro levels of listening.

The Limited Sense of Thinking about Listening

I have read and continue to read a great deal of the literature about listening. Sources like Steil and Bommelje's weekly online *ListeningLeader*, which extracts listening commentary from the popular culture and the press, is invaluable particularly with regards to institutional leadership. I also have a large collection of quotations about listening from Egyptian and Hebraic times forward, and have researched and written several papers on historical and philosophical approaches to listening (Purdy, 1998). The quotes do not make sense unless one realizes that aside from one essay by Plutarch, only brief statements about listening were published until the 20th century. While writing my chapters for the text, *Listening in Everyday Life* (co-edited with Deborah Borisoff), I surveyed most of the writing in the field. In addition, my roles as a member of the International Listening Association, and as an editorial assistant of the *International Journal of Listening*, have led me to read a lot of current listening research. From this overview, I can make some general conclusions about the field of listening.

In a nutshell, most modern thought about listening is severely limited by its grounding in cognitive psychology (for a review of this argument see Cronen, 1998). Unlike the communication field in general, listening has been slow to cut its attachment to the psychological, idealist philosophy that meaning is in people. If there is one "essence" in the broad experience of listening/communication it is that communication is about connection and relationship. Therefore, the study of the individual and how she/he makes meaning *alone* doesn't cut it. That is, if meaning is in people, then we must each make our own unique meaning. The emphasis on meaning leaves the results of our studies focused on the cognitive/interpretive level and generally ignores relationship, ethnicity, politics and culture. Of course, this is a generalization and there are exceptions, some of which I will discuss briefly.

Qualitative Research is Critical to Listening

One way to transcend the limitations of the cognitive/interpretivist perspective of listening is to adapt, as critical, a broad and encompassing sense of qualitative research. Until listening scholars begin to understand listening as a social, political and cultural process, as essentially about connection and relationship, we will continue in our present rut. What broader philosophical and cultural studies of listening tell us is that we are *already* connected in our social world through listening. As Fiumara illustrates (discussing Heidegger), to listen is to gather our world (1990, p. 1), so at any given time we are already living a shared social world gathered through our receptivity. Then within that world we foster and build relationships through interactions facilitated by and grounded in listening. (One would be tempted here to call this *active* listening, but listening is always a more or less consciously engaged activity and always active to some degree.)

I believe an open-ended project of qualitative research, what Denzin and Lincoln call a "generative form of inquiry" (p. x), would open new ways of understanding listening. Most critical research is cross-cultural research. It is important to move beyond the listening practices of our own ethnicity, society, and culture to understand how broad our understanding of listening *could* be. I have sketched some of this in my papers on listening and cultural consciousness (Purdy, 1982, 1995). We best understand our own cultural situation when we can get perspective from another experiential vantage point.

Some of the methods that are useful include (ordered from philosophical to concrete): phenomenology; hermeneutics; ethnography; historical; grounded research; case study; interview; narrative; discourse analysis; biography and autobiography; participatory and performance studies; and clinical approaches (for other methods see the range of methods represented in Cassell and Symon, 2004). My only challenge to this typical list is that phenomenology and its interpretive offshoots such as hermeneutics are the philosophical methods that ground all of the others, as well as being methods in their own right.

Qualitative Research in the Listening/communication Field

I am not aware of a plethora of qualitative research on listening. One of the more interesting methods for getting new ideas about listening has been reading the research of other fields (anthropology, sociology, music, philosophy, etc.) to see what has been said about listening. Some of us in the listening field were part of a project led by Witkin (see Witkin and Trochin's 1997 work on mapping constructs for listening) to carry out these explorations – the research wasn't limited to qualitative methods. The group's research did not turn up much qualitative research that related to listening. In my own work I have found a number of studies that are important to consider.

Two immediate studies that open new approaches are the study of "Listening and landscape among the Blackfeet" by Carbaugh (1999), and Adelmann's study (2001) of the listening repertory of participants in an educational setting. The Carbaugh study is a listening ethnography of the Blackfeet Native Americans. Its uniqueness is its descriptive method; it treasures the reported listening experience of the Blackfeet without imposing a modern cognitive perspective and hence finds something quite amazing in the experience of listening in and among the landscapes of the Western plains. Native Americans have a listening connection with the landscape itself. Adelmann, on the other hand, begins with an educational setting (a teacher training seminar) and maps the way ideas are gathered and used in the group process. The study is purely about the description of patterns of receptivity; how ideas are picked up and used through listening. Carbaugh is a great model for appreciating the different experience of listening in varied cultures and Adelmann is a model for tracking the way listening is used in social/organizational structures.

There also are many survey studies of listening, but most validate a few "theories" which are already assumed to be the patterns of listening behavior. Some candidates include listener styles, listening profiles and listener preferences. Solid, rigorous qualitative research should go back to the listening experience and attempt to understand and "validate" how these labels or concepts of listening fit within social and cultural context. We assume these models *are* the shape of listening experience and then precede to show how the cookies are cut out of the assumed social pattern rather than how the cookie cutter got to be this shape.

The broadest and most fascinating studies I have found are philosophical studies by Heidegger (1962), Fiumara (1990), Forester (1980), Gadamer (1976), Ricoeur (1981), Ihde (1976) and Smith (1979). They shed light on the cultural role of listening in Western culture and consciousness (the structure of our thinking and behaving), and hence show us the limits of our thinking about listening. Philosophy typically provides the most encompassing context for qualitative work. Two examples would include Gadamer's work which speaks of listening as a fusion of individual life horizons (contexts). This fusion/mediation through listening means we have an inexhaustible "source of possibilities of meaning (Gadamer, p. xix)." The second would be Fiumara's discussion of the originary meaning of listening in Western culture. She suggests that we might think of listening as midwifery, as helping to give birth to ideas in the mind of the other.

Qualitative Methods that Might be Most Useful for Listening

I think all of the *cultural* methods of qualitative research are useful, but especially those that study cultures or compare across cultures. Philosophical studies at times do give a cross cultural comparison of listening, but mostly they hold up a mirror so we can perceive our own culture. Some of the useful cultural methods include: historical and current first person ethnographies (narratives); and ethnographic (case) studies of other cultures (especially those that begin with the local experience as described by natives in their own linguistic and cultural context). For example, Zulick has done a fascinating study of listening and persuasion in early Hebraic civilization. Zulick, writing in *Rhetorica* (1992), discussed the act of persuasion in biblical Hebrew and noted that the hearer was assigned the role of rhetorical agent – the active party in a rhetorical interaction. She wrote that phrases such as "Hear, O Israel (Deuteronomy 5:1; 6:4)" "throw responsibility to the respondent, making the hearer rather than the speaker the deciding figure in a rhetorical act." Studies of ancient Egyptian culture show that the culture was very much structured by hierarchy and status; one listened to those who were in social and religious positions requiring reverence (Purdy, 1998).

Another ethnographic study is Fletcher's 1999 study of listening to police narratives. She studied the experience of being a cop (both male and female), but the process of learning how to listen to and collect narratives required learning about listening. She discovered over time that both silence and giving up control of the interview proved to be effective skills for her work.

Halley has carried out two International Listening Association programs collecting listening stories from US residents and others – this is the beginning of interesting work. I still have notes of listening stories and commentary from Hindu "mythology" that I gathered from expert sources in India and which needs to be developed into an article. Also, at the 2003 joint International Listening/Western Communication Association conference in Sweden there were the beginnings of programs to share cross-cultural experiences of listening; these efforts are to be encouraged.

I know this is not extensive, but I hope it offers direction for the critical importance of qualitative research in the study of listening, and also that it offers some suggestions on what has been done and what is left to be done.

Guidelines for Conducting Qualitative Research

There are guidelines for doing qualitative research. They are not absolutes, qualitative research is always a creative and flexible process, but they are useful for maintaining rigor and method:

1   One of the most important considerations in qualitative research is investigation of the assumptions that underlie the research. Qualitative research must be transparent if it is to be useful. In a recent qualitative research support group qualitative researchers were discussing their research. During the conversation, I probed for the research assumptions of each researcher. Researchers made statements like: "I want to change how we train people," "the organization needs to be changed," and "I want to get them to change the way they …" In qualitative research assumptions cannot be hidden if the research is to be well founded. These hidden assumptions were indicative of the intent of the researchers, but also indicated that the researchers needed to do qualitative (descriptive) research first to find out what was happening in their organizations before suggesting change. Some researchers add a section as a preface to

their study telling about assumptions or biases. Others add a section at the end where they either discuss personal biases about the research or report the perspectives of other researchers that might reveal different assumptions or interpretations.

2   In order to know what your assumptions are, you must interrogate yourself or have others help you ask questions to become aware of your assumptions. However, it is also very important to know the research context from literature searches across as many disciplines as might be useful. Equally important is to acquire firsthand experience of the culture being researched and to do a phenomenological description of the context.

3   Organize your literature search and then ask questions that are appropriate to the specific method being used. Asking questions will begin the focusing process necessary for conducting quality research. For example, if you are doing narrative research the questions, as in the Fletcher study mentioned above, would include broader methodological questions such as: "What are the ways of listening that will best gather the stories from the police culture I am researching?" Then, there are the specific research questions, such as: "Are the stories of female police officers different from those of male police officers?"

Another aspect of qualitative research include what one "must do" and "must not do" – some further guidelines for research if you will:

1   Consult and work with others. Many heads can make better sense of the cultural meaning of listening, of how to structure research and how to make sense of the results of research. You will find that many scholars and researchers are more than willing to help you with your research. Some will even offer to work with you.

2   Use the feedback from others, as well as your own intuition, to be as "rigorous" (as in critical and creative) as possible. Research that does not make a reasonable argument – and research is about making an argument – is not of much use. The argument is built as you present the literature review to show what has been done and what questions need to be answered. Then the research question(s) and how the research answers those question(s) is critical. Finally, the discussion of the research presentation interprets the results to argue for the interpretation the researcher has concluded is most meaningful.

3 Conduct a pilot study with a small sample, or in a limited context – a class, a family or a social group.
4 Continually question what you are doing throughout the research process and continue to ask others for their feedback and evaluation.

Things you should avoid doing include:

1 Don't work in isolation, research benefits from social interaction with other researchers.
2 Don't think your idea is not worthwhile. Talk over your ideas with other researchers in the area and let them help focus your research. Often you haven't seen similar research because it hasn't been done yet. You are breaking new ground.
3 Don't be afraid to fail. Great research is often the result of several stages of research where the questions, the understanding and the methods are refined leading to better results.

Conclusion

There has been a consistent bias against qualitative research in some areas of communication study. Unfortunately, listening is one of those areas where this research approach is yet to be embraced. In my auto-biographical and historical approach to research I have attempted to demonstrate that bias, but also to show the rationality and importance of privileging a qualitative approach to listening. Without the qualitative, contextual grounding of listening the quantitative research cannot be explained fully. Certainly qualitative and quantitative research complement each other, but without the richness of qualitative understanding, quantitative research is sterile and limited in its applicability. Finally, it is imperative to realize as well that there are many approaches to doing qualitative research and attempts to make qualitative research imitate quantitative research in its rigor are certainly self defeating.

QUESTIONS FOR DISCUSSION

1 What does listening mean to you?
2 How would you define listening? What concepts are central to your definition?
3 How would you describe your own listening and the listening of those around you?

4 Each of the first three questions are places for beginning to structure qualitative research, how would each lead to different thoughts about and approaches to studying listening?
5 One of my qualitative studies began by using others to help me collect descriptive data about the characteristics of listening. Each person was asked the question: "think of someone who is an effective listener, and then list 12 attributes of that listener." Do the same for an ineffective listener. Compare your results with others in your class, or with other research or listening books that describe an effective listener. How would the above results differ if the questions asked about "good" and "bad" listeners?
6 Research one of the core qualitative methods and conduct a mini-study using that method. For example, read a few articles about auto-ethnography and then do an ethnography of listening in some area of your life: listening in your family.

References

Adelmann, K. (2001). Listening and referring to voices: Students' repertory in educational settings. *International Journal of Listening*, 15, 38–67.

Babbie, E.R. (1999). *The basics of social research*. Englewood Cliffs, NJ: Wadsworth.

Carbaugh, D. (1999). "Just listen": "Listening" and landscape among the Blackfeet. *Western Journal of Communication*, 63, 3, 250–70.

Cassell, C., and Symon, G. (Eds.). (2004). *Essential guide to qualitative methods in organizational research*. Thousand Oaks, CA: Sage.

Cronen, V. (1998). Communication theory for the 21st century: Cleaning up the wreckage of the Psychology project. In J.S. Trent (Ed.). *Communication: Views from the helm for the 21st century*, pp. 177–83. Boston: Allyn & Bacon.

Denzin, N.K., and Lincoln, Y.S. (Eds.). (2000). *Handbook of qualitative research*, (2nd edn). Thousand Oaks, CA: Sage.

Denzin, N.K., and Lincoln, Y.S. (Eds.). (2005). *Handbook of qualitative research*, (3rd edn). Thousand Oaks, CA: Sage.

Fiumara, G.C. (1990). *The other side of language: A philosophy of listening*. (C. Lambert, Trans.) New York: Routledge.

Fletcher, C. (1999). Listening to narratives: The dynamics of capturing police experience. *International Journal of Listening*, 13, 46–61.

Forester, J. (1980). Listening: The social policy of everyday life (Critical theory and hermeneutics in practice). *Social Praxis*, 7–3/4: 219–32.

Gadamer, H. (1976). *Philosophical hermeneutics*. Berkeley: University of California Press.

Guardini, R. (1935). *Christliches bewusstsein: Versuche uber Pascal*. Leipzig: Hegner. Cited in J. Gebser (1995) *The ever-present origin*. (N. Barstad, and A. Mickunas, Trans.). Athens, OH: Ohio University Press.

Heidegger, M. (1962). *Being and time*. (J. Macquarrie, and E. Robinson, Trans.). New York: Harper and Row.

Idhe, D. (1976). *Listening and voice: A phenomenology of sound.* Athens, OH: Ohio University Press.

Ihde, D. (1986). *Experiential phenomenology: An introduction.* Albany, NY: SUNY Press.

Painter, J. (2007). Uses of Bayesian Statistics. Retrieved July 2007, from: http://www.tessella.com/Literature/Supplements/PDF/BayesianStatistics.pdf

Purdy, M. (1982). Styles of listening and structures of consciousness. *Journal of Communication Therapy,* 1, 1, 47–58.

Purdy, M. (1986, March). *Qualitative research methodology.* Paper presented at the International Listening Association, San Diego, CA.

Purdy, M. (1988, March). *Qualitative research and listening.* Paper presented at the International Listening Association, Scottsdale, AZ.

Purdy, M. (1989, February). *Issues in qualitative research.* Paper presented at ILA pre – conference on Research, Atlanta. (later published in Perspectives on listening research: Planning for the next generation, *International Listening Association,* 1991).

Purdy, M. (1995). *Listening and consciousness: The contributions of Jean Gebser.* Presentation at International Listening Association, Little Rock, AK, March.

Purdy, M. (1998, March). *Listening and consciousness: Historical roots.* Paper presented at the International Listening Association, Kansas City.

Rankin, P. T. (1928). The importance of listening ability. *English Journal* (College edn), 17, 623–30.

Ricoeur, P. (1981). *Hermeneutics and the human sciences.* (J.B. Thompson, Ed. and Trans). Cambridge: Cambridge University Press.

Smith, F.J. (1979). *The experience of musical sound.* New York: Gordon and Breach.

Witkin, B.R., and Trochin, W.W.K., (1997). Toward a synthesis of listening constructs: A concept map analysis. *International Journal of Listening,* 11, 69–87.

Zulick, M. D. (1992). The active force of hearing: The ancient Hebrew language of persuasion. *A Journal of the History of Rhetoric: Rhetorica,* 10, 4, 367–80.

3

Quantitative Research in Listening: Explication and Overview

Graham D. Bodie and Margaret Fitch-Hauser

In this chapter Bodie and Fitch-Hauser examine the role quantitative methods can play in listening research. They begin with a general overview of quantitative methods to orient the reader for a discussion of some of the quantitative listening research conducted in the past six decades and its contribution to our body of knowledge about listening. A final section suggests areas of vital importance for the future of listening research and theory.

Quantitative Research in Listening: Explication and Overview

Quantitative research attempts to quantify the relationship between two or more phenomena. While a qualitative researcher might ask, "What is the nature of lecture listening?" a quantitative researcher aims to be more specific in his or her examination of topics such as lecture listening. A more quantitatively oriented question concerning lecture listening might be, "How *much* are certain characteristics of the situation and the individual related to lecture listening?"

This does not imply the superiority of one method over the other. Rather, each method has its relative strengths and weaknesses. Qualitative research allows for deeper understanding and appreciation of phenomena, whereas quantitative research allows for more precise analysis and prediction. Choice of methodology should always be driven by theory and the nature of substantive research questions. These two methodologies are also similar in that they are both systematic attempts to examine concepts. In fact, having a system or following a process is a defining principle of research whether it is labeled quantitative or qualitative.

There are, however, appreciable differences between these two methods. Purdy (this volume) has offered his insights into qualitative research. The purpose of this chapter is to answer how quantitative methods can be used to study an abstract concept such as listening. In service of this aim, this chapter is divided into three main sections. First, we provide and dissect a definition of quantitative research and use an extended example to illustrate our points. If you have been exposed to an introductory methods class, this section might seem basic. Our goal is to ensure all readers have an idea of the language, logic, and limitations of quantitative research before we review the extant research that has utilized this perspective in the domain of listening; a brief overview of this research is the focus of our second main section. Finally, the chapter concludes by offering three areas ripe for future quantitative research.

Defining Quantitative Research

Before presenting and explaining a working definition of quantitative research, it is important to note this type of research is only useful to the extent that it answers theoretical and/or practical questions. Science, as a way of knowing, is driven by the prime component of understanding (see Berger, 1977). As the natural sciences were created to understand the natural world, the social sciences were created to understand the social world. Natural and social scientists alike are interested in "sense-making" – solving puzzles, understanding patterns, and investigating social problems (Bodie, 2009a). Thus, to the extent a researcher is interested in understanding a concept such as listening, she should be equipped with tools necessary to engage in this understanding. One set of tools available to the listening scholar is the broad realm of quantitative research. This type of research relies on (a) operationalization of empirical data which is (b) collected from a sample and translated into (c) numerical form that can then be (d) subjected to one or more statistical tests from which the data are (e) generalized to a larger population and (f) claims are made about the "true" nature of the phenomenon under study. In the next several sections we dissect this definition.

Operationalization of empirical data

Empirical data are observable units of analysis such as a conversation between two strangers or the listening patterns of college-aged males.

The first step in quantitative research is to choose an object of study (e.g., listening) that can be usefully narrowed to a manageable topic area (e.g., listening patterns of college-aged males) and observed in a laboratory or "natural" environment. Listening – like other phenomena such as communication, intelligence, and learning style – is an abstract concept. We cannot touch, taste, smell or otherwise measure listening directly. Instead, social scientists choose theoretically relevant operationalizations to study concepts of interest.

Critical to working with any concept that is both hypothetical in nature and very real as a life skill is the ability to operationalize it in a useful way. *Operationalization* is a way of making an abstract concept (like listening) more concrete and measurable. The ability to add a concrete dimension to the abstract is one of the advantages of quantitative research. Doing so allows researchers to clearly define the boundaries of a concept for a particular study. For example, by operationalizing effective listening as the score on a specific listening test, we have a concrete measure of "listening comprehension." This ability to achieve momentary clarity allows quantitative researchers to address very specific research questions.

The term most closely associated with operationalization is variable. Quantitative researchers most often talk about two types of variables. The *dependent variable* (DV) is the outcome of interest. A researcher interested in studying listening comprehension could operationalize this concept in several ways such as the amount of lecture material recalled after lecture exposure. An *independent variable* (IV) is any aspect of the environment or individual thought to have an influence on the DV. IVs can either be manipulated by the researcher (part of the environment) or be characteristic of the participants in a sample. In our case, we could manipulate the length of the lecture, the subject material presented in the lecture, and/or the credibility of the lecturer. Similarly, we could be interested in how much information is recalled by students of different genders, class ranks, or Grade Point Averages (GPAs). These latter variables – those intrinsically associated with participants and out of direct control of the researcher – are called classification IVs. This distinction is important because conclusions about causation are most strongly made when the researcher has direct control over manipulated variables; conclusions regarding causation with classification IVs are more speculative.

Since quantitative researchers depend on numerical data, they must rely on variable scaling, or the assignment of numbers to observations.

How a variable is scaled determines what types of statistical tests are appropriate. The most widely used classification system was introduced by Stevens (1946) and includes four types of scales: categorical (nominal scale); ranked (ordinal scale); and continuous (interval and ratio scales). When a variable is scaled as *nominal* independent categories are created and numbers are assigned arbitrarily to these categories. If we were interested in differences in listening comprehension based on biological sex, for example, we could assign all males in the sample the number one and all females in the sample the number two. These numbers do not have a meaningful numeric value but, instead represent a qualitative difference between individuals in the sample based on biological sex. *Ranked* data is said to have an *ordinal* scale. In our example, we could rank participants based on their listening comprehension score with those ranks corresponding to increasing/decreasing scores on our measure of comprehension. Operationalizing listening comprehension as the amount of information recalled after lecture exposure, however, provides a continuous measure of the concept; not only is a higher score greater than a lower score (information that ranking would provide), we also know how much greater. For instance, a score of 20 is five pieces of information more than 15. This difference is the same as the difference between 10 and 15, thus our scale is at the *interval* level. Very similar to interval level scales, a second type of continuous scale is a ratio scale. With a ratio scale it is possible to obtain a score of zero. In our running example, since an individual can recall zero pieces of information, our scale is a *ratio scale*. If we did not have a true zero point, as with semantic-differential (bipolar adjectives) or Likert scales (e.g., I was able to comprehend lots of information scored from Strongly agree – Strongly disagree), then our scale would only be at the interval level.

Populations, samples, and research design

After making decisions about concept operationalization, the next question a quantitative researcher must answer is, "Whose listening is of interest?" Suppose we are interested in learning the extent to which college students comprehend lecture material. Our population is college students – the specific group we are interested in studying. Since it is impossible for a researcher to study listening comprehension of all college students, a sample of people must be selected from that population (e.g., college students attending a Midwestern university). Once the population is narrowed down to a sample and variables have been determined, the researcher's next task is to determine the appropriate research strategy.

Two basic strategies or designs employed in quantitative research are post facto and experimental. *Post facto* research "begins with a measure of the dependent variable and then retroactively looks at preexisting subject independent variables and their possible influence on the dependent variable" (Sprinthall, 2003, p. 213). In other words, post facto research relies on classification IVs as opposed to IVs directly manipulated by the researcher. For example, we could be interested in how a person's typical communication style (e.g., dominant, dramatic, relaxed) is related to the ways in which he prefers to receive information (see later section on listening styles; Bodie and Villaume, 2003). To study this we could have participants fill out questionnaires that assess their general communication and listening styles. We would then run one or more types of statistical analyses to ascertain if communication and listening styles are associated. Although post-facto research is useful, it is often misinterpreted. *The only warranted conclusion one can make with this type of research is that there is a relationship between the variables.* It is theory that helps the researcher determine if a particular cause – effect sequence makes more sense than other possible sequences.

If researchers are concerned with causal relationships (as we often are in the field of listening) a more appropriate design is the *experiment*, offering full control over the IVs under question. Typically, we talk about experimental conditions within this type of research. If we chose to study the impact of lecture length on listening comprehension, then we would randomly assign participants into two groups.[1] One group would be exposed to a long lecture and the other group would be exposed to a short lecture; as with all other concepts, long and short are operationalized depending on theoretical or practical considerations. Using our same DV, we would look at the difference in the amount of information recalled between the groups. Given our groups do not differ on other characteristics, we could attribute the cause of this difference to lecture length.

---

[1]   It is important to note here that a true experiment requires that all participants are randomly assigned to conditions. As a subset of experimental design, quasi-experimental studies are those in which in tact groups are used. For instance, if a researcher used one introductory speech class as one condition and another class as the second condition, this would not be what is generally labeled a true experimental design. The reader is referred to Shadish, Cook, and Campbell (2002) for an in-depth treatment of experimental and quasi-experimental design.

Suppose we find students in the long lecture condition recall an average of 15 pieces of information, and students in the short lecture condition recall an average of 20 pieces of information. A cursory look at this data would suggest short lectures enable people to comprehend material better than long lectures. Instead of making an intuitive guess about the difference between two scores in the population of interest, however, researchers utilize statistical techniques to test the significance of the association between variables.

The use of statistical techniques to assess relationships between variables

When quantitative researchers begin a study they generally have an idea of the relationships they will find from the data. In our case, we may have a theory that allows us to hypothesize that short lectures will enable people to comprehend material better than long lectures. Although it is ideal to test this hypothesis directly, quantitative researchers generally use null hypothesis significance testing (NHST). The null hypothesis "is never proved or established, but is possibly disproved, in the course of experimentation" (Fisher, 1935, p. 19). This logic is consistent with the fact that although one can never establish proof for the existence of a claim in the social sciences, one can provide proof of its falsity (Popper, 1965; see also, Phillips, 2000). The null hypothesis is generally conceptualized as the hypothesis of no difference (in the case of comparing group means) or no association (in the case of establishing a relationship between groups).[2] At the most basic level, when we test the null hypothesis we are attempting to rule out random error as an explanation for the relationship between variables since our theory proposes some systematic source of variability, namely, the difference between the two groups. If you recall, the more we can control for the influence of other variables (e.g., by random assignment to condition), the more confident we can be that our result is the product of researcher manipulations or participant classifications.

---

[2]   The null hypothesis is not always represented as no difference or no association. The hypothesis of no difference/association has been labeled the "nill hypothesis" (Cohen, 1988) and is widely overused in the social sciences. However, for the sake of simplicity, we will refer to the null hypothesis in this sense. For further reading about the misuses of NHST, the reader is referred to Chow (1996), Cohen (1994), and Daniel (1998).

In our example, the null hypothesis is: lecture length has no effect on recall. In other words, the difference between the amount of information recalled by participants exposed to short versus long lectures is not different enough to conclude length of lecture has a systematic effect on listening comprehension. In most research, rejection of the null hypothesis is desired. If the null hypothesis is rejected, the researcher is warranted to accept the alternative hypothesis: length of lecture does have a systematic impact on the amount of information recalled. The more evidence gathered that an effect is due to some systematic variability, the greater confidence we have in our theory that produced this hypothesis.

Let's assume we have a theoretical rationale that proposes short lectures enable people to comprehend the material better than long lectures. To test this hypothesis let's suppose we collected data from 100 college students and that 50 students were randomly assigned to listen to a short or long lecture. After listening to their lecture, students were asked to take five minutes to recall as much of the lecture as they could. After this data is coded based on a researcher defined rubric, we find that the average (mean) recall score of the short lecture group was 20 pieces of information and the average recall score of the long lecture group was 15 pieces of information. After entering our data into a statistical program (e.g., SAS, SPSS), we subject it to statistical analyses that compare the means of these two groups (see later discussion on ANOVA for a more sophisticated treatment of group differences). The test statistic generated from this analysis will be some number that the computer program compares to a critical value. If the test statistic falls above this critical value, our result is considered "statistically significant" at some predetermined value. In most social sciences, that value is generally .05, and the significance level is generally labeled as $p \leq .05$ where p is the likelihood we have rejected the null hypothesis when that hypothesis is actually true in the population. In other words, at a .05 level of statistical significance, there is a 5 percent chance we made a mistake in attributing length of lecture to the differences in groups (Type I Error). This also means there is a 95 percent likelihood this result is not the product of random error; the difference between the groups is likely due to some systematic variation.[3]

---

[3] If a researcher does not find a statistically significant result, this does not automatically mean there is no difference between the groups that can be attributed to systematic variation. We may not have had enough people in our sample to generate a statistically significant result of a particular magnitude. According to Cohen (1988), the social sciences are traditionally

A few questions remain after we conclude our results are statistically significant. First, statistically significant does not necessarily mean practically significant or important. In fact, as critics of NHST have pointed out, given enough people, virtually any test of significance will likely be deemed statistically significant (Meelh, 1990). Cohen, Cohen, West, and Aiken (2003, p. 5) describe this:

> Statistical significance only provides information about whether the relationship exists at all, often a question of trivial scientific interest ... The level of statistical significance reflects the sample size, incidental features of the design, the sampling of cases, and the nature of the measurement of the dependent variable; it provides only a very pale reflection of the effect size.

Thus, we need some measure of practical significance that does not depend on these other factors.

Although not consistently reported, measures of effect size (e.g., d, f) are useful in the interpretation of results. An *effect size* is the magnitude of difference between variables. In our case, while the difference between 15 and 20 might be shown to be statistically significant, we should always look at how much variability in the recall scores can be attributed to the length of lecture. Similarly, confidence intervals provide estimates of the actual value of information likely to be recalled from the population given our experimental conditions. A confidence interval is a range of possible values within which the population parameter will fall a certain percent of the time (with $p \leq .05$, the percentage would be 95). Wide confidence intervals tell us our point estimate of the population (the mean of each sample group) is poor. Narrow confidence intervals tell us our point estimate of the population is better. The better our estimate, the more confidence we can have that an effect of a particular size exists in our population of interest.

Assuming our statistical test of significance allows us to reject the null hypothesis and our results have been interpreted as meaningful in some sense (by looking at the effect size, confidence intervals, etc.), our next step will be to generalize these findings to a larger population (for example, college students). In fact, one of the distinctions between

---

under powered; this means that even if there was a significant difference in the population, our study is not likely to detect it. Issues such as the trade off between significance level and power (Type II Error) are important to consider before conducting quantitative research.

qualitative and quantitative research is the ability to generalize beyond the sample studied; however, researchers must be careful. Since our sample was derived from a specific population it might not be warranted to conclude these results are applicable to, for example, all Americans (or even all college students). For instance, our college student sample is likely to be more educated, come from a more affluent background, and be younger than the average of all individuals in this country. If, however, our results are to be of any theoretical or pragmatic import, we must extend beyond those individuals directly tested. Considerations of sample size, the nature of sampling, and theory can aid in decisions about generalization (Shadish et al., 2002).

Summary

As this brief introduction has demonstrated, researchers interested in studying the nature of an abstract concept such as listening may choose to utilize quantitative methods. Such methods rely on empirical observations, operationalizations, variables, sampling, statistical techniques, and generalization. This next section gives an overview of general quantitative methods.

Types of Quantitative Methods

As implied above, there are several types of methods captured by the umbrella term "quantitative methods." In some research, scholars are interested in the relationship or association between variables. In other research (like our example of listening comprehension as influenced by lecture length), scholars are interested in the difference between two or more groups on some outcome variable. In all research, we are interested in how well our measurement instruments have captured our concept (Have we operationalized our concept in an appropriate way?). Several statistical measures have been developed to answer different realms of research questions. Three broad types are measures of association, measures of variability, and measures of reliability and validity.

The measures of association and variability we outline below are referred to as *inferential statistics* since we are interested in inferring information about a population based on data gathered from a sample.

All inferential statistics rely on descriptive statistics that describe the nature of the data. Descriptive statistics tell us information about the average or typical scores in a dataset as well as the variability of scores within that dataset. An important step in any statistical analysis is to inspect variable distributions including values of *central tendency* and values of *dispersion*. A typical measure of central tendency is the mean or arithmetic average of all scores; other common measures are the median (middle-most score) and the mode (most frequently occurring score). Measures of dispersion include the range (difference between the biggest and smallest score in a dataset), standard deviation (how much all scores in a distribution of scores typically deviate from the mean), variance (average of the squared deviations about the mean), and average deviation (average of the absolute value of difference between each data point and the mean).

Measures of association

When a researcher is interested in the relationship or association between two variables, she will most likely run an analysis from the correlation family. The most basic correlation statistic is the Pearson product-moment correlation coefficient which provides information about the linear relationship between two variables (bivariate relationship) scaled on the interval or ratio level. The *correlation coefficient* (symbolized as "r") ranges from −1.0 to +1.0 and describes the degree to which two variables vary together. If r is positive, the value of one variable gets larger as the other gets larger. If r is negative, the value of one variable gets larger as the other gets smaller. If r is close to 0, there is no systematic relationship between the variables; a high score on one variable is just as likely to be related to high and low scores on the other variable. The closer r is to +1 or −1, the more closely the two variables are related. Thus, r gives information about the direction and strength of a bivariate relationship.

Although the correlation coefficient is a useful value, what is often more interesting is r^2 – called the coefficient of determination – which represents the percent of variation in one variable related to variation in the other. The average score of a given variable always varies since there are a range of scores that have produced this average. When the variability of two variables collectively fluctuates to some degree, squaring the correlation coefficient tells us the amount of information about one variable that is contained in the other variable. For example, if we find a Pearson's *r* of .5 between listening comprehension and GPA, squaring this value gives us .25. Therefore, 25 percent of the information contained in listening comprehension scores can be explained by GPA, and 25 percent of the information contained in GPA can be explained by listening comprehension. In other words, the variation in listening comprehension scores would decrease by 25 percent if everyone in our dataset had the same GPA (and vice versa).

According to Cohen (1988), effect sizes in the social sciences are generally classified as small, medium, and large. If a study reports an r^2 of .01, the researcher has found a small effect; a value of .06 is considered a medium effect, and a value of .14 is considered a large effect. Our value of .25 would be considered a large effect by these standards.

A direct descendent of correlation is regression; in fact, studies that report results of a regression analysis usually begin by reporting *r* values. A regression analysis attempts to predict values of the DV when given values of one or more IV. If only one IV is specified, the researcher will use bivariate regression techniques. More common is multiple regression in which a DV is predicted from values of two or more IVs. If you understand the basic premise of correlation, then understanding regression is easier.

Any given participant in a research study can be described by his or her scores on relevant DVs and IVs. These scores can be graphed with a scatterplot – a graphical representation of where each person falls with respect to all variables of interest. An example of a scatterplot is show in Figure 3.1 which portrays what a correlation of .50 between listening comprehension and GPA would look like graphically. As seen in this figure, both the magnitude and direction of the relationship between listening comprehension and GPA can be gleaned just by inspecting the distribution of scores. Although one should rely on statistics to verify a relationship exists, simply looking at this graph suggests the two variables are positively and strongly related.

In ordinary least squares (OLS) regression,[4] there are an infinite number of lines that can represent a set of data points like the one presented in Figure 3.2. The job of OLS regression is to choose the "best fit" line which

---

[4]   Other regression techniques do exist but for simplicity sake they are not discussed in this chapter. The reader is referred to Cohen, Cohen, West, and Aiken (2003) for an in-depth exploration of correlation and regression techniques for social science research.

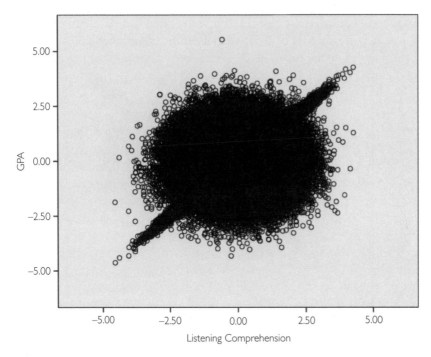

Figure 3.1   Scatterplot representing a correlation of .50 between listening comprehension and GPA

Notes: This data do not represent actual data gathered from actual college students but are simulated data based on preset values for illustrative purposes. The authors would like to thank James LeBreton of Purdue University with his assistance in accessing the SPSS syntax to generate this data.

is said to be BLUE (the best linear unbiased estimator) when certain assumptions are met (when these assumptions are not met, this type of regression analysis is not appropriate). *Best fit* refers to the line that reduces the squared residuals. A *residual* is the error that occurs due to the fact the model is predicting values of one variable based on the values of other variables; error comes from measurement error, unrepresented variance, and other sources. This best fit line is represented by:

$$\hat{Y} = b_0 + b_1 x_1 + b_2 x_2 + \dots b_n x_n$$

where $\hat{Y}$ is the predicted value of the dependent variable, b_0 is the value of Y when X = 0 (called the intercept), and $b_1 - b_n$ are values for the

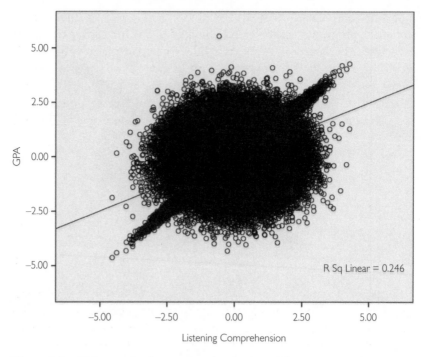

Figure 3.2 OLS regression line representing the "best fit" between listening comprehension and GPA for a correlation approximating .50
Notes: The actual correlation between these variables in this dataset is .496, $p < .001$.

respective independent variables when the other IVs are in the equation. Another way to understand $b_1 - b_n$ is that these values are the relative importance weights assigned to given IVs based on their ability to predict variability in the DV. For our two variable example, the line that best represents their relationship is presented in Figure 3.2. This line was generated by a statistical program (SPSS 16.0) that (conceptually) fits a series of lines to the data points in order to come up with the best prediction of our dependent variable of interest (listening comprehension) from the students' GPA. The program also provides values for the regression equation along with a measure of statistical significance and an R^2 value (effect size) that tells the researcher how much of the variance in the DV is accounted for by the set of IVs. Since there is only one IV in our example, R^2 is equivalent to the bivariate r^2 which, in our example, is .246, and the standardized regression coefficient is equal to the correlation coefficient.

In sum, by fitting a least squares line to a given set of data points, statistical programs estimate the value of a DV for each participant given values of one or more IVs and how well this equation does its job predicting. Also obtained from the analysis are relative importance estimates for each individual IV along with statistical significance for those values. From this information, the researcher can ascertain the specific IVs that contribute meaningfully to predicting scores on the DV and which ones are less important.

Testing differences between groups

Frequently, researchers are curious about the differences between groups of participants (as with our example of long versus short lectures and recall of information). Although these techniques are often described as exploring differences in means, they actually compare variability between and among the groups.

Suppose we wanted to know if men and women differ in their listening comprehension. The average score for men in the experiment and the average score for women in the experiment could be compared by a *t*-test. Although a thorough explanation of formulae for different types of t-tests is beyond the scope of this chapter, we should note here that variability in scores within the different groups are also taken into account for any t-test formula. If there are more than 2 groups, researchers use what is called an ANOVA.[5] ANOVA stands for analysis of variance, and the test compares the variability of a given DV between the groups versus the variability of a given DV within each group. In other words, ANOVA answers whether the groups vary more than individuals vary within the same group.

In our example, we are interested in answering whether the variability of men's scores significantly differs from the variability of women's scores. A test of statistical significance is run with the value of the *t*-test (*t*-value) or the value of the ANOVA (*F*-test). If the test statistic is greater than its critical value (determined from a table of critical values) then we conclude our result is statistically significant; we can conclude the groups differ more than they would by chance because the variability between the two groups was greater than the variability within each group (men differed from women more than individual men vary from individual men and individual women from individual women).

---

[5]   This test is called a MANOVA when dealing with more than one DV.

In other words, group scores on a DV were more discrepant than were individual scores on that DV in each group.

Assessing reliability and validity

The final issue to be addressed in this section concerns issues of reliability and validity; together these terms reference the quality of the link between a theoretical construct and its operationalization. Measures that are relatively free of random error are said to be reliable. Reliability is a necessary but not sufficient condition for score validity or the degree to which a test or instrument actually measures the construct it claims to measure. Since quantitative researchers rely on the operationalization of concepts into strictly defined variables, these issues are important. If we are not measuring what we claim to be measuring (validity), our results cannot be taken seriously. Similarly, even if our scales and surveys are accurately measuring the variables we set out to measure, if those scales and surveys are full of errors, then we cannot reliably assess our concept under question.

There are three basic methods for assessing reliability: test-retest, internal consistency, and intercoder reliability. With test-retest reliability, a researcher administers identical forms of a test across two or more time periods, usually several weeks or more apart. If the test is reliable, the scores reported at time one should be very highly correlated to later time periods. Internal consistency reliability is also concerned with self-report scales but its advantage is that a test only has to be administered once. Several types of internal consistency reliability are available including split-halves and alternate forms (see Johnson and Frandsen, 1963; Roach and Fitch-Hauser, 1984; Watson and Barker, 1988), but the most common in quantitative listening research is Cronbach's alpha – given by the symbol α. This statistic is derived from the correlations among individual items in a scale; thus, alpha typically increases as correlations among items increases.[6]

A higher order method of reliability analysis is called factor analysis. Although there are many variations of factor analysis (principle components, principle axis, exploratory, confirmatory, etc.), all of the techniques

---

[6]   Several variables affect Cronbach's alpha including the number of items in a scale. The reader is referred to Shevlin, Miles, Davies, and Salker (2000) for a good summary of how to interpret alpha coefficients.

under this label are used "when the researcher is interested in discovering which variables in the set form coherent subsets that are relatively independent of one another" (Tabachnick and Fidell, 2007, p. 607).

Suppose a researcher has a large set of items that measures several underlying aspects of listening behavior (e.g., verbal behavior, nonverbal behavior, affective components). The items designed to measure verbal components of listening should be more highly correlated with each other than they are with nonverbal components of listening. The most closely related items are said to compose *factors* "which reflect underlying processes that have created the correlations among [the items]" (Tabachnick and Fidell, 2007, p. 607). Watson, Barker, and Weaver (1995) used a form of this method to assess the factor structure of their listening instrument, the Listening Styles Profile, and Villaume and Weaver (1996) used factor analysis to assess the factor structure of two commercial tests of listening comprehension.

In addition to being a stable measure of a concept, a test also needs to be a valid measure of that construct. One type of validity is *face validity*, whether the test appears to appropriately measure the intended concept. However, this is not adequate as a full test of measurement validity. Validity can also be measured quantitatively. Two types of quantitatively determined validity are convergent and discriminant validity. *Convergent validity* measures the degree to which two or more attempts to measure the same concept are in agreement. If two listening tests are measuring the same aspect(s) of listening, scores on each should be highly related – they should have a high correlation. *Discriminant validity* is the degree to which a concept is different from other concepts – the degree to which there is a small correlation between a recently developed measure and established measures to which it should not be related. For example, if listening and reading are two distinct skills, the relationship between scores on a listening test and a reading test should be minimal.

Summary

The above discussion has been only a brief overview of quantitative methods; much more should be considered before engaging in research using these methods. This overview should, however, help the reader understand the extant research employing quantitative methodology, a review of which follows.

Quantitative Listening Research: An Overview

Listening has been identified as a hypothetical construct (Fitch-Hauser and Hughes, 1987). As such, the concept of listening is recognized as being abstract. Consequently, researchers have attempted to put boundaries around, or clarify just what the concept is and is not (Bodie, Worthington, Imhof, and Cooper, 2008). This theoretical work is important and provides the impetus for using certain methods to answer questions about the nature and correlates of listening. Unfortunately, it will not be possible to cover all of the quantitative research conducted over the past 60 or so years. The following sections will discuss only a small sample of that research.

Listening: The early years

Quantitative researchers generally trace the origins of listening research to the late 1940s and the work of Ralph Nichols whose main research interest was how students retain information in the classroom. Using factor analysis, Nichols (1948) made an early attempt to identify listening as a distinct concept by identifying "factors influencing classroom listening comprehension" (p. 161). College students in this study were asked to listen to a lecture then answer a series of multiple choice questions about its content. The multiple choice questions served as the measure of listening, defined as the ability to attend to information presented aurally. This groundbreaking research opened the door to further research by providing some specific measures of listening as well as identifying related constructs. One particularly influential study is represented by Spearritt's dissertation and subsequent monograph (1962) which showed listening emerged as a separate factor when a battery of tests (reading span, intelligence, general mental ability, etc.) was administered to a group of undergraduate students.

Of course, not all researchers were convinced that listening was a distinct ability. Kelly (1965) operationalized listening as an individual's score on two related tests of listening comprehension. His study found these measures of listening were strongly correlated to a test of general mental ability but only weakly correlated to each other. From these results he concluded listening comprehension was not a unique component of listening; instead, he concluded listening comprehension was more related to memory. This type of controversy led scholars such as Kittie Watson, Larry Barker, and Robert Bostrom in the 1970s and 1980s to attempt the development of more reliable and valid measures of listening comprehension. These researchers assumed listening is a set of skills related to, but distinct from, other abilities; the problem thus far was an inability to find a reliable and valid way to measure it.

The measurement of listening comprehension

The research conducted during the 1970s and 1980s conceptualized listening as a complex, multidimensional process. Although this was a shift from the unitary skill perspective, the research still equated listening with listening comprehension or a unique language comprehension skill that refers to the "active process of constructing meaning ... by applying knowledge to ... incoming sound" (Buck, 2001). In other words, listening was operationalized as a complex but interrelated set of abilities to attend to orally-presented information.

Quantitative researchers have put forth considerable effort developing a variety of listening tests. Four of the most popular are (1) the Brown-Carlsen Listening Comprehension Test (Brown and Carlsen, 1955), (2) the Sequential Tests of Educational Progress III Listening Test (STEP III) (Educational Testing Service, 1979), (3) the Kentucky Comprehensive Listening Test (Bostrom and Waldhart, 1980b, 1983), and (4) the Watson-Barker Listening Test (Watson and Barker, 1983, 1988, 2001).

Brown-Carlsen and STEP III

The Brown-Carlsen Listening Comprehension Test (Brown and Carlsen, 1955) was the first mass produced test of listening and claims to examine five components of listening comprehension: immediate recall; following directions; recognizing transitions; recognizing word meaning; and lecture comprehension. The STEP III (Educational Testing Service, 1979) is a general test of learning ability and recall. It includes a listening portion that attempts to test a single listening comprehension component.

Although popular, there are measurement concerns related with both the Brown-Carlesen and STEP tests. For example, correlations computed between the tests as well as with general tests of mental and reading ability found, "they are no more similar to each other than either is to a test of mental ability or to a test of reading ability" (Kelly, 1965, p. 142). A factor analytic study conducted by Fitch-Hauser and Hughes (1987) also disputed the validity of each test concluding, "[no] systematic pattern of loadings appeared in any of the factor analyses that corresponded to the pattern that the test authors had suggested" (p. 143). More recent measures have tried to rectify these deficiencies.

KCLT and WBLT

The Kentucky Comprehensive Listening Test (KCLT; Bostrom and Waldhart, 1980b, 1983) and the Watson-Barker Listening Test (WBLT; Watson and Barker, 1983, 1988, 2001) were both designed to measure listening comprehension across five dimensions. The KCLT was structured to test (1) short-term listening, (2) listening with rehearsal, (3) interpretive listening, (4) lecture listening, and (5) overcoming distractions (Bostrom, and Waldhart, 1983). The WBLT was structured to test: (1) evaluating message content; (2) understanding meaning in conversations; (3) understanding and remembering information in lectures; (4) evaluating emotional meanings in messages; and (5) following instructions and directions (Watson and Barker, 1988). Both measurement instruments have reported acceptable reliability (Bostrom, 1984; Roberts, 1986) and internal validity (Bostrom, 1990; Roberts, 1988). Additionally, Applegate and Campbell (1985) found correlations between scores on each test; however, the results indicated neither test "is exhaustive [nor] all-encompassing" (p. 9). Perhaps the most comprehensive projects addressing the reliability and validity of these two tests involved executing factor analysis to statistically determine the factorial validity of the two listening tests.

Fitch-Hauser and Hughes (1987) sought to address the reliability and validity of these two tests by comparing each test to a factor structure designed around the components each test reported to measure. Unfortunately, neither test adhered to this structure; thus the external validity of the tests was reported as questionable. The authors concluded the tests are either "testing something in addition to listening [or] the tests are tapping more listening constructs than they claim" (p. 146). Extending these findings, Villaume and Weaver (1996) conducted first and second order factor analyses on both the KCLT and the WBLT. Each of the tests ultimately indicated a lack of external validity, which mirrored prior concerns (see Roberts, 1988). However, as Villaume and Weaver suggest, perhaps by administering both tests or constructing a test that combines the best elements of the KCLT and the WBLT a better test of listening comprehension can be developed. This work has yet to be done.

Although the majority of research using the KCLT and WBLT has been devoted to reliability and validity issues, there are several studies that attempt to determine characteristics of good and poor listeners as defined by scores on these tests. For instance, Bommelje, Houston, and Smither (2003) researched the relationship between personality and listening in an attempt to identify the personality characteristics of good listeners, defined as individuals with high scores on the WBLT. Using scores on the WBLT and the Hogan Personality Inventory (HPI), the researchers found weak, but statistically significant relationships between listening and two personality dimensions identified by the HPI, success in school and caring. In an attempt to clarify the relationship, the researchers employed OLS regression using the HPI elements as IVs, and the WBLT total score as the DV. The results yielded a small, but statistically significant relationship between listening comprehension and the HPI element of "caring." This result linking personality and listening opens the door for further research in this area.

The main importance of this and other, similar studies (e.g., Bostrom, 1990) involving personality and listening is the support they give to Worthington's (2003) conclusion that "the listening process does not occur in a vacuum" (p. 81). Several studies show pre-existing conditions within the listener have an impact on listening behavior and comprehension (see, Bodie et al., 2008; Imhoff, this volume). Consequently, if a measure of listening identifies the relationship between listening and those pre-existing conditions, the listening test has a degree of validity.

Other scholars question the validity of listening tests because they are "measures of the acquisition of information" (Bostrom, 1990, p. 24). Although "[retention] of information is a reasonable goal of listeners" (Rasmuson, 1987, p. 114), the measurement of this goal falls short of tapping into the cognitive realm of the listening process. Attempts to remedy this problem have come from the research of Powers and colleagues into the concept of *listening fidelity*.

Listening fidelity (LF) refers to "the degree of congruence between the cognitions of a listener and the cognitions of a source following a communication event" (Mulanax and Powers, 2001, p. 70). Rather than having participants recall specific aspects of a verbal message, LF measures listening comprehension as one's ability to draw a geometrical figure explained by a confederate. The accuracy with which participants replicate the figure gives a measure of the degree to which the participant was able to understand the confederate at a fundamental level; since the same explanation is shown to all participants, the influence of basic communication fidelity (see Powers and Lowry, 1984) is controlled. As argued by Powers and Bodie (2003), "[this] approach to the measurement of listening skill is as fundamental to the listening process as a measure of hearing and the necessary starting point in establishing a theoretically sound measure of competence in listening" (p. 24). Mulanax and Powers (2001) claim concurrent validity of the measure based on its correlation with receiver apprehension (see below for an explanation of receiver apprehension), and Fitch-Hauswer, Powers, O'Brien, and Hanson (2007) provide evidence that LF is a measure of fidelity by reporting (a) LF scores vary as a function of potential fidelity of a message as well as (b) significant correlations between the measure of LF and scores on the WBLT.

Where this test can be most readily criticized is in its ecological validity: does it measure some aspect of listening that can be translated into practical advice for the listener? Perhaps studies that attempt to replicate results found with basic communication fidelity (Powers and Lowry, 1984) where individuals have a goal and attempt to communicate this goal to a confederate (Powers and Spitzberg, 1986) will show some level of correspondence and increase our confidence in LF results.

Another line of research that seems promising has been recently advanced by Janusik (2005, 2007). Janusik has proposed a model of listening grounded in the work of Baddeley (1986) on working memory. In testing her model, she has explored the relationship between a measure of conversational listening span and three other span measures based in working memory. By identifying a significant relationship between her measure of conversational listening and other cognitively-based measures, she was able to support the perspective that listening is a cognitive process; this validates the supposition that her measure taps some concept called listening. The most important extension this research provides is that the measure assesses listening within the context of conversation; from a communication perspective this is the core feature of listening (Bodie, 2009b). This is important because it moves the study of listening comprehension beyond "the correct/incorrect measure used by traditional listening tests" (Janusik, 2007, p. 149) which may measure memory as opposed to listening per se.

The above is far from a comprehensive review of listening assessment tests. Researchers in education, second language learning, linguistics, psychology, and discourse studies, just to name a few, all have much to say about listening comprehension. Given the multi-disciplinary nature of listening, it is no surprise that tests tend to measure listening in slightly nuanced ways leading one to question the ability to ever capture the true and complete essence of listening (see Buck, 2001, Chapter 4, for a similar argument). Most test designers would agree, however, that a set of skills comprising "listening" exists. Indeed, authors of listening comprehension tests set out with a particular framework that offers a theoretical conceptualization of the skills comprising listening. The constructs deemed central to listening within this framework are then operationalized by creating test items that seem to provide some level of face validity. Researchers then seek to demonstrate reliability of different test sections and validity of the test as a whole. Researchers and others interested in listening must keep in mind there are dozens of tests of listening comprehension available for individuals of different ages and abilities. The reader is referred to Buck (2001) for a review of these tests and a more thorough treatment of his systematic approach to developing listening tests. Moreover, working with listening assessment is only one way researchers have used quantitative methods.

Listening as more than mere comprehension

Janusik's recent work attempts to shift the study of listening from measuring "mere recall" to measuring listening as a process. Her research builds on past efforts to demonstrate listening is either related or similar to elements of memory but still a distinct and separate skill. Early attempts by Bostrom and Bryant (1980) and Bostrom and Waldhart (1980a) compared listening with memory and found listening and memory comprised different constructs. Specifically, they found short-term memory and short-term listening were different. In this research, the authors (see also Bostrom, 1996) posit, like memory, listening includes short-term and long-term components. The research supported this hypothesis by showing evidence for three types of listening based upon specific listening tasks. These three types of listening were short-term, short term with rehearsal, and long-term. Their research also supports the conclusion that the three types of listening are independent of each other. That is, being an effective "short-term listener" did not correlate with being an effective "long-term listener."

Other research has found correlations between listening and reading (Caffrey, 1953), listening and receiver apprehension (Fitch-Hauser, Barker, and Hughes, 1990; Roberts, 1988), and listening and cognitive complexity (Beatty and Payne, 1984). All of these studies suggest listening is more than the recall of orally-presented information. This same line of thinking led Thomas and Levine (1994) to test three models of listening, all of which included verbal recall, listening, and listening behaviors. The model that best fit the data posited "verbal recall ability was antecedent to listening, and listening was antecedent to gaze, nods, and [short back channel responses]" (p. 119). Although this study sparked a short but heated debate (Bostrom, 1996; Thomas and Levine, 1996), further research to extend these findings is lacking. Similarly, a model forwarded by Goss (1982) has yet to be fully tested or expanded since its introduction.

Although less common than correlational studies, some have used experimental methods to study listening. For example, Fitch-Hauser (1984) focused on the role of inference-making in story recall. Her study provides evidence that existing mental constructs or schema aid listeners in making sense of their social world. As stated by Fitch-Hauser (1990), listeners "use some type of plan or blueprint to interpret, store, and recall information" (p. 77). This conclusion was based on manipulating the content of messages (the IV) and testing what participants "remembered" hearing (the DV). Interestingly, subjects "remembered" things not present in the stimulus stories. In other words, they inferred information so the reconstructed story fit their schema.

In sum, as the research discussed in this section suggests, listening is more than just the comprehension of a message. In order to truly understand listening as a process, we must also understand how listening and aspects of information processing – like memory – work together to allow a listener to receive a message, interpret it, process and store it, and ultimately recall a message that in someway resembles the original message (see Imhof, this volume).

Variables that impact and are impacted by listening

Other conceptualizations of listening propose that certain listening traits influence information acquisition (listening comprehension) and motivate individuals to listen (or not to listen) (Roberts, 1988). Studies conceptualizing listening in this manner either treat listening as an IV or a DV, whereas research on listening comprehension focuses solely on listening as a DV. In other words, listening preferences or beliefs can influence comprehension or other communication-related phenomena. Likewise, listening comprehension might influence motivation to listen. Research of this type attempts to answer questions such as, how individuals come to have certain listening preferences and how listening preferences are related to other individual differences. In addition, this research focuses on how these variables are likely to influence listening comprehension.

Several personality-type measures have been developed by quantitative scholars attempting to understand listening. These measures are usually developed as self-report instruments and administered with other tests in order to establish concurrent and discriminant validity. Several concepts and their associated measures will be reviewed below, namely listening styles, willingness to listen, receiver apprehension, and interaction involvement.

Listening styles, preferences, and conceptualizations

Based on Shiffrin and Schneider's (1977) claim that people tend to listen in a habitual manner, Langer (1980) proposed that individual's may be prone to utilize one particular listening style regardless of the situation. This theoretical work led Watson, Barker, and Weaver (1995) to develop the Listening Styles Profile (LSP-16), a sixteen-item self-report scale that allows respondents to characterize their preferences, concerns and emphases while listening to other people. In an exploratory factor analysis of several items, Watson, Barker and Weaver (1995) reported a four-factor solution identifying four sets of listening concerns oriented about people, action, content, and time; each scale contains four items.

People-oriented listeners usually try to find common ground among interlocutors and remain nonjudgmental. These individuals can be characterized as caring, understanding, and concerned about the "emotional states" of others (Watson, Barker and Weaver, 1995, p. 5). Typically labeled relationally-oriented, people-oriented listeners are often sought for their emotional support skills.

Content-oriented listeners often listen for complex information, and thoroughly evaluate the content of a message before drawing conclusions. This style is characterized by a preference to listen to highly credible sources and the tendency to ask questions to gain more information. Likewise, content-oriented listeners are generally unbiased because of their willingness to listen to both sides of an argument (Barker and Watson, 2000).

Action-oriented listeners have a preference for focused and organized information. This type of listener is bothered by disorganization and can come across as overtly critical. Individuals utilizing this style are often labeled task-oriented, and are often contrasted with people-oriented listeners (Barker and Watson, 2000).

Time-oriented listeners tend to verbalize the limited amount of time they are wiling or able to devote to listening. Individuals operating under this style, more than the other three styles, are more likely to interrupt others and signal disinterest via nonverbal cues such as looking at clocks or watches (Barker and Watson, 2000).

Research conducted with the LSP-16 has shown preference for a particular listening style or a set of styles is correlated with other individual difference variables including sex, gender, personality, and communication-related traits. Luttrell (1992) reported that men show a preference for action-oriented listening, while females show a preference for the people-oriented style. As we discussed above, however, statistical significance should not be the only criterion for judging difference. In Lutrell's study, sex explained less than 1 percent of the variance in reports of the action-oriented style. With the people-oriented style, sex explained roughly 10 percent of the variability in scores. This sex main effect was also qualified by a significant interaction between biological sex and psychological gender. In the case of people-oriented listeners, sex-typed males reported the lowest while sex-typed and aschematic (showing both agentic and communal orientations) females reported the highest levels of this preference. Moreover, inspection of means suggest that cross-sex-typed males and females report quite similar levels of this listening preference. In fact, Lutrell's results suggest that sex-typing might be driving most of the differences between the sexes in terms of listening styles. Johnston, Weaver, Watson, and Barker (2000) provide evidence for this gender-based explanation; they report individuals possessing a communal orientation (more traditionally characterized as feminine) prefer a person-centered listening style, while individuals embracing an agentic orientation (more traditionally characterized as masculine) prefer a more task-oriented listening style (a combination of action- and content-orientations).

Another focus of listening styles research attempts to discover personality traits that might underlie these preferences. Utilizing Eysenck's framework, Weaver, Watson, and Barker (1996) found extroverts preferred a people-centered style, neurotics were more prone to be concerned with time constraints when listening, and psychotics embraced a socially callous listening style. Working from the Five Factor model, Worthington (2003) hypothesized relationships between personality elements identified by the Keirsey Temperament Sorter (KTS) and listening styles. To test her hypotheses, Worthington ran correlations between the four listening styles identified by the LSP-16 (people, action, content, time) and the four personality types identified by the KTS (extraversion/introversion, sensor/intuitor, thinker/feeler, judger/perceiver). The data analysis supported three of the four hypothesized relationships by producing statistically significant correlations between three listening styles and personality types. Specifically, significant, but weak, correlations were reported between a people LS and extraversion, intuiting, and feeling. Content LS correlated with judging and thinking. Action LS was weakly, but significantly correlated with sensing, thinking, and judging. Finally, although the fourth hypothesis was not supported, the results indicated a relationship between Time LS and introversion, thinking, and sensing.

Having found support for the hypothesized relationships between LS and personality, Worthington wanted to understand the relationship more clearly, so she submitted the data to a canonical correlation analysis.[7] This analysis revealed that the vast majority (79 percent of the variance) of the systematic relationship between the four listening styles and four personality categories can be explained by the interaction of people LS and the personality categories. This result seems to indicate personality characteristics associated with the People LS have a tremendous impact on how people listen. In turn, when combined with the findings of the gender-based research discussed above that shows People LS and communal gender orientation are correlated, the findings may imply listening is strongly influenced by a combination of personality and gender schematicity. Clearly, there is still much for us to learn about listening through this type of research.

---

[7] Canonical correlation is a multivariate technique that assesses the degree of association between two sets of variables. This is an extension of the bivariate case discussed above. See Tabachnick and Fidell (2007) for a general overview.

Another important line of research using the LSP-16 has been spearheaded by Bodie and Villaume (2003; Villaume and Bodie, 2007), and questions the scoring procedures of the scale. Traditionally, respondents who score in the upper tertile for one of these four orientations are identified as having the corresponding characteristic listening style. Many individuals cannot be characterized as having one listening style because they score highly on more than one listening orientation (Watson, Barker, and Weaver, 1995). Taking this knowledge under consideration, Bodie and Villaume (2003) proposed an alternative scoring method for the LSP whereby participants' scores on the listening orientations were treated as continuous variables (interval level scaling). Utilizing the multivariate technique known as canonical correlation (the same method used by Worthington, 2003), the authors found three patterns of association between the set of four listening style orientations measured by the LSP and a set of communicator style and apprehension variables.

First, people-centered listening is manifested in a relationally-oriented speaking style characterized by a low level of dyadic communication apprehension. Second, the combination of high content- and action-orientations is associated with an attentive, precise style of arguing the issues that tends to leave an impression on people. Finally, the combination of high action- and time-orientations (and to a lesser extent people-orientation) with low content-orientation is associated with higher apprehension toward receiving information, lower dyadic communication apprehension, and a dramatic, animated and forceful style that dominantly asserts one's goals/concerns.

Since this was the first use of this technique with the LSP-16, a second study was conducted that included several other individual difference variables (e.g., Eysenck's BIG THREE, interaction involvement, interpersonal communication motives, gender role) to test the robustness of these findings (Villaume and Bodie, 2007). Results indicated a similar pattern of listening styles is found regardless of the variables under question adding validity to the newly formed scoring method for the LSP. Of course, the method employed by Bodie and Villaume does not remedy the issue of low internal consistency estimates for each LSP subscale (Bodie and Worthington, in press). Ongoing research is seeking to remedy this issue by proposing a new version of the LSP-16 that will consistently produce reliability estimates more indicative of a "good" scale (Nunnally, 1978).

The only other scale that attempts to measure listening styles was published in 2003 by Pearce, Johnson, and Barker. This scale has respondents rate the extent to which they engage in certain listening behaviors or preferences (e.g., I ask questions when I don't fully understand a speaker's message; I want to listen to what others have to say when they are talking). Scores are tallied on these items and respondents are placed into one of three listening styles: active; involved; or passive. The 2003 study reports efforts to establish reliability by using factor analysis and test-retest methods. However, the report of convergent validity only references qualitative means. As previously mentioned, qualitative methods do not provide a true test of convergent validity, thus opening this scale up for future validation research.

Although not called a measure of listening style, a recent study conducted by Imhof and Janusik (2006), reports a measure of listening concepts. This measure has individuals report the extent to which they believe 65 activities associated with listening (e.g., hearing, observing, evaluating) are similar to what they think of as "listening." The authors' claim this measure can be used to test different models of the listening process to determine the extent to which, for instance, listening concepts determine listening behavior. In other words, how individuals conceptualize listening is likely to influence how they go about processing information in different situations. Their 2006 study reports the first use of the scale as well as preliminary evidence of its factor structure. Future research should confirm this structure and provide further evidence of its validity.

Willingness to listen

Willingness to listen was originally conceptualized as the "other half" of the willingness to communicate (WTC) construct developed by McCroskey and his colleagues. Since the WTC scale (McCroskey, 1992; McCroskey and Richmond, 1987) was solely focused on an individual's propensity to speak in certain situations, Roberts and Vinson (1989) sought to develop a similar scale that assessed an individual's motivation to listen. The original scale was modified (Roberts and Vinson, 1998) and preliminary evidence gathered of its reliability and validity. Unfortunately, there has been no published research on this scale in nearly 10 years, although Richmond and Hickson (2001) claim a modified version of this scale is reliable and valid for use in the public speaking classroom.

Receiver apprehension

Receiver apprehension refers to a fear of inadequately processing or psychologically adjusting to spoken discourse (Wheeless, 1975). Two measures have been created to test receiver apprehension. The first (RAT; Wheeless, 1975) includes 20-self report items referencing how the individual generally feels while listening rated on 5-point scales. Beatty, Behnke, and Henderson (1980) provided preliminary evidence that this 20-item scale achieved adequate internal consistency and test-retest reliability as well as correlated significantly with an established measure of anxiety, which lends credence to its concurrent validity. A revised 16-item version (RRAT; Wheeless and Scott, 1976) includes fewer items in each of the three conceptual categories proposed by its definition: situations where messages are encountered; generalized affective responses to categories of messages; and cognitive reactions to message-processing tasks.

A meta-analysis conducted in 1990 by Preiss, Wheeless, and Allen organized 28 manuscripts into five categories.[8] Based on this analysis, the authors found receiver apprehension to be negatively related to listening comprehension, information processing capacity, information processing effectiveness, and education level and positively related to information processing anxiety. Although these relationships make conceptual sense, this study is over 15 years old and some of the operationalizations of the DVs seem speculative; more importantly, all of the data is self report which introduces a method bias to the results. Thus, future research in this area is certainly warranted.

Interaction involvement

The last concept, interaction involvement (II), is defined as "the extent to which an individual participates with another in conversation" (Cegala, Savage, Brunner, and Conrad, 1982, p. 230). Involvement in

---

[8]   Lipsey and Wilson (2001) explain that "meta-analysis can be understood as a form of survey research in which research reports, rather than people, are surveyed" (p. 1). The techniques involved allow the researcher to make generalizable claims across a greater number of individuals and explore potential moderators for the effects between variables. Readers are referred to Hunter and Schmidt (2004) for a thorough treatment of meta-analysis.

conversation has been shown to predict others' perceptions of a speaker's communication effectiveness (Downs, 1985); this makes sense given that individuals low on II are less attentive to others and less able to determine effective conversational strategies (Cegala, 1981, 1984).

The scale that measures this construct, the Interaction Involvement Scale (IIS), assesses three II components. *Responsiveness* is the tendency for an individual to respond appropriately during conversations. *Perceptiveness* is one's ability to "read" or assign meaning to other's behavior. Finally, *attentiveness* refers to the aspect of II most closely related to listening; this is validated by an inspection of the items that measure this factor (e.g., "My mind wanders during conversations and I often miss parts of what is going on"; "I listen carefully to others during a conversation"). In the third study in the Cegala et al. (1982) report, the authors attempt to correlate the three aspects of II with nonverbal indicants of listening (e.g., eye gaze, body focused gesturing) while individuals were not engaged in a speaking turn. These results did not reach conventional levels of significance for any of the listening variables. Two later studies (Villaume and Cegala, 1988; Villaume, Jackson, and Goldsmith Schouten, 1989) have, however, found that low involved conversation partners have more difficulty responding to ongoing conversation, an indication of a lack of skill or motivation to listen.

Summary

This section has summarized the relevant research on four individual differences proposed in the quantitative listening research: listening preference; willingness to listen; receiver apprehension; and interaction involvement. This research has individuals self-report about their listening behaviors, preferences, motivations, and/or abilities and looks at relationships between these preferences and other variables (which are usually also self-reported). Such research helps us more clearly understand listening as a complex process. By conducting quantitative research of this type, we expand our theoretical base by furthering the boundaries of understanding the dimensions of listening. Another aspect of expanding theory is examining the effect of a construct in specific situations.

Applied Research in Listening

The research discussed so far has looked very generally at listening. Many researchers have chosen to look not at listening as the unit of study, but the use and impact of listening in specific areas. The final area of quantitative research we will discuss looks at how the skill of listening affects outcomes in several applied areas of practice.

Health and healthcare

One applied area that has received attention is medicine. An early study in this area looked at the listening habits of first year medical students. Watson, Lazarus, and Thomas (1999) administered the Listening Preference Profile[9] to students in a *Foundations of Medicine* class. The researchers were interested in whether listening preference would change as the students went through the class. The study results indicated a large number of medical students experienced a change in their listening preference during the first year of medical school. Specifically, they found subjects who tested as people-oriented listeners at the beginning of the semester reported listening avoidance or no listening preference by the end of the semester. No significant change occurred in the other categories. These results indicate that something about the setting, whether it is listening burnout from listening to lectures or a shift from an empathic to a diagnostic orientation, has an impact on listening behavior. The authors propose the results of this study be used to help train medical students in the communication skills necessary for the successful practice of medicine. However, before this can happen, further research needs to identify what elements contribute to the change in listening preferences. Moreover, specific skills needed to effectively listen in the medical field must also be uncovered and placed within a coherent theoretical framework.

Several lines of research that might aid such efforts have explored the impact of physician–patient communication (of which listening is included) on outcomes such as emotional health, symptom resolution,

[9]   The Listening Preference Profile and the Listening Styles Profiles are similar instruments. The test authors chose to use preferences rather than styles for their "business" version of the scale which includes one more item per factor than the "research" version of the scale. The reader is referred to Barker and Watson (2000) for this scale.

physiological measures, pain control, and medication compliance. One meta-analysis reported effective physician communication was positively correlated with beneficial health outcomes (Stewart, 1995). Although listening was not isolated in these studies, given the importance of listening to effective communication, it follows that this skill likely has a unique impact on health.

Consistent with this line of reasoning, research by Cegala and his colleagues suggests listening is important in the medical interview. The category of talk labeled "information verifying" includes "fidelity-enhancing utterances" (Cegala, 1997, p. 186) and is most closely related to what literature typically defines as an effective listening strategy, namely providing feedback that one has understood another. One additional and particularly relevant aspect of the physician's ability to listen reflects the notion that listening involves "filling in gaps" provided by the use of indirect communication strategies of patients (Cegala, McNeilis, and McGee, 1995; see also Fitch-Hauser, 1984). Of course, the patient's relative listening abilities are also important, which has been recognized in recent research as well (e.g., Post, Cegala, and Miser, 2002).

Other research in this area points out the economic as well as the health benefits of listening in the medical context. For example, Lee (2000) found physicians fail to identify the patient's reason for visiting in 77 percent of medical interviews primarily because physicians interrupt 69 percent of patients within 18 seconds of the patient beginning to speak. It is no wonder many patients report their doctors lack concern and empathy (Korsch, Gozzi, and Francis, 1968; Lane, 1983; Schulman, 1978; Zimmerman and Arnold, 1990)! As one would expect, patients with health care practitioners who use more patient-centered communication, including listening, are more satisfied with their practitioners and their overall medical care (Wanzer, Booth-Butterfield, and Gruber, 2004). In fact, Wanzer et al. (2004) report effective listening, including showing empathy, is a predictor of patient satisfaction. Consequently, these patients are less likely to sue their physicians. Research in 1992 revealed two-thirds of malpractice cases were linked to communication problems (Hickson et al., 1992).

These findings have led some researchers to wonder why the medical community has failed to focus more on listening training, particularly in light of research that reveals listening contributes to the quality of health care without putting additional time pressure on the physician. Hausman (2001) found when both the physician and patient engaged in active listening the patient's compliance increased. This finding is even more important in light of research that indicates cancer patients are more satisfied with their oncologists when those physicians engage in shared decision-making strategies that include active listening (Brown et al., 2002). The type of patient – physician interaction described in these findings is called biopsychosocial. This type of approach includes expressing empathy, involving patients in decision-making, asking open-ended questions, and listening attentively. Research has shown physicians who use a biopsychosocial approach with patients take no more time per average office visit and have the added bonus of a more satisfied patient who is more willing to follow prescribed treatment (duPre, 2000).[10]

Listening and social support

Similar to the importance of listening to satisfaction in the healthcare setting, the perception that support is available and the reception of quality support when facing everyday hassles and major life stressors have both been linked to numerous beneficial outcomes including overall health and well-being (e.g., Burleson and MacGeorge, 2002; Dunkel-Schetter, Blasband, Feinstein, and Herbert, 1992; Herzberg, Hammen, Burge, Daley, Davila and Lindberg, 1999; Lakey and Lutz, 1996; Wethington and Kessler, 1986). Theorists within and beyond the communication discipline have developed sophisticated models of supportive people, supportive messages, and supportive interactions in order to map the causal mechanisms earlier work had implied by this link. Unfortunately, our scholarship is fragmented, at best, with respect to the role of listening in supportive interactions (Bodie, 2009a).

One important line of research has been conducted by Burleson and his colleagues for over 30 years (see Burleson, 2003 for a review). Stemming from constructivism – a general theory of communication skill (Burleson and Bodie, 2008) – research on supportive communication has consistently shown that messages high in person centeredness, the explicit recognition and legitimization of thoughts and feelings about a stressor, are functionally more sophisticated than messages low

---

[10]   We would like to acknowledge the help of Chris Bond with locating the research associated with this section.

in this quality (that is, messages that implicitly or explicitly deny and delegitimize the other person's thoughts and feelings or tell them how he or she *should* feel).

Unfortunately, even when experiencing major life difficulties, individuals often receive unhelpful or even harmful support. For example, Dunkel-Schetter and Wortman (1982) report potential support providers believe cancer "patients should avoid thinking or talking about negative aspects of their situation and try to be as cheerful and optimistic as possible" (p. 82). Dakof and Taylor (1990) found, in general, victims of major life stressors having been exposed to (a) inappropriate responses (e.g., minimization, criticizing), (b) individuals who fail to express concern, empathy or affection, and (c) avoidance from one or more network members including medical professionals. Similarly, Perrine (1993) reports potential support providers have a greater tendency to want to solve problems than to engage in supportive listening behaviors (the adage, think before you speak comes to mind here). In other words, informal help providers may avoid listening to the distressed other due to burnout or anxiety; this may lead the distressed other to feel worse rather than better.

In research with the bereaved, Lehman, Ellard, and Wortman (1986) found the two most "helpful" listening behaviors are (1) providing the opportunity to ventilate, and (2) presence ("being there"). These same behaviors are likely to be perceived as helpful in other supportive contexts. Generally, supporters who are effective listeners provide more direct eye contact, are receptive to disclosures, and ask more follow-up questions (Miller, Berg, and Archer, 1983). Does the reception of unhelpful support or the reception of helpful support, however, result from "good" or "bad" listening in supportive interactions? Unfortunately, there is no direct empirical evidence of this claim, certainly an area for future research.

Evidence can be found, however, in research conducted by Suzanne Jones and her colleagues (Jones, 2004; Jones and Guerrero, 2001; Jones and Wirtz, 2006). This research shows creating a warm support environment through the use of nonverbal behaviors such as close proximity, forward lean, facial expressiveness, and gaze (that ios, nonverbal immediacy; Andersen, 1985) is considered, in addition to high person-centered messages, by support recipients as high quality emotional support. Thus, both verbal and nonverbal elements of a support provider's emotional support attempts are likely to impact the feelings, coping behavior, personal relationships, and even physical health of the recipient

(Albrecht and Goldsmith, 2003; Cohen and Wills, 1985; Goldsmith, 2004; Uchino, 2004). The specific impact of listening, in all its manifestations, is indeed open for theoretical speculation and empirical scrutiny.

An additional line of research relevant to listening and social support is outlined by Bodie and Burleson (2008). Their dual-process theory of supportive message outcomes proposes the variables found to moderate effects of support messages (e.g., sex of provider, need for support) do so either by influencing the message recipient's ability and/or motivation to systematically process these messages or by serving as environmental cues that quickly trigger responses to the message. In other words, it is how a supportive message is processed that determines its outcomes. By borrowing a general model of message reception from the persuasion literature, Bodie and Burleson have provided listening scholars with a way to understand how message processing plays out in the realm of social support. Future research using this model is likely to also shed light into message reception more generally (see also Bodie, 2009a).

Juror decision making

Another example of applied research can be found in Worthington's (2001) work on juror listening preference and the assignment of negligence and the size of damages awarded. In this research, Worthington used listening preference as the IV to address the question of whether listening preference has any relationship with juror decisions. High people preference had a significant impact on the perceived level of negligence and time preference had a significant impact on the amount of damages awarded. This study adds to our knowledge about the impact of listening preference but the results can also be used by trial attorneys when evaluating potential jurors.

Listening and salesperson performance

The final area of applied research we will explore happens in the context of salesperson performance which is generally couched within a larger literature on adaptive selling behavior. *Adaptive selling* is the process whereby a salesperson adjusts his or her selling techniques, strategies, and communication based on feedback garnered from interpersonal listening or "the cognitive process of actively sensing, interpreting, evaluating, and responding to the verbal and nonverbal messages of present or potential customers" (Castleberry and Shepherd, 1993, p. 36). Adaptive selling behavior is typically measured by the ADAPTS scale developed by Spiro and Weitz (1990) and interpersonal listening is typically measured by the Interpersonal Listening in Personal Selling (ILPS) scale (Castleberry, Shepherd, and Ridnour, 1999). The ILPS has achieved evidence of reliability and validity in a number of studies and high levels of interpersonal listening are positively correlated with job satisfaction, sales performance, adaptability, and age.

Similarly, Drollinger, Comer, and Warrington (2006) have developed the Active Empathetic Listening Scale (AEL). Based on Rogerian psychology and listening models that include empathy as a component of motivation to listen, the AEL measures three components of listening: sensing; processing; and responding. In three studies, Drollinger and colleagues determined the factor structure using confirmatory methods and convergent validity by correlating AEL subscales with measures of perspective taking, empathetic concern, and a measure of active listening; nomological validity was fostered by correlating scale items with theoretically meaningful concepts, namely: trust; relationship skills; and selling performance effectiveness. These finding mirror the work of Castleberry and colleagues and, thus, studies testing the concurrent validity of these scales to each other are warranted. Both lines of research show the importance of listening, conceptualized as an ability to understand, empathize with and adapt to clients, in a sales environment. This work is promising both theoretically and practically and should thrive in the near future.

Summary

As this section has shown, quantitative research can be used to identify how a theoretical concept is used in a concrete world. This type of research helps us test a form of face validity of a concept. By seeing how the concept works in the "real world" we can support our argument that a hypothetical construct truly does have impact and relevance to everyday life.

Listening Research and the Future

This chapter has provided only a glimpse of quantitative methods in listening research. In the six decades that scholars have studied this critical communication competency, we have raised more questions than we have answered. Consequently, this area should provide many questions and hypotheses for future researchers (great news for undergraduate and graduate students looking for research paper, thesis, and dissertation topics!). For example, as briefly mentioned above, research into the antecedents of listening such as verbal recall or accuracy in listening is one fruitful area for future scholars to engage. Drawing from suggestions offered in the past (Bodie, Janusik, and Välikoski, 2008) and inserting our own opinions about the future of listening research, the following sections suggest areas ripe for new thinking, methods, and theory.

Discovering the relationship between listening and other constructs

Researchers have only begun to look at the relationship between listening and other variables. For example, just three published papers (Bommelje, Houston and Smither 2003; Villaume and Bodie, 2007; Worthington, 2003) examine the relationship between listening and personality. To date, no one has explored how personality and listening style contribute to the development of one's general communication behavior. This communication behavior may include such constructs as verbal aggressiveness, willingness to listen, or apprehension. Villaume and Bodie (2007) come the closest to this goal; however their research is correlational in nature and does not address issues of causation. If listening is a critical component of communication, we must explore how the myriad of constructs that influence communication impact listening. In addition, we need to further define the role and function of listening in the communication process.

At an even more general level, it is important to continually theorize and develop ways to test how listening is different from other means of information processing. Although much of the early work was concerned with listening and reading comprehension, how listening is manifest in, as well as can be distinguished from, discourse processing, sentence comprehension, and other, related constructs is an important endeavor. This type of theoretical work should reach beyond discipline specific efforts and has wide appeal throughout the academy (e.g., Bodie et al., 2008).

Developing and testing listening theory

Similar to this last call, a critical need for future research is to focus more specifically on developing and testing listening theory. Theory is important to any type of research because it provides us with explanations of the phenomenon as well as boundaries or guidelines for what the phenomenon is or is not (Bodie, in press). For example, should memory be considered part of the listening process? If so, we must be able to distinguish between what constitutes listening and what constitutes memory. In order to answer such questions it will be necessary for scholars to develop and rigorously test sophisticated models of listening. Thomas and Levine (1994) began this process over 10 years ago, and Janusik's current work is a contemporary step in the right direction. More work needs to be done, however, that goes beyond looking at listening as a linear progression from recall to listening behaviors or as simply a cognitive construct.

Halone, Cunconan, Coakley, and Wolvin (1998) suggest listening is comprised of at least five factors: cognitive; affective; behavioral/verbal; behavioral/nonverbal; and behavioral/interactive. This research is a good example of multi-method research. This quantitative study was developed with insight gained from qualitative investigations into how individuals conceptualize listening (Coakley, Halone, and Wolvin, 1996; Halone, Wolvin, and Coakley, 1997; Wolvin, Coakley, and Halone, 1995). Although such a "grounded" approach has its advantages, it also calls into question the validity of a listening model based on individual perceptions of the process as opposed to drawing from theories in areas such as cognitive psychology and linguistics. Despite this limitation, the reader is encouraged to investigate these issues. This multi-method project moves us in the right direction by attempting to provide a theoretically meaningful conceptualization of the multidimensional nature of listening, one that can be shared among those who develop tests of listening competence and related listening constructs.

Developing and testing measures of listening

As indicated in the section on listening tests, all existing listening tests are flawed. The good news: there is room for more test development research! For instance, given the laboratory approach taken by most listening assessment scholars, listening tests might overestimate an individual's effectiveness in situations where they are not prompted to listen at an optimal level (e.g., conversation in a noisy cafeteria; see Buck, 2001). Habitual listening patterns are important as well, thus testing listening in more realistic circumstances is a fruitful area for future research.

Another important area of test and scale development lies within the realm of cross-cultural listening research. Several scholars have recently made the call for listening researchers to pay more attention to cross-cultural variability in listening perceptions, styles, and processing (e.g., Imhof and Janusik, 2006; Valikoski, Ilomaki, Maki, and Janusik, 2005); thus, a further area for future investigation might be labeled cross-cultural listening research. Ultimately, more research needs to be done in this area so we can more fully understand the impact of culture on individual differences in listening.

Conclusion

Quantitative research allows us to clarify abstract concepts, test for reliability and validity, test relationships, and identify needs and best practices. Without quantitative research, we would remain in the world of the abstract and have difficulty expanding the boundaries of our knowledge about specific concepts. Additionally, we would not be able to generalize our discoveries to larger populations.

Several techniques were offered in the first section of this chapter and extended examples were used to illustrate how these techniques might be used to study listening. The research reviewed, although not exhaustive, should have provided a relatively concrete picture of what quantitative listening scholars do – develop and test theory in order to understand the effects of listening and the impact of individual and situational variables on the listening process. Much more work is needed, and a few specific areas were offered as examples of this need.

Certainly, to get a broad picture of an abstract concept such as listening, we need both qualitative and quantitative research. Mixing methods is particularly important as we continue to expand what we know about listening as a critical communication competency and as we continue to develop our theories of this process. Of course we know that a theory is never complete; the only way, however, to expand the boundaries of our understanding of listening is to engage in credible research that addresses intriguing questions.

QUESTIONS FOR DISCUSSION

I   What is quantitative research? How can an abstract concept such as listening be studied with quantitative methods? What types of questions can quantitative research answer more appropriately than qualitative research? What types of questions are not easily answered by quantitative research?

2   Why is theory important to quantitative research?
3   Name three major types of quantitative methods. What types of questions are these methods appropriate for answering?
4   What are the main ways quantitative researchers have operationalized listening? What are the positive and negative aspects of these operationalizations?
5   Make a list of behaviors you think describe a "good" listener. Looking back at the research presented in this chapter, are your notions of good listening verified by the empirical research? Which ones are? From whose research does this come? Which ones are not? How could you devise a study to test your theory of good listening?
6   What are some questions about listening you feel need to be addressed using a quantitative method? Why do you feel this type of method is most appropriate?
7   Of the areas of future research we identify, which is the most important for the field of listening? Why? Are there other areas we have not addressed in this chapter that are important for the advancement of listening research? Make a case for your additions.

References

Albrecht, T.L., and Goldsmith, D.J. (2003). Social support, social networks, and health. In T.L. Thompson, A.M. Dorsey, K.I. Miller and R. Parrott (Eds.). *Handbook of health communication*, pp. 263–84. Mahwah, NJ: Erlbaum.

Andersen, P.A. (1985). Nonverbal immediacy in interpersonal communication. In A. W. Siegman and S. Feldstein (Eds.). *Multichannel integrations of nonverbal behavior*, pp. 1–36. Hillsdale, NJ: Erlbaum.

Applegate, J.S., and Campbell, J.K. (1985, March). *A correlation analysis of overall and sub-test scores between the Watson-Barker and the Kentucky Comprehensive Listening Tests*. Paper presented to the annual meeting of the International Listening Association, Orlando, Florida.

Baddeley, A.D. (1986). *Working memory*. New York: Oxford University Press.

Barker, L.L. and Watson, K. W. (2000). *Listen Up. How to improve relationships, reduce stress, and be more productive by using the power of listening*. New York: St. Martins Press.

Beatty, M.J., Behnke, R.R., and Henderson, L.S. (1980). An empirical validation of the receiver apprehension test as a measure of trait listening anxiety. *Western Journal of Speech Communicaiton*, 44, 132–36.

Beatty, M.M. and Payne, S. (1984). Listening comprehension as a function of cognitive complexity. *Communication Monographs*, 51, 85–9.

Berger, C.R. (1977). The covering law model in communication inquiry. *Communication Quarterly*, 25, 7–19.

Bodie, G.D. (2009a). Evaluating listening theory: Development and illustration of five criteria. *International Journal of Listening*, 23, 81–103.

Bodie, G.D. (2009b). *The understudied nature of listening in interpersonal communication*. Paper presented at the annual convention of the National Communication Association, Chicago, IL.

Bodie, G.D., and Burleson, B.R. (2008). Explaining variations in the effects of supportive messages: A Dual-Process framework. In C. Beck (Ed.). *Communication Yearbook 32*, pp. 355–98. London: Taylor & Francis.

Bodie, G.D., and Villaume, W.A. (2003). Aspects of receiving information: The relationship between listening preferences, communication apprehension, receiver apprehension, and communicator style. *International Journal of Listening*, 17, 47–67.

Bodie, G.D. and Worthington, D.L. (in press). Revisiting the Listening Styles Profile (LSP-16): A confirmatory factor analytic approach to scale validation and reliability estimation. *International Journal of Listening*.

Bodie, G.D., Janusik, L.A., and Välikoski, T-R. (2008). Priorities of listening research: Four interrelated initiatives. A white paper sponsored by the research committee of the International Listening Association. Retrieved on June 2, 2009 from www.listen.org.

Bodie, G.D., Worthington, D.L., Imhof, M., and Cooper, L. (2008). What would a unified field of listening look like? A proposal linking past perspectives and future endeavors. *International Journal of Listening*, 22, 103–22.

Bommelje, R., Houston, J., and Smither, R. (2003). Personality characteristics of effective listeners: A five factor perspective. *International Journal of Listening*, 17, 32–46.

Bostrom, R.N. (1984). Research Update. Lexington, KY: Kentucky Listening Research Center.

Bostrom, R.N. (1990). Measuring individual differences in listening. In R.N. Bostrom (Ed.). *Listening behavior: Measurement and application*, pp. 15–24. New York: Guilford.

Bostrom, R.N. (1996). Memory, cognitive processing, and the process of "listening" – A reply to Thomas and Levine. *Human Communication Research*, 23, 298–305.

Bostrom, R.N. and Bryant, C. (1980). Factors in the retention of information presented orally: The role of short-term listening. *Western Journal of Speech Communication*, 44, 137–45.

Bostrom, R.N., and Waldhart, E.S. (1980a). Components in listening behavior: The role of short-term memory. *Human Communication Research*, 6, 222–7.

Bostrom, R.N., and Waldhart, E.S. (1980b). *The Kentucky Comprehensive Listening Test*. Lexington, KY: The University of Kentucky.

Bostrom, R.N., and Waldhart, E.S. (1983). *The Kentucky Comprehension Listening Test*. Lexington, KY: The University of Kentucky.

Brown, J.I. and Carlsen, G.R. (1955) *Brown-Carlsen Listening Comprehension Test*. New York: Harcourt, Brace, and World, Inc.

Brown, R.F., Butow, P.N., Henman, M, Dunn, S.M., Boyle, F., and Tattersall, M.H.N. (2002). Responding to the active and passive patient: Flexibility is the key. *Health Expectations*, 5, 236–45.

Buck, G. (2001). *Assessing listening.* Cambridge, UK: Cambridge University Press.

Burleson, B.R. (2003). Emotional support skill. In J.O. Greene and B.R. Burleson (Eds.). *Handbook of communication and social interaction skills*, pp. 551–94. Mahwah, NJ: Erlbaum.

Burleson, B.R., and Bodie, G.D. (2008). Constructivism and interpersonal processes. In W. Donsbach (Ed.). *The international encyclopedia of* communication, vol 3, pp. 950–54. Oxford: Blackwell.

Burleson, B.R., and MacGeorge, E.L. (2002). Supportive communication. In M.L. Knapp and J.A. Daly (Eds.), *Handbook of interpersonal communication* 3rd edn, pp. 374–424. Thousand Oaks, CA: Sage.

Caffrey, J.G. (1953). Auding ability as a function of certain psychometric variables. Unpublished PhD dissertation, University of California at Berkeley.

Castleberry, S.B., and Shepherd, C.D. (1993). Effective interpersonal listening and personal selling. *Journal of Personal Selling and Sales Management*, 13, 35–49.

Castleberry, S.B., Shepherd, C.D., and Ridnour, R. (1999). Effective interpersonal listening in the personal selling environment: Conceptualization, measurement, and nomological validity. *Journal of Marketing Theory and Practice*, 8, 30–8.

Cegala, D.J. (1981). Interaction involvement: A cognitive dimension of communicative competence. *Communication Education*, 30, 109–21.

Cegala, D.J. (1984). Affective and cognitive manifestations of interaction involvement during unstructured and competitive interactions. *Communication Monographs*, 51, 320–38.

Cegala, D. (1997). A study of doctors' and patients' communication during a primary care consultation: Implications for communication training. *Journal of Health Communication*, 2, 169–94.

Cegala, D.J., McNeilis, K.S., and McGee, D.S. (1995). A study of doctors' and patients' perceptions of information processing and communication competence during the medical interview. *Health Communication*, 7, 179–203.

Cegala, D.J., Savage, G.T., Brunner, C.C., and Conrad, A.B. (1982). An elaboration of the meaning of interaction involvement: Toward the development of a theoretical concept. *Communication Monographs*, 49, 229–48.

Chow, S.L. (1996). *Statistical significance: Rationale, validity, and utility.* Newberry Park, CA: Sage.

Coakley, C.G., Halone, K.K., and Wolvin, A.D. (1996). Perceptions of listening ability across the life-space: Implications for understanding listening competence. *International Journal of Listening*, 10, 21–48.

Cohen, J. (1988). *Statistical power analysis for the behavioral sciences* 2nd edn. New York: Academic Press.

Cohen, J. (1994). The world is round (p < .05). *American Psychologist*, 49, 997–1003.

Cohen, J., Cohen, P., West, S.G., and Aiken, L.S. (2003). *Applied multiple regression/correlation analysis for the behavioral sciences* 3rd edn. Mahwah, NJ: Erlbaum.

Cohen, S., and Wills, T.A. (1985). Stress, social support, and the buffering hypothesis. *Psychological Bulletin*, 98, 310–57.

Dakof, G.A., and Taylor, S.E. (1990). Victims' perceptions of support attempts: What is helpful from whom? *Journal of Personality and Social Psychology*, 58, 80–9.

Daniel, L.G. (1998). Statistical significance testing: A historical overview of misuse and misinterpretation with implications for the editorial policies of educational journals. *Research in the Schools*, 5, 2, 23–32.

Downs, V.C. (1985). Interaction involvement as a predictor of perceived social style: An empirical test of dialogic communication assumptions. *Communication Research Reports*, 2, 62–7.

Dunkel-Schetter, C. and Wortman, C.B. (1982). The interpersonal dynamics of cancer: Problems in social relationships and their impact on the patient. In H.S. Friedman and M.R. DiMatteo (Eds.), *Interpersonal issues in healthcare*, pp. 349–80. New York: Academic Press.

Dunkel-Schetter, C., Blasband, D., Feinstein, L., and Herbert, T. (1992). Elements of supportive interactions: When are attempts to help effective? In S. Spacapan and S. Oskamp (Eds.), *Helping and being helped: Naturalistic studies*, pp. 83–114. Newbury Park, CA: Sage.

Drollinger, T., Comer, L.B., and Warrington, P.T. (2006). Development and validation of the active empathetic listening scale. *Psychology and Marketing*, 23, 161–80.

Educational Testing Service. (1979). *STEP III Manual and Technical Report*. Menlo Park, CA: Addison-Wesley Publishing Company.

Fisher, R.A. (1935). *The design of experiments*. Edinburgh: Oliver & Boyd.

Fitch-Hauser, M. (1984). Message structure, inference making, and recall. In R.N. Bostrom (Ed.). *Communication Yearbook 8*, pp. 378–92. Beverly Hills, CA: Sage.

Fitch-Hauser, M. (1990). Making sense of data: Constructs, schemas, and concepts. In R. N. Bostrom (Ed.). *Listening behavior: Measurement and application*, pp. 76–90. New York: Guilford.

Fitch-Hauser, M.E., and Hughes, A. (1987). A factor analytic study of four listening tests. *The Journal of the International Listening Association*, 1, 129–47.

Fitch-Hauser, M.E., Barker, D.A., and Hughes, A. (1990) Receiver apprehension and listening comprehension. *Journal of the Southern Communication Association*, 56, 62–71.

Fitch-Hauser, M.E., Powers, W.G., O'Brien, K., and Hanson, S. (2007). Extending the conceptualization of listening fidelity. *International Journal of Listening*, 21, 81–91.

Goldsmith, D.J. (2004). *Communicating social support*. New York: Cambridge University Press.

Goss, B. (1982). Listening as information processing. *Communication Quarterly*, 30, 304–7.

Halone, K.K., Cunconan, T.M., Coakley, C.G., and Wolvin, A.D. (1998). Toward the establishment of general dimensions underlying the listening process. *International Journal of Listening*, 22, 12–28.

Halone, K.K., Wolvin, A.D., and Coakley, C.G. (1997). Accounts of effective listening across the life-span: Expectations and experiences associated with competent listening practices. *International Journal of Listening*, 11, 15–38.

Hausman, A. (2001). Taking your medicine: Relational steps to improving patient compliance. *Health Marketing Quarterly*, 19, 49–71.

Herzberg, D.S., Hammen, C., Burge, D., Daley, S.E., Davila, J., and Lindberg, N. (1999). Attachment cognitions predict perceived and enacted social support during late adolescence. *Journal of Adolescent Research*, 14, 387–404.

Hickson, G.B., Clayton, P.B., Giethen, P.E., and Sloan, F.A. (1992). Factors that prompted families to file medical malpractice claims following prenatal injuries. *JAMA*, 267, 2359–2363.

Hunter, J.E., and Schmidt, F.L. (2004). *Methods of meta-analysis: Correcting error and bias in research findings* (2nd edn). Newbury Park, CA: Sage.

Imhof, M., and Janusik, L. A. (2006). Development and validation of the Imhof-Janusik Listening Concepts Inventory to measure listening conceptualization differences between cultures. *Journal of Intercultural Communication Research*, 35, 79–98.

Janusik, L.A. (2005). Conversational listening span: A proposed measure of conversational listening. *The International Journal of Listening*, 18, 14–30.

Janusik, L.A. (2007). Building listening theory: The validation of the conversational listening span. *Communication Studies*, 58, 139–56.

Johnson, F.C., and Frandsen, K. (1963). Administering the Brown-Carlsen Listening Comprehension Test. *Journal of Communication*, 13, 38–45.

Johnston, M.K., Weaver, J.B., III, Watson, K.W., and Barker, L.L. (2000). Listening styles: Biological or psychological differences? *International Journal of Listening*, 14, 32–46.

Jones, S.M. (2004). Putting the person into person-centered and immediate emotional support: Emotional change and perceived helper competence as outcomes of comforting in helping situations. *Communication Research*, 32, 338–60.

Jones, S. M., and Guerrero, L. K. (2001). Nonverbal immediacy and verbal person-centeredness in the emotional support process. *Human Communication Research*, 4, 567–96.

Jones, S.M., and Wirtz, J. (2006). How does the comforting process work?: An empirical test of an appraisal-based model of comforting. *Human Communication Research*, 32, 217–43.

Kelly, C.M. (1965). An investigation of the construct validity of two commercially published listening tests. *Speech Monographs*, *32*, 139–43.

Korsch, B.M., Gozzi, E.K., and Francis, V. (1968) Doctor-patient interaction and patient satisfaction. *Pediatrics*, 42, 5, 885–70.

Lakey, B., and Lutz, C.J. (1996). Social support and preventive and therapeutic interventions. In G.R. Pierce, B.R. Sarason and I.G. Sarason (Eds.), *Handbook of social support and the family*, pp. 435–65. New York: Plenum Press.

Lane, S.D. (1983). Compliance, satisfaction, and physician-patient communication. In R. Bostrom (Ed.), *Communication Yearbook 7*, pp. 772–99. Beverly Hills, CA: Sage.

Langer, E. (1980). Rethinking the role of thought in social interaction. In H. Harvey, W. Ickes, and R. Kidd (Eds.), *New direction in attribution research* vol. 2, pp. 35–58. Hillsdale, NJ: Erlbaum.

Lee, J. (2000). 10 ways to communicate better with patients. *Review of Opthamology*, 7, 10, 38–42.

Lehman, D.R., Ellard, J.J., and Wortman, C.B. (1986). Social support for the bereaved: Recipients' and providers' perspectives on what is helpful. *Journal of Consulting and Clinical Psychology*, 54, 438–46.

Lipsey, M.W., and Wilson, D.B. (2001). *Practical meta-analysis: Applied social research methods series 49*. Thousand Oaks, CA: Sage.

Luttrell, E. S. (1992) Listening preferences as a function of sex and gender-role self-perception. Unpulished master thesis, Auburn University, Auburn, AL.

McCroskey, J.C. (1992). Reliability and validity of the willingness to communicate scale. *Communication Quarterly*, 40, 16–25.

McCroskey, J.C., and Richmond, V.P. (1987). Willingness to communicate. In J.C. McCroskey and J.A. Daly (Eds.), *Personality and interpersonal communication*, pp. 119–31. Newbury Park, CA: Sage.

Meelh, P.E. (1990). Why summaries of research on psychological theories are often uninterpretable. *Psychological Reports*, 66, 195–244.

Miller, L.C., Berg, J.H., and Archer, R.L. (1983). Openers: Individuals who elicit intimate self-disclosure. *Journal of Personality and Social Psychology*, 44, 1234–44.

Mulanax, A., and Powers, W. (2001). Listening fidelity: Development and relationship to receiver apprehension and locus of control. *International Journal of Listening*, 15, 69–78.

Nichols, R.G. (1948). Factors in listening comprehension. *Speech Monographs*, 15, 154–63.

Nunnally, J.C. (1978). *Psychometric theory* (2nd edn). New York: McGraw-Hill.

Pearce, C.G., Johnson, I.W., and Barker, R.T. (2003). Assessment of the Listening Styles Inventory: Progress in establishing reliability and validity. *Journal of Business and Technical Communication*, 17, 84–113.

Perrine, R.M. (1993). On being supportive: The emotional consequences of listening to another's distress. *Journal of Social and Personal Relationships*, 10, 371–84.

Phillips, D.C. (2000). *The expanded social scientist's bestiary: A guide to fabled threats to, and defenses of, naturalistic social science*. Lanham, MD: Rowman & Littlefield.

Popper, K. (1965). *Conjectures and refutations* (2nd edn). New York: Basic Books.

Post, D.M., Cegala, D.J., and Miser, W.F. (2002). The other half of the whole: Teaching patients to communicate with physicians. *Family Medicine*, 34, 344–52.

Powers, W.G., and Bodie, G.D. (2003). Listening fidelity: Seeking congruence between cognitions of the receiver and the sender. *International Journal of Listening*, 17, 19–31.

Powers, W.G., and Lowry, D.N. (1984). Basic communication fidelity. In R.L. Bostrom (Ed.). *Communication competence*, pp. 57–71. Beverly Hills, CA: Sage.

Powers, W.G., and Spitzberg, B. (1986). Basic communication fidelity and image management: A new approach. *Communication Research Reports*, 3, 110–13.

Preiss, R.W., Wheeless, L.R., and Allen, M. (1990). Potential cognitive processes and consequences of receiver apprehension: A meta-analytic review. *Journal of social Behavior and Personality*, 5, 2, 155–72.

Rasmuson, T.R. (1987). The effects of pausing and listening ability on retention of a spoken message. *The Journal of the International Listening Association*, 1, 114–28.

Richmond, V.P. and Hickson, M. III. (2001). *Going public: A practical guide to public talk*. Boston: Allyn & Bacon.

Roach, D.A., and Fitch-Hauser, M.E. (1984, April). *A comparison of three modes of administering listening tests*. Paper presented to the fifth annual convention of The International Listening Association, Scottsdale, AZ.

Roberts, C.V. (1986) A validation of the Watson-Barker Listening Test. *Communication Research Reports*, 3, 115–19.

Roberts, C.V. (1988). The validation of listening tests: Cutting the Gordian knot. *The Journal of the International Listening Association*, 2, 1–19.

Roberts, C.V., and Vinson, L. (1989, November). *Willingness to listen: Another dimension of a multifaceted process*. Paper presented at the Speech Communication Association Convention, San Francisco, CA.

Roberts, C.V., and Vinson, L. (1998). Relationship among willingness to listen, receiver apprehension, communication apprehension, communication competence, and dogmatism. *International Journal of Listening*, 12, 40–56.

Schulman, E.D. (1978). *Intervention in human services* (2nd edn). St. Louis: Mosby.

Shadish, W.R., Cook, T.D., and Campbell, D.T. (2002). *Experimental and quasi-experimental designs for generalized causal inference.* Boston: Houghton Mifflin.

Shevlin, M., Miles, J.N.V., Davies, M.N.O., and Salker, S. (2000). Coefficient alpha: A useful indicator of reliability? *Personality and Individual Differences,* 28, 229–37.

Shiffrin, R., and Schneider, W. (1977). Controlled and automatic human information processing, II: Perceptual learning, automatic attending, and a general theory. *Psychological Review,* 84, 127–90.

Spearritt, D. (1962). *Listening comprehension: A factorial analysis.* Series Number 76. Melbourne: Australian Counsel for Educational Research.

Spiro, R.L. and Weitz, B.A. (1990). Adaptive selling: Conceptualization, measurement, and nomological validity. *Journal of Marketing Research,* 27, 61–9.

Sprinthall, R.C. (2003). *Basic statistical analysis* (7th edn). Boston: Allyn and Bacon.

Stevens, S.S. (1946). On the theory of scales of measurement. *Science,* 103, 677–80.

Stewart, M.A. (1995). Effective physician-patient communication and health outcomes: A review. *Canadian Medical Association Journal,* 152, 1423–33.

Tabachnick, B.G. And Fidell, L.S. (2007). *Using multivariate statistics* (5th edn). Boston: Pearson.

Thomas, L.T., and Levine, T.R. (1994). Disentangling listening and verbal recall: Related but separate constructs? *Human Communication Research,* 21, 103–27.

Thomas, L.T., and Levine, T.R. (1996). Further thoughts on recall, memory, and the measurement of listening: A rejoinder to Bostrom. *Human Communication Research,* 23, 306–8.

Uchino, B.N. (2004). *Social support and physical health: Understanding the health consequences of relationships.* New Haven, CT: Yale University Press.

Valikoski, T.R., Ilomaki, I., Maki, E., and Janusik, L.A. (2005). Conversational listening span: A comparative study of American and Finnish students. *Prologos (Premier Journal of the Finnish Communication Association),* 1, 88–108.

Villaume, W.A., and Bodie, G.D. (2007). Discovering the listener within us: The impact of trait-like personality variables and communicator styles on preferences for listening style. *International Journal of Listening,* 21, 102–23.

Villaume, W.A., and Cegala, D.J. (1988). Interaction involvement and discourse strategies: The patterned use of cohesive devices in conversation. *Communication Monographs,* 55, 22–39.

Villaume, W.A., Jackson, J., and Goldsmith Schouten, T. (1989). Issue-event extensions and interaction involvement text-based and meaning-based discourse strategies *Human Communication Research,* 15, 407–27.

Villaume, W.A., and Weaver, J.B. (1996). A factorial approach to establishing reliable listening measures from the WBLT and the KCLT: Full information factor analysis of dichotomous data. *International Journal of Listening*, 10, 1–20.

Wanzer, M., Booth-Butterfield, M., and Gruber, K. (2004). Perceptions of health care providers' communication: Relationships between patient-centered communication and satisfaction. *Health Communication*, 16, 363–84.

Watson, K.W., and Barker, L.L. (1983). *Watson-Barker Listening Test*. Tega Cay: SC: SPECTRA, Inc.

Watson, K.W., and Barker, L.L. (1988). Listening Assessment: The Watson-Barker Listening Test. *The Journal of the International Listening Association*, 2, 20–32.

Watson, K.W., and Barker, L.L. (2001). *Watson-Barker Listening Test*. Tega Cay: SC: SPECTRA, Inc.

Watson, K.W., Barker, L.L., and Weaver, J.B. (1995). The listening styles profile (LSP16): Development and validation of an instrument to assess four listening styles. *International Journal of Listening*, 9, 1–13.

Watson, K.W., Lazarus, C.J., and Thomas, T. (1999). First-year medical students' listener preferences: A longitudinal study. *International Journal of Listening*, 13, 1–11.

Weaver, J.B., III, Watson, K.W., and Barker, L.L. (1996) Individual differences in listening styles: Do you hear what I hear? *Personality and Individual Differences*, 20, 381–7.

Wethington, E., and Kessler, R.C. (1986). Perceived support, received support, and adjustment to stressful life events. *Journal of Health and Social Behavior*, 27, 78–89.

Wheeless, L. (1975). An investigation of receiver apprehension and social context dimensions of communication apprehension. *The Speech Teacher*, 24, 3, 261–8.

Wheeless, L., and Scott, M.D. (1976, April). *The nature, measurement and potential effects of receiver apprehension*. Paper presented at the meeting of the International Communication Association, Portland, OR.

Wolvin, A.D., Coakley, C.G., and Halone, K.K. (1995). A preliminary look at listening development across the life-span. *International Journal of Listening*, 9, 62–83.

Worthington, D.L. (2001). Exploring juror's listening processes: The effect of listening style preference on juror decision making. *International Journal of Listening*, 15, 20–37.

Worthington, D.L. (2003). Exploring the relationship between listening style preference and personality. *International Journal of Listening*, 17, 68–87.

Zimmerman, R. and Arnold, W.E. (1990) Physicians' and patients' perceptions of actual versus ideal physician communications and listening behaviors. *Journal of the International Listening Association*, 4, 143–64.

Part III

Listening as a Cognitive and Relational Activity

4

What is Going on in the Mind of a Listener? The Cognitive Psychology of Listening

Margarete Imhof

In this chapter Imhof discusses the mental activities which are involved in listening. She brings together empirical research from cognitive psychology and psycholinguistics to illustrate the complexity of the listening process. She centers on a model of information processing which looks at listening as the intentional selection, organization, and integration of verbal and nonverbal aspects of acoustic information. Consequently, the text looks at how hearing and listening are different and what kinds of activities a listener engages in as he or she makes sense of the sound waves which meet the ear. The following questions are addressed: How do we separate and select concurring information? What is the role of all the information which accompanies the words and which we receive along with the speech input, such as the facial expression or hand gestures? Do we need to learn how to listen or would the ability to listen to sounds and languages come naturally? What are the competencies that a listener needs in order to handle the more or less structured stream of information that comes without full stops and commas and very often in half sentences and poorly articulated words? What does a listener do with what he or she hears? How does the listener create the message? How would one know that one listened well?

Listening as a Dimension of Cognitive Psychology: Listening as a Mental Activity

Cognitive psychology can be viewed as an umbrella for a collection of theories that consider processes through which humans acquire, interpret, remember, and make use of information. The pertaining research focus is on the "mental processes and activities used in perceiving, remembering, thinking, and understanding, as well as the act of using those processes" (Ashcraft, 2006, p. 11) and takes into account how and why humans select information, organize information into a coherent and meaningful structure, integrate information into the existing structure of prior knowledge, and use it for a decision on an appropriate reaction. In addition to the qualitative and quantitative changes of a person's mental representations and cognitive structure as a result of information processing, cognitive psychologists also look at how these changes can be objectively measured, for example in terms of response characteristics and outcome performance. Furthermore, it is of interest how the events and results of human information processing are influenced by the characteristics both of the individual and the message (Mayer, 1999, 2003; Pressley, 2000).

From the perspective of cognitive psychology, listening is first and foremost conceptualized as an act of information processing (Cutler and Clifton, 1999), notwithstanding any additional communicative and social purposes an instance of listening might serve (Janusik, 2002; Wolvin and Coakley, 1996). Within the framework of cognitive psychology, listening can be defined as the process of selecting, organizing, and integrating information (Imhof, 2004b). Listening involves processing information from various internal and external sources, as the verbal information may be complemented and modified by prior knowledge, context information, situational variables, body language, and nonverbal paralinguistic messages. While hearing, which is a necessary precursor of listening, occurs automatically, listening is an intentional and controlled process which requires attentional capacity, expends energy, depletes self-regulatory strength (Schneider and Shiffrin, 1977; Shiffrin and Schneider, 1977), and requires information processing across several modalities, such as acoustic and visual signals. Figure 4.1 represents a model of the listening process from the perspective of cognitive psychology drawing on Mayer's (1996, 1999) SOI model of information processing.

Considering the array of activities involved, it becomes evident that a listener is required to actively perform and monitor a sequence of recurring steps in order to prepare for listening, to adequately perceive and handle the information, and to later act on the information (Imhof, 1998, 2003b). Listening requires a functioning self-regulatory system with comprehensive attention and working memory capacity (Janusik, 2004), because the relevant stimuli are temporally distributed, which means that they are transient and not available for further reference. In order to illustrate the task demands involved in the problem of listening, the individual steps of the listening process will be detailed in the

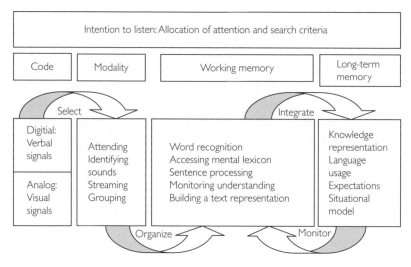

Figure 4.1   Model of listening in terms of cognitive psychology

remainder of the text. In order to present the research, the individual activities are discussed in linear succession for readability; this is not meant to suggest that they necessarily occur in a strictly linear or serial sequence (Hagoort, 2005).

Cognitive Processes Involved in Listening: Listening as a Composite Activity

A necessary precedent of listening is hearing which involves the perception of sound waves by the eardrums. The human information processing system is built in a way that not all stimuli which have been registered are also fully processed (Anderson, 2004; Ashcraft, 2006). Only part of the incoming information will be attended to and, as a consequence, transferred to what is called the working memory for further and conscious processing. Listening is initiated as an act of intentional allocation of attention to a series of acoustic events which has an intelligible structure, such as speech or music. (It would not be an incident of listening if a tree fell on the ground and we heard the noise). The issues here are how this intention is generated and in which way it has an impact on the subsequent processing characteristics.

Create and maintain an intention for listening: What is a person listening for?

Since the ear is always open to receive sound waves, even as we sleep, we can use the acoustic modality to constantly monitor the world around us. We are accustomed to a certain type of acoustic envelope, and as long as nothing special happens in the environment, we know that we are safe. Sound is typically the result of sudden changes which need to attract our attention immediately and solicits an orientating response which is data driven and involuntary (Cohen, 1993) and occurs without intentional control (Styles, 2006). Cherry (1953) describes the "Cocktail Party Effect" which basically means that we turn towards a conversation when we hear our name (or some other highly relevant information) mentioned, even if this event takes place in a multi-source environment and in some distance. While the explanations for this phenomenon are still being tested (Styles, 2006), the phenomenon illustrates how sound is used for orientation of attention in space. Hearing happens automatically without a conscious decision; it operates rapidly, and consumes little if any conscious resources (Ashcraft, 2006, p. 149).

In contrast to this, the initiation of listening is associated with a completely different mode of perception, namely one which presumes "a planned, goal-directed course of action" (Cohen, 1993, p. 6), because listening implies that a person has made a "conscious choice about to whom, what, and when she wanted to listen" (Barker and Watson, 2000, p. 70). For example, a person may be busy preparing food in the kitchen while the radio is playing in the background. The two activities usually do not interfere with each other. As a certain phrase catches the person's attention (for example, a news item on an airplane crash), the person interrupts her work and makes sure she gets the information on whether this was the plane a friend was on or not. This decision to direct the attention to this particular item determines the transition from hearing to listening. From this moment on, the act of listening follows a deliberate decision, uses conscious resources and drains the pool of attentional capacity (Ashcraft, 2006, p. 149).

The intention that was framed for listening has an impact on the way that the information is processed. Anderson and Pichert (1978) experimented with different instructions for text comprehension and found that a specific perspective that was imposed on a comprehender yielded different patterns of retention and recall. So, for example, when subjects listened to a text from the perspective of a prospective homebuyer, they retained different details as compared to subjects who listened to the same text from the perspective of a prospective burglar. Considering the fact that a homebuyer and a burglar are likely to have quite different preferences when it comes to the characteristics of a house, this finding is probably not really exciting. What is remarkable, however, is the fact that participants, when they had to shift perspectives for recall, retrieved significantly fewer details and were unable to reconstruct details which had been perceived as irrelevant before (Flammer and Tauber, 1982). So, it can be concluded that the intention which guides an act of listening serves as a filter for the incoming information and facilitates retention of relevant information while irrelevant information is discarded or compromised.

Select information: How does a listener tell information from noise?

Segregation of acoustic information   At the basis of any listening process is the problem of selecting acoustic information from the environment. This is by no means a trivial endeavor because the listener is exposed to a mix of sound waves due to the fact that "events in the real world overlap and 'compete'" (Handel, 1989, p. 209). The cognitive system needs to disentangle the "messy" input of simultaneous and therefore interfering events in order to keep apart the sounds emitted by the voice of the person next to us from the voice in the radio, and the motor sounds of the car in which we carry on this particular conversation. Selecting and segregating sources of auditory information requires a flexible and adaptable processing system: "Noise would quickly bring most artificial language processing systems to their knees (if they had knees) under the sorts of conditions in which people communicate successfully everyday" (Oden, Rueckl, and Sanocki, 1991).

Distinction between language and non-language acoustic stimuli   Initially, as the acoustic stimuli reach the sensory register, the listener may or may not allocate attention to them and transmit them to further processing (Anderson, 2004; Atkinson and Shiffrin, 1968). Any information which does not receive attention at this point cannot be retrieved at a later stage in the process. In this first step, the human information processor analyzes physical aspects of any acoustic input (Koelsch, Gunter, Friederici, and Schröger, 2000) in order to distinguish between non-language and language signals. Language sounds carry distinct acoustic characteristics, such as frequency, relative changes in frequency, pitch, and rhythm (Pisoni, 1987) which facilitate auditory streaming and segregating the incoming sound waves into perceptual groups (Summerfield and Culling, 1992) using auditory Gestalt principles of similarity, proximity, common fate, and continuity (Bregman, 1978, 1981, 1990; Styles, 2005).

Phonetic processing   The listener uses the (implicit) knowledge about the phonology of a language to categorize the sounds and performs "a sharp division into categories in labeling and an enhanced discrimination between category relative to within category" (Tartter, 1998, p. 273). For example, we identify a sound as either /ba/ or /da/, no matter how clearly the physical realization of the sounds actually is presented. The listener has an implicit knowledge as to which sounds and which sequence of sounds to expect and which sounds have a zero probability to occur in certain positions. So, if someone says "ŋ ose" (with an initial /ŋ/ - sound as, for example, the end position in "sing"), a listener will always report that he heard a person say "nose", because an English speaking listener would not expect the /ŋ/ sound in the initial position of any word and therefore correct the acoustic input according to the phonetic rules of the respective language (Tartter, 1998).

As a rule, the listener accommodates for rather broad variations in the sound structure of speech with a considerable degree of flexibility (Lively, Pisoni, and Goldinger, 1994; Norris, McQueen, and Cutler, 2003; Scott, 2005). This is why we still perceive and make meaning of sounds in spite of rather generous phonetic distortions as we listen to speakers who feature a heavy accent or dialect (Cutler, Smits, and Cooper, 2005), or who are not able to produce a standard pronunciation for any reason (as, for example, very young children, persons speaking while chewing gum).

The listener readily repairs an incomplete sound structure and constructs a meaningful message as Warren (1970) illustrated in his experiments on the phoneme restoration effect. Subjects listened to the following sentences each of which was missing a sound at the point indicated by the asterisk:

It was found that the *eel* was on the axle.
It was found that the *eel* was on the shoe.
It was found that the *eel* was on the orange.
It was found that the *eel* was on the table.

When asked what they had just heard, subjects had no difficulty to respond with *wheel, heel, peel, meal*, in accordance with the general context of the sentence.

Cross-modal processing in listening   The cognitive system also takes into account information that appears across or in conjunction with other modalities, for example, vision and touch (Guttman, Gilroy, and Blake, 2005; Styles, 2006). As in the ventriloquist effect, we mislocate the source of speech at the apparent visual location of the speaker's puppet. More frequently, however, cross-modal information processing takes place when a listener is confronted with nonverbal parts of a message, such as facial and hand gestures (Goldin-Meadow, 2003). It is, however, not only the obvious gesture that has an impact on listening. Research suggests that the movements of the head help the listener to structure and sequence speech. When natural movements of the head are missing, the listener finds it more difficult to understand speech (Yehia, Kuratate, and Vatikiotis-Bateson, 2002). McGurk and MacDonald (1976) looked at lip movements and found that when a mismatch between the acoustic and the visual input occurs, the percept is modified in order to resolve the conflict. So, for example, when a person hears /ga/ and lip-reads "ba" the resulting percept is reported as /da/ which is phonetically halfway between the two conflicting stimuli (Bertelson, Vroomen, and de Gelder, 2003).

To summarize, the first step in information processing in listening consists of a rapid sequence of analyses which result in the identification and categorization of the stimuli and which represent the "raw material" for further processing.

Organize information: How does a listener know what it all means?

The step of organizing information requires that meaningful units are identified, meaning is assigned to the identified units, and that the meaningful units are organized into a representation of the text base.

Word recognition   No sooner has the listener managed to segregate and identify the linguistic input, than the listener assigns meaning to the information. In order to accomplish this, the listener needs to structure the acoustic input into meaningful units. This is an active and construc- tive process, because spoken language does not feature distinctive spaces between words and sentences, as this would be the case in writ- ing (Cutler, 1999), nor can spontaneous speech generally be expected to provide well-formed, coherent, and grammatically correct verbal input (Inhoff and Connine, 1995). The listener uses intonation, pauses, and emphases, so-called prosodic features, to detect and isolate the relevant words and phrases, for example, rising and falling tones, and distribu- tion of pauses and stresses across an utterance.

Structure and content of the mental lexicon   For word recognition, the lis- tener accesses the mental lexicon right away in order to assign meaning to the percepts. These are not necessarily identical with individual words, since some percepts consist – technically speaking – of a colloca- tion of several words (for example, expressions like "few and far between", "how are you?"). In any case, to complete word recognition, the listener needs to assign meaning to the identified linguistic units by accessing the inner or mental lexicon and selecting the appropriate entry. Models of the mental lexicon have developed from strictly hierarchical and content based models of semantic memory (Collins and Quillian, 1969) to spreading activation network models (Collins and Loftus, 1975), and complex propositional models which hold that the mental lexicon comprise a variety of aspects (Ashcraft, 2006; Crocker, Pickering and Clifton, 2000; Gaskell and Marslen-Wilson, 1997; Jay, 2003). Most cogni- tive psychologists agree that the mental lexicon contains semantic infor- mation which includes the declarative knowledge and the defining characteristics associated with the word. Knowing a word certainly entails the "ability to define it, the ability to recognize situations for using it, knowledge of its alternative meanings, the ability to recognize inappropriate uses of the word" (Miller, 1999, p. 3). In addition, the lis- tener keeps information on word frequency, morphological characteris- tics, and the grammatical function of a word in the mental lexicon (Pickering, Clifton, and Crocker, 2000). Brain studies show that if the listener is exposed to less frequently used words or to words which deviate from the established context either semantically, grammatically, or morphologically, the event related potentials are more pronounced than when the matching and expected word occurs (Brown and Hagoort,

2000; Kutas, Federmeier, and Sereno, 1999; Kutas and Hillyard, 1980; Osterhout and Holcomb, 1995; van Petten and Kutas, 1990, 1991).

Beyond the conceptual information, the mental lexicon comprehends procedural knowledge and a pictorial representation, relational context, and also biographical and episodic information (Anderson, 2004; Jay, 2003) which can be used as a listener assigns meaning to the percepts.

For instance, as a listener processes the following sentence: "He bought himself a good knife," he or she needs to choose from several entries for "good", as in "a good girl", "a good friend", "a good citizen" or "a good time" (Miller, 1999). It is now important to identify what "good" is supposed to mean in the current context and what the pertaining characteristics are. The listener associates procedures that characterize a "good" knife, considers the shape, the kinesthetic qualities of the article, and maybe remembers an episode in which he had used a "good" knife and accidentally cut his finger with it. Given that this information is available as the listener processes the sentence, the next evident step is to make a decision on which information to select and which to neglect for further processing. If the sentence occurs in a conversation between chefs, one might want to continue about qualities of knives, which would be an inappropriate decision if the situation was an interrogation of a person who is accused of violence involving a knife.

Sentence processing Models of lexical access and word recognition are complemented by models of sentence processing. In order to make coherent sense of speech, the listener must define a surface structure of an utterance in terms of who or what is the agent and what is the action performed on what or whom, where, when, how? If a listener is presented with the following sentence (Vonk, 1985, p. 208): "Harry did not trust Albert because he was so suspicious," he or she needs to decide if the subordinate clause ought to be related to Harry or to Albert. This can be resolved in a variety of ways, as, for example, using prior knowledge of the individuals involved or contextual information that is currently available. The context makes it possible for a listener to assign meaning even to corrupted utterances, such as: "Do you know where … yes … wait … I have it."

The role of working memory in listening A listener rarely ever processes individual sentences or singular events. When acoustic information consists of a sequence of information, more specific comprehension skills and extensive short term memory are required, because the listener needs to relate the different parts of the utterance to each other, for instance to resolve prepositional phrases and to make necessary inferences (Cain, 2006; Gathercole and Baddeley, 1993). The phonological loop and the central executive functions of working memory are instrumental in monitoring comprehension and organizing the input in a meaningful way (Baddeley, 2006; Cain, 2006). The capacity of working memory has been shown to play an important role for text comprehension in reading (Cain, Oakhill, and Lemmon, 2004; Just and Carpenter, 1992). Cain (2006) reports that poor readers do not necessarily have an impaired memory for facts but that they make fewer inferences which are necessary to fully understand the meaning of a story as opposed to being able to recall its surface.

The challenge for the listener is to effectively store the information contained in the text as he or she generates the text representation so that it can be accessed and corrected later if necessary. Research on so-called "garden path sentences" has shown that people differ in the ability to recognize sentences which require a revision of the initial interpretation or a reinterpretation of the established relationships altogether. For example, a sentence like: "The daughter of the German teacher ...," may be interpreted as "the daughter of the teacher who is German" or as "the daughter of the teacher who teaches German." The resolution of this ambiguity will only be successful if more context information is available and if the listener has the capacity to store the choice of possible interpretations long enough in working memory to reconsider the validity of the initial interpretation.

The text representation   The final result of this step is described in terms of a text representation that can be used as the basis for a more comprehensive situational model. The text representation forms the "interconnected network of idea units ... expressed in a message" (Singer, 1994, p. 479) and stands for the essential result of the information processing. It is the necessary condition for a full understanding and lends itself to the construction of the situational model. The issue of how the nature of the text representation can be described has raised considerable theoretical debate. The controversy is about whether the representation of the text is to be modeled as an abstract, propositional structure (Kintsch, 1998) or as a rather concrete mental illustration (Dörner, 2005; Garnham and Oakhill, 1996; Johnson-Laird, 1983; Stanfield and Zwaan, 2001). As of now, results from experimental research seem to support the notion that the human information processor is quite flexible here and that it may depend on discourse characteristics, for example, content, if a more abstract or a more concrete representation is more viable (Perrig and Kintsch, 1985).

Integrate information: How does a listener create the big picture of the message?

The situational model is constructed in the final necessary step (Johnson-Laird, 1983; Kintsch, 1998; Zwaan and Singer, 2003) and forms the basis for a possible subsequent response. In the situation model, the listener creates "a representation of what the text is about" (van Oostendorp and Bonebakker, 1999).

Inferences   In order to arrive at this situation model, the listener uses inferences to supplement the text and fill information gaps inherent in the message. Inferences can be defined as a class of cognitive processes which generate new information using both existing knowledge and currently incoming information (Ashcraft, 2006; van der Meer, 1995). Inferences are typically rule-based or knowledge-based (Garnham, 1989) and play a role on different levels of speech comprehension (Rickheit, Schnotz, and Strohner, 1985). *Semantic inferences* simply serve to complete the structure of an utterance, as for example, to identify the referent for a pronoun or to restore a compromised word. Semantic inferences are based on the (implicit) knowledge of all aspects of the language, including the culturally framed conventions of usage (Clark, 1996). So, for example, when we listen to a story in which a dinner is mentioned that supposedly was a "total disaster", we probably would not make the inference that anyone was injured or poisoned, but that most likely someone goofed in the kitchen – if anything at all happened beyond a minor social hiccup. Whereas if we listen to a story saying that "the old Christmas tree lights rescued from the loft for the umpteenth time caused an electrical disaster", we rightly conclude in the situational model that something serious happened, although the intensifying adjective "total" is missing in the second utterance (Aitchison, 2003, p. 159f.).

Listeners generate *bridging inferences* as they add details to what they have just heard in order to establish links between sentences and to create a coherent story that makes sense in the real world.

If a listener is presented with the following story (Bishop, 1997):

(1)   John was at the beach.
(2)   He stepped on some broken glass.
(3)   He had to go to the hospital.

a semantic inference would be based on the knowledge of syntactical rules, such as the inference that "he" in sentence (3) refers back to "John" in sentence (1). A bridging inference is made, when the listener draws on his general or world knowledge in order to establish coherence (Kintsch, 1998; Singer, 1994), for example, when the listener makes the inference that John was walking on the beach with bare feet and that he hurt himself on the broken glass.

For an *elaborative inference*, a listener would use information from other sources, such as prior knowledge and knowledge of conversational or cultural conventions. The foundation for these inferences is the principle that text comprehension is driven by an automatic "search-after-meaning" (Graesser, Singer, and Trabasso, 1994, p. 371) which motivates the listener to construct the situation model in a way that allows a meaningful response. For example, when a listener is presented with a sentence such as: "Peter does not get drunk every night any more," he or she assumes that Peter must have had a serious drinking problem. Elaborative inferences typically contain constructions of space, time, protagonist, causality, and intentionality, for example, ideas about goals and motives of the agents, personal dispositions and emotional states of the persons involved, to name the most prominent categories (Barquero, 1999; Graesser and Zwaan, 1995; Rinck, 2000; Zwaan and Radvansky, 1998) which are almost automatically generated and monitored during text comprehension (Therriault, Rinck, and Zwaan, 2006).

Neural correlates of the situation model   Recent research suggests that the situational model has indeed a neural correlate. It was found that the pattern of brain activation of listeners when they listened to a sentence which described a concrete event corresponded to the activation pattern that would be expected when the comprehender had actually perceived the situation in an interaction with the real world (Kaschak et al., 2005). Experiments which require restructuring of spatial information represented in the mental model showed that searching for the relevant information takes longer if the target item is located "further" away from the current position so that it makes sense to conclude that the mental model is thought of as some kind of searchable mental image.

Monitoring structure building Language comprehension can be conceptualized as a structure building process which combines the incoming information (or what was made of it) and information that had been retrieved from long-term memory. It is generally agreed that in order to accomplish this part of the listening task, the comprehender uses both top-down and bottom-up processes to construct a meaningful situational model (Gernsbacher, 1990; Kintsch, 1989, 2005). Gernsbacher (1990) proposes that the language comprehender starts organizing the incoming information immediately (as opposed to taking in the full utterance before assigning meaning) and proceeds from there to construe the mental model and to monitor its development. The "principle of immediacy of interpretation" (Anderson, 2004, p. 391) is supported by experiments which tested the "Advantage of First Mention"-effect: Language comprehenders react faster to references to information that occurs at the beginning of a sentence and they retain more of this information. It is, however, a serious problem for theory-building that the supporting data were almost exclusively collected in experiments which involve reading rather than listening, so some caution might be appropriate as results are being generalized. In particular, the different functions of the parts of working memory involved (the phonological loop for listening and the spatio-visual sketch pad for reading) may play a role in determining how fast and how efficiently structure building will occur. The listener also may experience more interferences as he or she takes into account the knowledge and the impression which the speaker makes in the situation (Krauss and Pardo, 2006). It is a further problem for the listener to regularly update the situation model as more information is coming in (Zwaan and Madden, 2004) and to distinguish between valid and invalid information in the process.

Conditions for Listening: Influences on Listening

As the listening process is described in some detail, it needs to be recognized that the process and product of listening depend on the constellation of variables pertaining to the listener, the speaker/the source, the message and the situation, and the mutual interactions (see Figure 4.2). This mindmap can be used both to illustrate differential effects in

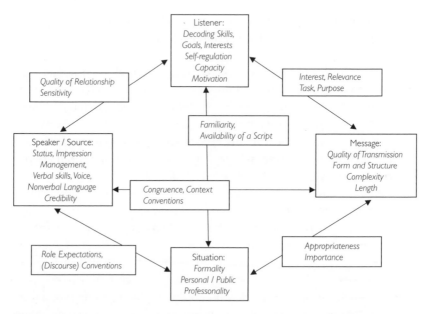

Figure 4.2   Mindmap of variables pertaining to a comprehensive model of listening

listening behavior and to generate hypotheses about causes, effects, and covariation of processes involved in listening.

Characteristics of the listener: What does the listener add to the message?

The process and the product of listening – as any other information processing would – depend very much on the listener characteristics. The most relevant aspects are the linguistic competences across the life span (Cain, 2006; Imhof, 2002; McDevitt and Ford, 1987; Nieding, 2006), prior knowledge (Kintsch, 1989; Kintsch and Franzke, 1995; Penno, Wilkinson and Moore, 2002; Whitney and Waring, 1991; Woloshyn, Paivio, and Pressley, 1994) and practice (Caillies, Denhière, and Jhean-Larose, 1999), the cultural background and appreciation for listening (Imhof and Janusik, 2006; Kiewitz, Weaver, Brosius, and Weimann, 1997), self-regulation and self-monitoring competences (Vohs and Ciarocco, 2004), and goals, motivation and emotions (Butcher and Kintsch, 2003; Carpenter, Miyake and Just, 1995; Graesser, Singer and Trabasso, 1994; Lorch, Klusewitz, and Lorch, 1995; Guthrie, Wigfield, Barbosa, et al., 2004). While it was found that people have systematically different preferences for input modalities (Kürschner, Schnotz, Eid, and Hauck, 2005), it is still an issue open to research what exactly the implications of these preferences are in terms of cognitive processes. In a study on reading Narvaez, van den Broek, and Barron-Ruiz (1999) found that "readers adjust their inferential activities to reflect a particular reading purpose" and go on to conclude that this "contradicts the view that inference generation during reading is a purely automatic, text-driven process" (p. 493). If this is true for reading, it is rather plausible to assume that the same type of adjustment is present in listening. The pertaining experimental evidence, however, is still to be delivered.

Characteristics of the speaker/of the source: How does the source have an impact on how a person listens?

As the listener makes meaning of a sequence of acoustic information, the process and product are influenced by the way that the source is perceived. Specifically in interpersonal exchanges, the way that the partner is perceived, and the hypotheses which the listener forms about the speaker have an effect on the way the message is understood (Habermann, 1996; Schober and Brennan, 2003). The listener takes into account what he or she sees, hears, and knows of the speaker, the interpretation of the speaker (What type of person is he or she? Well-meaning? An expert? A self-presenter?) and the definition of the relationship between him- or herself and the speaker (Who is this person for me? Who does this person think I am?). The message is viewed in the light of the nonverbal messages which accompany the utterance, for example, listening to someone say "I am fine" with a wavering, breaking voice may elicit a different reaction than listening to someone say the same with a firm voice. Knapp and Hall (2002) review empirical evidence for the various dimensions of nonverbal communication (see also Wolvin and Coakley, 1996) and how listeners may or may not be aware of its influence on the communication process. In spite of the inherent ambiguity of nonverbal signals, they are powerful means for conveying meaning and they are used across all cultures (Argyle, 1988). Some of the nonverbal behavior is regulated by presentation rules, as for example the obligation to smile (LaFrance and Hecht, 1999), while other aspects of nonverbal behavior are strongly associated with the verbal expression, as some languages seem to have a 'script' for hand gestures that typically go with the words as is visible in native Italian speakers.

The concept of the speaker or the source of the oral information has an impact on the listener's behavior. When we know that a speaker is putting on the friendly face, we react differently than when we feel that the smile is authentic. The credibility, the assumed motivation of the speaker, the expertise which a listener associates with the source of the information are other obvious aspects that change the way in which a message is processed.

Speakers in their turn use the nonverbal expressions of the listeners to monitor their speech: "In fact, speakers need listeners' signals to do their job well" (Pasupathi, Stallworth, and Murdoch, 1998, p. 2). If the listener(s) stopped providing nonverbal feedback, the speaker would be irritated and discomposed in a short period of time.

Characteristics of the situation: What does the context add to the listening process?

The impact of the situation on both behavior and mental processes is yet another issue (Herrmann, 1982). Van Dijk (1999) proposes to "define contexts as the structure of all properties of the social situation that are systematically relevant for the production, comprehension, or functions of discourse and its structures" (p. 130). Giles and Coupland (1991) offer a framework within which they organize the situational facets which affect the style of changes in the communication and in particular in the listening behavior. The two main categories that determine a situation are the participants involved and the surrounding scene. On the part of the participants, the individual and the relationships need to be considered. If the person acts as "the person" or as a member or representative of a social category, communication behavior will vary accordingly. The person's behavior will be accounted for in terms of both stable and temporary features which are expressed through personality, interests, appearance on the one hand, and moods, emotional states, etc., on the other hand.

Aspects of the situation calibrate the listener orientation (Imhof, 2004a) and have an influence on the expectations for listening behavior. This was demonstrated in a study where participants had to select characteristics of good and poor listening behavior of individuals in different situations (professional context, instruction context, personal conversation) and with different status roles (superior, symmetric, subordinate) and in different cultural environments (Germany, USA) (Imhof, 2003a, 2004b). Participants would expect listeners in a subordinate role to confirm their attention and to keep eye-contact throughout the conversation while a listener in a superior role would not be expected to do so.

For a listener in a superior position it is more important to be open-minded and non-judgmental, while he or she would get away with fidgeting or doing something else besides the conversation. Also, in contrast to participants from Germany, participants from the US would insist that the listener gives feedback, for example, by nonverbal signs, that he feels responsible for the speaker – listener relationship throughout the conversation. Asking questions is considered part of the pattern of good listening behavior in a professional context, but significantly less so in an educational setting.

Research (Knapp and Hall, 2002) shows that the intensity of facial gestures is higher in low-status listeners than in higher status listeners. Women also tend to display a wider range of facial gestures than men, especially when communicating with men (Hall, 1984). Rummer (1996) reports an interesting study on how the experimental manipulation of a situation changes the characteristics of speech production. When participants retell a story of an observed burglary, the results are quite different in terms of speaking fluency, accuracy, emotional involvement, and added embellishments, depending on whether they are supposed to report to the police or whether they are instructed to tell their story to a neighbor. The question remains open if people actually listen differently, too, and how this could be described.

The effect of the situation also has been demonstrated in terms of systematic interferences which occur, for example, when listeners need to process information in a noisy environment. When people listened to descriptions of others in the presence of noise, their accounts of what they have heard was more extreme (for example, less recall of mitigating information) than in situations which were more conducive to listening (Baron, David, Brunsman, and Inman, 1997).

Characteristics of the message: How does the form of the message affect its content?

The final aspect under consideration here is the message itself and its characteristics because there is evidence for the assumption that we adjust the way of information processing to make it appropriate for the material at hand (Weaver, Bryant, and Burns, 1995). Research has shown that variables such as text difficulty (Müsseler, Rickheit, and Strohner, 1985), the way text is organized by different levels of headings and signals (Murray and McGlone, 1997; Lorch, Lorch, and Inman, 1993; Young, 1994), structure (Mannes and Kintsch, 1987; Speer and Clifton, 1998) and coherence (Kintsch and Kintsch, 1995), the way that text is combined with visuals (Moreno and Mayer, 2000, 2002) and gestures (Goldin-Meadow, 2003), text length, the task that is associated with text (Broekkamp, van Hout-Wolters, Rijlaarsdam, and van den Bergh, 2002), make a difference to the outcome performance that is typically measured in terms of reproduction rates or recall (for a more comprehensive overview see Butcher and Kintsch, 2003). The problem with these research studies is that they are very often based on reading comprehension and additionally that the texts used are of low ecological validity. Graesser, Millis, and Zwaan (1997) call the experimental texts "textoids," because the material is, more often than not, constructed in a highly artificial way in order to control for certain variables which are focused in the study. There are, however, interesting findings which indicate that the nature and the texture of the verbal message makes a difference in the processing results. The issue of if and how this applies to oral information is still under investigation.

Issues for Further Research

Research on listening from the perspective of cognitive psychology is still growing, because most literature focuses on written text (Alexander and Jetton, 2003). Cognitive psychologists and psycholinguistics have teamed up to study speech perception (for example, as documented in Cutler, 2005) and text and discourse comprehension (Graesser, Gernsbacher, and Goldman, 2003), but the complete picture of listening has yet to be pieced together from diverse research paradigms within cognitive psychology, such as attention and perception, from studies on mental models and comprehension, with additional contributions from an array of other disciplines within psychology, such as personality and social psychology. The research which exists encompasses a wide range of methodological approaches so that it is not an easy task to integrate the findings or to conduct a meta-analytical study of the many dimensions of listening. It has been proposed that listening research needs to be integrated into a unifying framework fostering theory building in the field (Bodie, Worthington, Imhof, and Cooper, 2008).

Therefore, the most urgent issue for research on listening is to develop adequate and specific methods and instruments. So far, what we see is that some studies in text comprehension include acoustic material, some studies present reading material sequentially – which is in some aspects more like listening than like reading – while other work looks at text comprehension without making the distinction between written and acoustic material. In this context, it appears important to realize that listening and reading are not identical twins, although it has been proposed that information is processed as a set of abstract propositions independent of the input modality (Bradley and Forster, 1987; van der Meer, 1996). If the latter assumption were true, results from research on reading comprehension could be generalized, mutatis mutandis, to listening comprehension. This presumption, however, is in contrast to research results which describe the wide array of modality specific effects and mental activities (Cohen, 1993; Cowan, 1995; Neumann, van der Heijden, and Allport, 1986) which are "unique to listening" (Buck, 2001, p. 31) and which make a difference in the raw data which are generated from speech perception as opposed to print decoding (Danks and End, 1987). We find functional differences between the processing of auditory and visual information on all levels, namely on the level of perception, word recognition, sentence parsing, and discourse comprehension. These differences can be accounted for in terms of working memory, of retrieval, and of long-term storage, as, for example, acoustic signals are temporally distributed, as opposed to the spatial distribution of visual stimuli, acoustic information lasts longer in the phonological loop of working memory than visual information lasts in the spatio-visual sketch pad part of the working memory. In addition, brain research has shown that different areas of the brain are activated during the processing of when oral and written language (Brown and Hagoort, 2000; Price, Indefry, and van Turennout, 1999).

The demand for analyzing reading and listening separately is supported by practical considerations. We need the research in order to obtain a more specific idea of what we can teach as we teach listening, because it is evident that strategies which can be applied to reading material (Pressley, 2000; Pressley and Afflerbach, 1995) are not applicable to acoustic material (for example, refer back to a difficult passage, underline and mark important words). If strategy use is supposed to have an impact on retention, the feasibility of specific strategies and the effect of the differential availability of the strategies need to be empirically investigated. To have a more specific basic knowledge on how listening works and how it is affected by certain strategies is certainly important as it comes to consider the issue of how listening can be taught and assessed (Buck, 2001; Imhof, 1998, 2004b; Janusik, 2002; Rost, 1990). At this point, the latest, we need to realize that listening is not even a fraternal twin of reading, but rather another cousin with specific characteristics from the language skills family.

Suggestions for practical observation and research

1   Observe your listening day and reflect on who you listened to, how well you listened and why.
2   Observe a conversation (recorded or live) and describe the nonverbal signals carefully. Then analyze the relationship between the nonverbal and the verbal communication: What does the nonverbal part of the communication say?
3   Describe a conflict or misunderstanding which you have perceived in a communication recently. Drawing on the research: What could be the possible contributions of the listener in creating and/or aggravating the misunderstanding? Do you see any alternatives to avoid situations like this in the future?
4   How do you know that you have listened well?

QUESTIONS FOR DISCUSSION

1   Where in the listening process do you see potential for improvement by training?
2   Where in the listening process would you expect traps and barriers which cause misunderstanding or communication breakdowns?
3   How would you describe a "good" listener? What does this person do that a "poor" listener would not be able or fail to do?
4   Drawing on the research findings: What could you as a listener do in order to improve on the efficiency of information processing in selected situations, for example, as in class or in a meeting?
5   What would your recommendation be to a speaker in order to make his speech listener-friendly in selected situations, for example, as in public speaking situations, in teaching situations, or in small group interactions?

References

Aitchison, J. (2003). *Words in the mind*. Oxford: Blackwell.

Alexander, P.A., and Jetton, T. (2003). Learning from traditional and alternative texts: New conceptualizations for the information age. In A.C. Graesser, M.A. Gernsbacher, and S.R. Goldman (Eds.). *Handbook of discourse processes*, pp. 199–241. Mahwah, NJ: Lawrence Erlbaum.

Anderson, J.R. (2004). *Cognitive psychology and its implications*. New York: W.H. Freeman and Company.

Anderson, R.C., and Pichert, J. W. (1978). Recall of previously unrecallable information following a shift in perspective. *Journal of Verbal Learning and Verbal Behavior*, 17, 1–12.

Argyle, M. (1988). *Bodily communication*. London: Methuen.

Ashcraft, M.H. (2006). *Cognition*. Upper Saddle River, NJ: Pearson Education.

Atkinson, R.C., and Shiffrin, R.M. (1968). Human memory: A proposed system and its control processes. In W.K. Spence, and J.T. Spence (Eds.). *The psychology of learning and motivation: Advances in research and theory*, Vol. 2, pp. 89–195. New York: Academic Press.

Baddeley, A. (2006). Working memory: An overview. In S. J. Pickering (Ed.). *Working memory and education*, pp. 1–31. Amsterdam: Elsevier.

Barker, L.L., and Watson, K.W. (2000). *Listen up*. New York: St. Martin's Press.

Baron, R.S., David, J.D., Brunsman, B.M., and Inman, M. (1997). Why listeners hear less than they are told: Attentional load and the teller-listener extremity effect. *Journal of Personality and Social Psychology*, 72, 826–38.

Barquero, B. (1999). Mentale Modelle von mentalen Zuständen und Handlungen der Textprotagonisten [Mental models of mental states and actions of text protagonists]. *Zeitschrift für Experimentelle Psychologie*, 46, 243–8.

Bertelson, P., Vroomen, J., and de Gelder, B. (2003). Visual recalibration of auditory speech identification: A McGurk aftereffect. *Psychological Science*, 14, 592–7.

Bishop, D.V. (1997). *Uncommon understanding: Development and disorders of language comprehension in children*. Hove: Psychology Press.

Bodie, G.D., Worthington, D., Imhof, M., and Cooper L.O. (2008). What would a unified field of listening look like? A proposal linking past perspectives and future endeavors. *International Journal of Listening*, 22, 103–22.

Bradley, D.C., and Forster, K.I. (1987). A reader's view of listening. In U.H. Frauenfelder, and L.K. Tyler (Eds.). *Spoken word recognition*, pp. 103–34. Amsterdam: Elsevier Science Publishers.

Bregman, A.S. (1978). The formation of auditory streams. In J. Requin (Ed.). *Attention and Performance VII*, pp. 63–75. Hillsdale, NJ: Lawrence Erlbaum Associates.

Bregman, A.S. (1981). Asking the "What For" question in auditory perception. In M. Kubovy, and J.R. Pomerantz (Eds.). *Perceptual organization*, pp. 99–118. Hillsdale, NJ: Erlbaum.

Bregman, A.S. (1990). *Auditory scene analysis*. Cambridge, MA: MIT Press.

Broekkamp, H., van Hout-Wolters, B.H.A.M., Rijlaarsdam, G., and van den Bergh, H. (2002). Importance in instructional text: Teachers' and students' perceptions of task demands. *Journal of Educational Psychology*, 94, 260–71.

Brown, C., and Hagoort, P. (2000). On the electrophysiology of language comprehension: Implications for the human language system. In M.W. Crocker, M. Pickering, and C. Clifton (Eds.). *Architectures and mechanisms for language processing*, pp. 213–37. Cambridge: Cambridge University Press.

Buck, G. (2001). *Assessing listening*. Cambridge: Cambridge University Press.

Butcher, K.R., and Kintsch, W. (2003). Text comprehension and discourse processing. In A.F. Healy, and R.W. Proctor (Eds.). *Handbook of psychology, vol. 4 Experimental psychology*, pp. 575–95. Hoboken, NJ: John Wiley & Sons.

Caillies, S., Denhière, G., and Jhean-Larose, S. (1999). The intermediate effect: Interaction between prior knowledge and text structure. In H. van Oostendorp, and S.R. Goldman (Eds.). *The construction of mental representations during reading*, pp. 151–68. Mahwah, NJ: Lawrence Erlbaum.

Cain, K. (2006). Children's reading comprehension: The role of working memory in normal and impaired development. In S.J. Pickering (Ed.). *Working memory and education*, pp. 61–91. Amsterdam: Elsevier.

Cain, K., Oakhill, J., and Lemmon, K. (2004). Individual differences in the inference of word meanings from context: The influence of reading comprehension, vocabulary knowledge, and memory capacity. *Journal of Educational Psychology*, 96, 671–81.

Carpenter, P.A., Miyake, N., and Just, M.A. (1995). Language comprehension: Sentence and discourse processing. *Annual Review of Psychology*, 46, 91–120.

Cherry, E.C. (1953). Some experiments on the recognition of speech with one and two ears. *Journal of the Acoustical Society of America*, 25, 975–9.

Clark, H.H. (1996). *Using language*. Cambridge: Cambridge University Press.

Cohen, R.A. (1993). *The neuropsychology of attention*. New York: Plenum Press.

Collins, A.M., and Loftus, E.F. (1975). A spreading-activation theory of semantic processing. *Psychological Review*, 82, 407–28.

Collins, A.M., and Quillian, M.R. (1969). Retrieval time from semantic memory. *Journal of Verbal Learning and Verbal Behavior*, 8, 240–7.

Cowan, N. (1995). *Attention and memory: An integrated framework*. Oxford: Oxford University Press.

Crocker, M.W., Pickering, M., and Clifton, C. (2000). *Architectures and mechanisms for language processing*. Cambridge: Cambridge University Press.

Cutler, A. (1999). Prosodische Struktur und Worterkennung bei gesprochener Sprache [Prosodic structure and word recognition in speech]. In

A.D. Friederici (Ed.). *Enzyklopädie der Psychologie, Themenbereich C Theorie und Forschung, Serie III Sprache, Band 2 Sprachrezeption*, pp. 49–83. Göttingen: Hogrefe.

Cutler, A. (Ed.). (2005). *Twenty-first century psycholinguistics: Four cornerstones.* Mahwah, NJ: Lawrence Erlbaum.

Cutler, A., and Clifton, C. (1999). Comprehending spoken language: A blueprint of the listener. In C.M. Brown, and P. Hagoort (Eds.). *The neurocognition of language*, pp. 123–66. Oxford: Oxford University Press.

Cutler, A., Smits, R., and Cooper, N. (2005). Vowel perception: Effects of non-native language vs. non-native dialect. *Speech Communication*, 47, 32–42.

Danks, J.H., and End, L.J. (1987). Processing strategies for reading and listening. In R. Horowitz, and S.J. Samuels (Eds.). *Comprehending oral and written language*, pp. 271–94. London: Academic Press.

Dörner, D. (2005). Verstehen verstehen [Understanding understanding]. *Zeitschrift für Psychologie*, 213, 187–92.

Flammer, A., and Tauber, M. (1982). Changing the reader's perspective. In A. Flammer, and W. Kintsch (Eds.). *Discourse processing*, pp. 379–91. Amsterdam: North-Holland Publishing Company.

Garnham, A. (1989). Inference in language understanding: What, when, why and how. In R. Dietrich, and C.F. Graumann (Eds.). *Language processing in social context*, pp. 153–72. North-Holland: Elsevier.

Garnham, A., and Oakhill, J. (1996). The mental models theory of language comprehension. In B.K. Britton, and A.C. Graesser (Eds.). *Models of understanding text*, pp. 313–39. Mahwah, NJ: Lawrence Erlbaum.

Gaskell, A.G., and Marslen-Wilson, W.D. (1997). Integrating form and meaning: A distributed model of speech perception. *Language and Cognitive Processes*, 12, 613–56.

Gathercole, S.E., and Baddeley, A.D. (1993). *Working memory and language.* Hove: Lawrence Erlbaum Associates.

Gernsbacher, M.A. (1990). *Language comprehension as structure building.* Hillsdale, NJ: Lawrence Erlbaum Associates.

Giles, H., and Coupland, N. (1991). *Language: Contexts and consequences.* Milton Keynes: Open University Press.

Goldin-Meadow, S. (2003). *Hearing gesture: How our hands help us think.* Cambridge, MA: The Belknap Press of Harvard University Press.

Graesser, A.C., and Zwaan, R.A. (1995). Inference generation and construction of situation models. In C.A. Weaver, S. Mannes, and C.R. Fletcher, (Eds.). *Discourse comprehension*, pp. 117–39. Hillsdale, NJ: Lawrence Erlbaum.

Graesser, A.C., Gernsbacher, M.A., and Goldman, S.R. (Eds.).(2003). *Handbook of discourse processes.* Mahwah, NJ: Lawrence Erlbaum.

Graesser, A.C., Millis, K.M., and Zwaan, R.A. (1997). Discourse comprehension. *Annual Review of Psychology*, 48, 163–89.

Graesser, A.C., Singer, M., and Trabasso, T. (1994). Constructing inferences during narrative text comprehension. *Psychological Review*, 101, 371–95.

Guthrie, J.T., Wigfield, A., Barbosa, P., Perencevich, K.C., Taboada, A., Davis, M.H., Scafiddi, N.T., and Tonks, S. (2004). Increasing reading comprehension and engagement through concept-oriented reading instruction. *Journal of Educational Psychology*, 96, 403–23.

Guttman, S.E., Gilroy, L.A., and Blake, R. (2005). Hearing what the eye sees. *Psychological Science*, 16, 228–35.

Habermann, G.M. (1996). Inferential miscommunication and language learning. *Alberta Modern Language Journal*, 32, 2, 13–26.

Hagoort, P. (2005). Broca's complex as the unification space for language. In A. Cutler (Ed.). *Twenty-First century psycholinguistics: Four cornerstones*, pp. 157–72. Mahwah, NJ: Lawrence Erlbaum.

Hall, J.A. (1984). *Nonverbal sex differences. Communication accuracy and expressive style*. Baltimore: Johns Hopkins University Press.

Handel, S. (1989). *Listening: An introduction to the perception of auditory events*. Cambridge: MIT Press.

Herrmann, T. (1982). *Sprechen und Situation* [Speaking and situation]. Berlin: Springer.

Imhof, M. (1998). What makes a good listener? – Assessment of listening behavior in instructional settings. *International Journal of Listening*, 12, 81–108.

Imhof, M. (2002). In the eye of the beholder – Children's perception of good and poor listening behavior. *International Journal of Listening*, 16, 40–56.

Imhof, M. (2003a). The social construction of the listener: Listening behaviour across situations, perceived listener status, and cultures. *Communication Research Reports*, 20, 369–78.

Imhof, M. (2003b). *Zuhören – Psychologische Aspekte auditiver Informationsverarbeitung* [Listening – Psychological Aspects of auditory information processing]. Göttingen: Vandenhoeck & Ruprecht.

Imhof, M. (2004a). Who are we as we listen? Individual listening profiles in varying contexts. *International Journal of Listening*, 18, 36–45.

Imhof, M. (2004b). *Zuhören und Instruktion - Empirische Zugänge zur Verarbeitung mündlich vermittelter Information* [Listening and instruction – Empirical approaches to modes of oral information processing]. Münster: Waxmann.

Imhof, M., and Janusik, L.A. (2006). Development and validation of the Imhof-Janusik Listening Concepts Inventory to measure listening conceptualization differences between cultures. *Journal of Intercultural Communication Research*, 35, 79–98.

Inhoff, A.W., and Connine, C. (1995). Perceptual similarity and salience in the accessing of lexical meaning. In R.F. Lorch, and E.J. O'Brien (Eds.). *Sources of coherence in reading*, pp. 73–89. Hillsdale, NJ: Lawrence Erlbaum.

Janusik, L.A. (2002). Teaching listening: What do we do? What should we do? *International Journal of Listening*, 16, 5–39.

Janusik, L.A. (2004). Researching listening from the inside out: The relationship between conversational listening span and perceived communicative competence. Digital dissertations, UMI Proquest. Available at: http://www.lib.umi.com/dissertations.

Jay, T.B. (2003). *The psychology of language*. Upper Saddle River, NJ: Prentice Hall.

Johnson-Laird, P.N. (1983). *Mental models: Towards a cognitive science of language, inference, and consciousness*. Cambridge, MA: Harvard University Press.

Just, M.A., and Carpenter, P.A. (1992). A capacity theory of comprehension: Individual differences in working memory. *Psychological Review*, 99, 122–49.

Kaschak, M.P., Madden, C.J., Therriault, D.J., Yaxley, R.H., Aveyard, M., Blanchard, A.A., and Zwaan, R.A. (2005). Perception of motion affects language processing. *Cognition*, 94, 79–89.

Kiewitz, C., Weaver, J.B., Brosius, H.-B., and Weimann, G. (1997). Cultural differences in listening style preferences: A comparison of young adults in Germany, Israel, and the United States. *International Journal of Public Opinion Research*, 9, 233–47.

Kintsch, E., and Kintsch, W. (1995). Strategies to promote active learning from text: Individual differences in background knowledge. *Swiss Journal of Psychology*, 54, 141–51.

Kintsch, W. (1989). The representation of knowledge and the use of knowledge in discourse comprehension. In R. Dietrich, and C.F. Graumann (Eds.). *Language processing in social context*, pp. 185–209. North-Holland: Elsevier.

Kintsch, W. (1998). *Comprehension: A paradigm for cognition*. Cambridge: Cambridge University Press.

Kintsch, W. (2005). An overview of top-down and bottom-up effects in comprehension: The CI perspective. *Discourse Processes*, 39, 125–8.

Kintsch, W., and Franzke, M. (1995). The role of background knowledge in the recall of a news story. In R.F. Lorch, and E.J. O'Brien (Eds.). *Sources of coherence in reading*, pp. 321–33. Hillsdale, NJ: Lawrence Erlbaum.

Knapp, J.A., and Hall, M.L. (2002). *Nonverbal communication in human interaction*. London: Thomson Learning.

Koelsch, S., Gunter, T., Friederici, A.D., and Schröger, E. (2000). Brain indices of music processing: "Nonmusicians" are musical. *Journal of Cognitive Neuroscience*, 12, 520–41.

Krauss, R.M., and Pardo, J.S. (2006). Speaker Perception and Social Behavior: Bridging Social Psychology and Speech Science. In P.A.M. Van Lange (Ed.). *Bridging social psychology: Benefits of transdisciplinary approaches*, pp. 273–8). Mahwah, NJ: Lawrence Erlbaum Associates Publishers.

Kürschner, C., Schnotz, W., Eid, M., and Hauck, G. (2005). Individuelle Modalitätspräferenzen beim Textverstehen [Individual modality preferences in text comprehension]. *Zeitschrift für Entwicklungpsychologie und Pädagogische Psychologie*, 37, 2–16.

Kutas, M., and Hillyard, S.A. (1980). Reading senseless sentences: Brain potentials reflect semantic incongruity. *Science*, 207, 203–5.

Kutas, M., Federmeier, K.D., and Sereno, M.I. (1999). Current approaches to mapping language in electromagnetic space. In C.M. Brown, and P. Hagoort (Eds.). *The neurocognition of language*, pp. 359–92. Oxford: Oxford University Press.

LaFrance, M., and Hecht, M.A. (1999). Option or obligation to smile: The effects of power and gender on facial expression. In P. Philippot, R.S. Feldman, and E.J. Coats (Eds.). *The social context of nonverbal behavior*, pp. 45–70. Cambridge: Cambridge University Press.

Lively, S.E., Pisoni, D.B., and Goldinger, S.D. (1994). Spoken word recognition: Research and theory. In M.A. Gernsbacher (Ed.), *Handbook of psycholinguistics*, pp. 265–301. San Diego, CA: Academic Press.

Lorch, R.F., Klusewitz, M.A., and Lorch, E.P. (1995). Distinction among reading situations. In R.F. Lorch, and E.J. O'Brien (Eds.). *Sources of coherence in reading*, pp. 375–98. Hillsdale, NJ: Lawrence Erlbaum.

Lorch, R.F., Lorch, E.P., and Inman, W.E. (1993). Effects of signalling topic structure on text recall. *Journal of Educational Psychology*, 85, 281–90.

Mannes, S.M., and Kintsch, W. (1987). Knowledge organization and text organization. *Cognition and instruction*, 4, 91–115.

Mayer, R.E. (1996). Learning strategies for making sense out of expository text: The SOI model for guiding three cognitive processes in knowledge construction. *Educational Psychology Review*, 8, 357–71.

Mayer, R.E. (1999). Designing instruction for constructivist learning. In C.M. Reigeluth (Ed.). *Instructional-design theories and models*, Vol. II, pp. 141–59. Mahwah, NJ: Lawrence Erlbaum.

Mayer, R.E. (2003). *Learning and instruction*. Upper Saddle River: Pearson Education.

McDevitt, T.M., and Ford, M.E. (1987). Processes in young children's communicative functioning and development. In M.E. Ford, and D.H. Ford (Eds.). *Humans as self- constructing living systems: Putting the framework to work*, pp. 145–75. Hillsdale, NJ: Lawrence Erlbaum Associates.

McGurk, H., and MacDonald, J. (1976). Hearing lips and seeing voices. *Nature*, 264, 746–8.

Miller, G.A. (1999). On knowing a word. *Annual Review of Psychology*, 50, 1–19.

Moreno, R., and Mayer, R.E. (2000). A coherence effect in multimedia learning: The case for minimizing irrelevant sounds in the design of multimedia instructional messages. *Journal of Educational Psychology*, 92, 117–25.

Moreno, R., and Mayer, R.E. (2002). Verbal redundancy in multimedia learning: When reading helps listening. *Journal of Educational Psychology*, 94, 156–63.

Murray, J.D., and McGlone, C. (1997). Topic overviews and the processing of topic structure. *Journal of Educational Psychology*, 89, 251–71.

Müsseler, J., Rickheit, G., and Strohner, H. (1985). Influences of modality, text difficulty, and processing control on inferences in text processing. In G. Rickheit, and H. Strohner (Eds.). *Inferences in text processing*, pp. 247–71. Amsterdam: Elsevier.

Narvaez, D., van den Broek, P., and Barron-Ruiz, A. (1999). The influence of reading purpose on inference generation and comprehension in reading. *Journal of Educational Psychology*, 91, 488–96.

Neumann, O., van der Heijden, A.H.C., and Allport, A.D. (1986). *Visual selective attention: Introductory remarks*. Bielefeld: Center for interdisciplinary research.

Nieding, G. (2006). *Wie verstehen Kinder Texte* [How do children understand texts]? Lengerich: Pabst.

Norris, D., McQueen, J.M., and Cutler, A. (2003). Perceptual learning in speech. *Cognitive Psychology*, 47, 204–38.

Oden, G.C., Rueckl, J.G., and Sanocki, T. (1991). Making sentences make sense, or words to that effect. In G. B. Simpson (Ed.). *Understanding word and sentence*, pp. 285–303. Amsterdam: Elsevier Science Publishers.

Osterhout, L., and Holcomb, P.J. (1995). Event-related potentials and language comprehension. In M.D. Rugg, and M.G.H. Coles (Eds.). *Electrophysiology of mind: Event-related brain potentials and cognition*, pp. 171–215. New York: Oxford University Press.

Pasupathi, M., Stallworth, L.M., and Murdoch, K. (1998). How what we tell becomes what we know: Listener effects on speakers' long-term memory for events. *Discourse Processes*, 26, 1–25.

Penno, J.F., Wilkinson, I.A.G., and Moore, D.W. (2002). Vocabulary acquisition from teacher explanation and repeated listening to stories: Do they overcome the Matthew effect? *Journal of Educational Psychology*, 94, 23–33.

Perrig, W., and Kintsch, W. (1985). Propositional and situational representations of text. *Journal of Memory and Language*, 24, 503–18.

Pickering, M.J., Clifton, C., and Crocker, M.W. (2000). Architectures and mechanisms in sentence comprehension. In M.W. Crocker, M.J. Pickering, and C. Clifton (Eds.). *Architectures and mechanisms for language processing*, pp. 1–28. Cambridge: Cambridge University Press.

Pisoni, D.B. (1987). Auditory perception of complex sounds: Some comparisons of speech vs. nonspeech signals. In W.A. Yost, and C.S. Watson (Eds.). *Auditory processing of complex sounds*, pp. 247–56. Cambridge: Cambridge University Press.

Pressley, M. (2000). What should comprehension instruction be the instruction of? In M.L. Kamil, P.B. Mosenthal, P.D. Pearson, and R. Barr (Eds.). *Handbook of reading research*, Vol. III, pp. 545–61. Mahwah, NJ: Lawrence Erlbaum.

Pressley, M., and Afflerbach, P. (1995). *Verbal protocols of reading*. Hillsdale, NJ: Lawrence Erlbaum.

Price, C., Indefry, P., and van Turennout, M. (1999). The neural architecture underlying the processing of written and spoken word forms. In C. M. Brown, and P. Hagoort (Eds.). *The neurocognition of language*, pp. 211–40. Oxford: Oxford University Press.

Rickheit, G., Schnotz, W., and Strohner, G. (1985). The concept of inference in discourse comprehension. In G. Rickheit, and H. Strohner (Eds.). *Inferences in text processing*, pp. 3–49. Amsterdam: Elsevier Publishers.

Rinck, M.(2000). Situationsmodelle und das Verstehen von Erzähltexten: Befunde und Probleme [Situation models and understanding of narrative texts: Findings and problems]. *Psychologische Rundschau*, 51, 115–22.

Rost, M. (1990). *Listening in language learning*. New York: Longman.

Rummer, R. (1996). *Kognitive Beanspruchung beim Sprechen* [Cognitive load in speech production]. Weinheim: Beltz.

Schneider, W., and Shiffrin, R.M. (1977). Controlled and automatic human information processing: I. Detection, search, and attention. *Psychological Review*, 84, 1–66.

Schober, M.F., and Brennan, S.E. (2003). Processes of interactive spoken discourse: The role of the partner. In A.C. Graesser, M.A. Gernsbacher, and S.R. Goldman (Eds.). *Handbook of discourse processes*, pp. 123–64. Mahwah, NJ: Lawrence Erlbaum Associates.

Scott, S.K. (2005). The neurobiology of speech perception. In A. Cutler (Eds.). *Twenty-first century psycholinguistics: Four cornerstones*, pp. 141–56. Mahwah, NJ: Lawrence Erlbaum.

Shiffrin, R.M., and Schneider, W. (1977). Controlled and automatic human information processing: II. Perceptual learning, automatic attending, and a general theory. *Psychological Review*, 84, 127–90.

Singer, M. (1994). Discourse inference processes. In M.A. Gernsbacher (Ed.). *Handbook of psycholinguistics*, pp. 479–515. San Diego: Academic Press.

Speer, S.R., and Clifton, C. (1998). Plausibility and argument structure in sentence comprehension. *Memory and Cognition*, 26, 965–78.

Stanfield, R.A., and Zwaan, R.A. (2001). The effect of implied orientation derived from verbal context on picture recognition. *Psychological Science*, 12, 153–6.

Styles, E.A. (2005). *Attention, perception and memory*. Hove: Psychology Press.

Styles, E.A. (2006). *The psychology of attention*. Hove: Psychology Press.

Summerfield, Q., and Culling, J.F. (1992). Auditory segregation of competing voices: absence of effects of FM or AM coherence. In R.P. Carlyon, C.J. Darwin, and I.J. Russel (Eds.). *Processing of complex sounds by the auditory system: Proceedings of the Royal Society Discussion Meeting*, December 4–5, 1991, pp. 63–72. Oxford: Clarendon.

Tartter, V.C. (1998). *Language and its normal processing*. London: Sage Publications.

Therriault, D.J., Rinck, M., and Zwaan, R.A. (2006). Assessing the influence of dimensional focus during situational model construction. *Memory and Cognition*, 34, 78–89.

Van der Meer, E. (1995). Gedächtnis und Inferenzen [Memory and inferences]. In D. Dörner, and E. van der Meer (Eds.). *Das Gedächtnis*, pp. 341–80. Göttingen: Hogrefe.

Van der Meer, E. (1996). Gesetzmäßigkeiten und Steuerungsmöglichkeiten des Wissenserwerbs [Functions and control in knowledge acquisition]. In F.E. Weinert (Ed.). *Enzyklopädie der Psychologie: Themenbereich D Praxisgebiete, Serie I Pädagogische Psychologie, Band 2 Psychologie des Lernens und der Instruktion*, pp. 209–48. Göttingen: Hogrefe.

van Dijk, T.A. (1999). Context models in discourse processing. In H. van Oostendorp, and S.R. Goldman (Eds.). *The construction of mental representations during reading*, pp. 123–48. Mahwah, NJ: Lawrence Erlbaum.

van Oostendorp, H., and Bonebakker, C. (1999). Difficulties in updating mental representations during reading news reports. In H. van Oostendorp, and S. Goldman (Eds.). *The construction of mental representations during reading*, pp. 319–39. Mahwah, NJ: Lawrence Erlbaum.

van Petten, C., and Kutas, M. (1990). Interactions between sentence context and word frequency in event-related brain potentials. *Memory and Cognition*, 18, 380–93.

van Petten, C., and Kutas, M. (1991). Electrophysiological evidence for the flexibility of lexical processing. In G.B. Simpson (Ed.). *Understanding word and sentence*, pp. 129–74. Amsterdam: Elsevier Science Publishers.

Vohs, K.D., and Ciarocco, N.J. (2004). Interpersonal functioning requires self-regulation. In R.F. Baumeister, and K.D. Voss (Eds.). *Handbook of self-regulation. Research, theory, and applications*, pp. 392–407. New York: The Guilford Press.

Vonk, W. (1985). The immediacy of inferences in the understanding of pronouns. In Rickheit, G., and Strohner, H. (Eds.). *Inferences in text processing*, pp. 205–18. Amsterdam: Elsevier Publishers.

Warren, R.M. (1970). Perceptual restorations of missing speech sounds. *Science*, 167, 392–3.

Weaver, C.A., Bryant, D.S., and Burns, K. (1995). Comprehension monitoring: Extensions of the Kintsch and van Dijk model. In C.A. Weaver, S. Mannes, and C.R. Fletcher (Eds.). *Discourse comprehension*, pp. 177–93. Hillsdale, NJ: Lawrence Erlbaum.

Whitney, P., and Waring, D.A. (1991). The role of knowledge in comprehension: A cognitive control perspective. In G.B. Simpson (Ed.). *Understanding word and sentence*, pp. 199–216. Amsterdam: Elsevier Publishers.

Woloshyn, V.E., Paivio, A., and Pressley, M. (1994). Use of elaborative interrogation to help students acquire information consistent with prior knowledge and information inconsistent with prior knowledge. *Journal of Educational Psychology*, 86, 79–89.

Wolvin, A.D., and Coakley, C.G. (1996). *Listening*. Madison: Brown & Benchmark.

Yehia, H.C., Kuratate, T., and Vatikiotis-Bateson, E. (2002). Linking facial animation, head motion and speech acoustics. *Journal of Phonetics*, 30, 555–68.

Young, L. (1994). University lectures – macro-structure and micro-features. In J. Flowerdew (Ed.). *Academic Listening: Research perspectives*, pp. 159–76. Cambridge: Cambridge University Press.

Zwaan, R.A., and Madden, C.J. (2004). Updating situation models. *Journal of Experimental Psychology: Learning, Memory, and Cognition*, 30, 283–8.

Zwaan, R.A., and Radvansky, G.A. (1998). Situation models in language comprehension and memory. *Psychological Bulletin*, 123, 162–85.

Zwaan, R.A., and Singer, M. (2003). Text comprehension. In A.C. Graesser, M.A. Gernsbacher, and S.R. Goldman (Eds.). *Handbook of discourse processes*, pp. 83–121. Mahwah, NJ: Lawrence Erlbaum Associates.

5

Listening: A Dialogic Perspective
James J. Floyd

In this chapter Floyd suggests that important aspects of listening can extend beyond the boundaries of specific listening types or purposes. In standard approaches to listening, four types of listening are often presented as constituting the various purposes of listening. Thus one can engage in "discriminative listening" (listening to distinguish the aural and visual stimuli); "comprehensive listening" (listening to understand the message); "therapeutic listening" (giving someone who is troubled an opportunity to talk through his/her problem); and "critical listening" (analyzing and evaluating messages) (Wolvin and Coakley, 1996, pp. 156–355).

Without denying the importance and usefulness of these listening purposes, this chapter discusses dialogic listening as a general approach to listening, or one that applies to nearly all listening situations and purposes. The basic idea in this chapter is that listeners, as well as speakers, can adopt one of two contrasting attitudes or approaches to listening in practically any situation. The underlying idea of the *dialogic* approach is that, in any communication situation, there is a relational, or interpersonal, dimension (see Brockreide, 1968); communication always involves people interacting with other people. And the overall nature and quality of one's listening can be affected significantly by that person's attitude/approach toward the other person or persons involved in any situation – from the dyadic, to conversations among people, to small group communication, to listening in public and mediated settings.

Therefore, the discussion in this chapter centers upon the contrast between a *dialogic* attitude/approach and a *monologic* attitude/approach to listening. The key idea of the chapter is that dialogic listening represents a more productive and even more ethical approach to listening than does a monological approach. The chapter presents and discusses each or the two approaches, with examples; discusses difficulties that listeners might encounter in attempting to listen dialogically; and discusses possible solutions to these problems.

The author attempts to provide you with an alternative that you might decide to use in your own listening efforts, hopefully leading to more productive and satisfying listening in almost any communication setting.

The Nature of Dialogue

The word "dialogue" appears to have a variety of meanings for "both laymen and scholars" (Johannesen, 2002, p. 55). One may think of it as consisting of any situation in which there is an exchange between two or more people. At other times it is viewed as a theatrical term used to describe the difference between an uninterrupted speech (monologue) and the exchanging of lines, as in a conversation (dialogue). In other situations it describes any kind of extended discussion over some issue or topic, as in "a public dialogue."

As I am using the term in this chapter, however, dialogue represents communication characterized "by such qualities as mutuality, open-heartedness, directness, honesty, spontaneity, frankness, lack of pretense, nonmanipulative intent, communion, intensity, and love in the sense of responsibility of one human for another" (Johannesen, 1971, p. 375). The "essential movement" in dialogic communication "is turning toward, outgoing to and reaching for the other" (1971, p. 375). As Johannesen further explains it, we should think of dialogue "as a stance, orientation, or bearing in communication rather than as a specific method, technique, or format." In this sense, dialogue refers more to an "attitude" toward or spirit of communication (2002, p. 58). In contrast, the opposite, or antithesis, of dialogue, is monologue, any form of communication which "seeks to command, coerce, manipulate, conquer, dazzle deceive, or exploit (Johannesen, 1971, p. 377).

Perhaps the key to understanding the essential nature of this approach/orientation is to think of the dialogic communicator as one who attempts to minimize the tendency toward selfishness and the manipulation of others, for monologue either ignores those selfish tendencies or intentionally *strives* to accomplish selfish, manipulative purposes. Either approach (dialogue or monologue) can potentially occur in any kind of communication setting. Johannesen (2002, p. 65) contends, for example, that while dialogue easily relates to "private, interpersonal communication settings," public communication (speeches, essays, editorials, and mass media appeals) can have "sincere dialogical attitudes." Indeed public speakers often do have dialogic or monologic attitudes and approaches to their listeners.

Another approach to understanding the basic nature of communication as dialogue is to consider it as a philosophical construct, such as

Weaver's analysis of Plato's conception of the non-lover, the evil lover, and the noble lover (Weaver, 1985, pp. 5–26). While the non-lover represents a person who speaks or listens without passion or personal involvement, the evil and the noble lover represent philosophical attitudes and approaches that closely parallel monologue and dialogue (See Johannesen, 2002, pp. 65–6). The evil or monologic communicator "is not motivated by benevolence toward the beloved, but by selfish appetite." This "base" speaker (lover) "influences us in the direction of what is evil," a speaker whose goal is "exploitation" (Weaver, 1985, pp. 10–11).

In contrast, the noble lover is similar to the descriptions of a dialogic communicator in that he or she has "mastered the conflict within his own soul by conquering appetite and fixing his attention on the intelligible and divine." This true, noble, lover "follows the beloved in reverence and awe," expressing a love that exhibits "no jealousy or meanness toward the loved one" but endeavors by all means "to lead him in the likeness of the god whom they both honor." In this way, says Weaver, love is converted from "the exploitative to the creative" (pp. 13–14).

The Importance of Dialogic Listening

Any examination of the characteristics of dialogue and monologue makes it clear that either approach to communication should apply to listeners as well as to speakers. Importantly, as Wolvin and Coakley stress, listening "is very much a communication function" (1996, p. 108). And as Ogden and Richards indicate in *The Meaning of Meaning* (1956), we need to pay attention to the listener function in communication as much as we attend to the speaker function:

> It is certainly true that the preoccupation with 'expression' as the chief function of language has been disastrous … Speech does imply a listener…. Thus Dittrich, the holder of one of the few recognized Chairs of the subject, wrote in 1900: 'For linguistic science it is fundamental that language is an affair not merely of expression but also of impression, that communication is of its essence, and that in its definition this must not be overlooked. (Ogden and Richards, 1956 p. 231).

Charles Larson (2007) provides a related justification for applying the concepts of dialogue and monologue to listening as well as speaking. Focusing on the need for evaluation, his approach to persuasion emphasizes the role of the receiver. He writes, for example, that "we live in a world in which persuasive messages of various types continually compete for our attention, our beliefs, and our actions." He goes on to say that, since "we spend far more time receiving persuasion than sending persuasion," we need to focus on becoming "more critical and responsible" listeners, consumers "of persuasive messages" (p. 2). This echoes the earlier writing of Ralph G. Nichols (1987, p. 24), who reminded us that "persuadees listening to what appears to be persuasive speech benefit greatly by concentrating upon the evaluative function of the listening process." More specifically, he urged us to discern speaker motivation, hidden motives, a desire for "personal gain," the speaker's use of support, and his or her use of fallacious reasoning (p. 24).

These statements suggest, then, a dual aspect to dialogic listening. The first aspect relates to ways in which one can actually listen dialogically rather than monologically. The second suggests the need – as a listener – to recognize and to distinguish between speakers who are dialogic and those who are monologic in their approach to communication. Listeners attempting to succeed in either aspect of dialogic listening – listening dialogically and distinguishing between dialogic and monologic speakers – must understand and utilize the skills necessary to meet either goal.

How to Listen Dialogically

Johannesen's "characteristics of dialogue" do not apply exclusively to either speaking or listening but, instead, to the nature of dialogic communication in general. But since the discussion here concerns effective dialogic listening, we can consider those dialogic characteristics as they relate specifically to listening. The characteristics include: authenticity; inclusion; confirmation; presentness; spirit of mutual equality; and supportive climate (2002, pp. 58–60).

Authenticity suggests that one should attempt to listen without deception. Providing feedback that is insincere; pretending interest in a speaker's ideas and feelings when not actually caring; feigning interest in a person's problems, activities, etc. while not actually interested or concerned would suggest a lack of authenticity. In contrast, an authentic listener would attempt to respond honestly, avoid jumping to conclusions, provide honest feedback, suspend judgment of the speaker, and avoid any form of "using" the other person for selfish and/or concealed reasons. Ideally, the speaker should be able to talk to you as you are, not an artificial, disguised version of yourself.

Inclusion requires the listener to make every effort to place him or herself in the speaker's position. It involves not being a detached, disinterested observer but attempting to understand and appreciate where the speaker is coming from. It requires an effort to understand the speaker before making evaluations/judgments. And it encourages the listener to provide feedback that invites the speaker to agree or disagree and or to correct the listener's interpretations. The goal of listening inclusively is to improve communication by actively attempting to understand the speaker as much as possible.

The idea of confirming the other suggests that a dialogic listener should accept the speaker (the other) as a person of worth simply because he or she is a human being. For some this may seem unrealistic, even too idealistic. But this characteristic does not mean that one should accept everyone as equally good, kind, productive, honest, likeable or even personally acceptable. It does mean that one makes a serious attempt to respond to all people as having value simply because they are human. Thinking of others as objects (see Buber, 1958, pp. 11–15) or roles has a dehumanizing effect and does not belong to dialogic listening.

The concept of presentness applies to attention, meaning that one actively attends to the speaker and continues to stay with him/her (sustaining attention). One can be in a room, sitting next to or across from the speaker but not really present. One's attention and thoughts can be elsewhere. Thus, the dialogic listener always attempts to go far beyond a mere physical presence to active involvement, interest, and attentiveness. A spirit of mutual equality, like confirmation, clearly does not suggest that all people are equal. Instead, it requires one to attempt to listen to the other from an orientation of equality in the sense that everyone has the right to communicate freely and openly. Allowing one's biases to determine that some people and/or their ideas are inherently inferior (or superior) will tend to limit or destroy the chance for successful dialogic listening. Experience amply demonstrates that people are capable of wisdom and folly, regardless of who they are or what they have accomplished. A spirit of equality implies that one should encourage others to speak without prior evaluation or other restrictions. After understanding someone, the listener certainly has the right to evaluate, accept, or reject the other's ideas. But it is far less clear that we can or should attempt to evaluate another's feelings.

A supportive climate results from the cumulative effect of the dialogic listener's effort to reflect the characteristics of listening authentically, inclusively, with confirmation, with presentness and in a spirit of equality. These characteristics, taken together, will help establish a supportive communication climate.

Problems with Dialogic Listening

While dialogic communication (listening and speaking) has strong appeal at the level of theory and ethics, as a practical matter it poses problems, especially for the listener who wishes to choose dialogue over monologue as a basic approach to listening.

For in spite of the apparent desirability and superiority of dialogue, practical problems can arise, making the successful practice of dialogic listening more difficult than it may appear. The basic characteristics of dialogue (briefly discussed here as they relate to listening), while quite possibly inspiring, hardly give any specific direction as to what one actually does when attempting to listen dialogically. There appear to be no explicit rules or instructions. Indeed, the underlying idea that dialogue represents an attitude toward or spirit of communication strongly implies that the individual must attempt to understand and apply dialogic ideas and concepts to his or her speaking or listening without having explicit rules or directives to follow.

The problem of empathy

Dialogic listening and speaking present problems similar to those raised by the concept of empathic communication. While empathy is easy enough to set forth, to advocate and discuss in broad philosophical terms, the actual practice and application of empathy proves challenging and difficult. Feeling what another person feels, experiencing *with* another, while inviting and desirable may be impossible in actual practice. Arnett and Nakagawa and John Stewart, respectively, argue against empathy as a viable concept. Arnett and Nakagawa maintain, for example, that the highly questionable assumptions that support empathic listening should lead to "alternative formulations" (1983, p. 374). Similarly,

Stewart (1983, p. 380) contends that "the empathic paradigm breaks down when its conceptual coherence or underlying assumptions are subject to critical scrutiny."

Specifically, Stewart argues that, regardless "of the view of empathy that one adopts, it becomes necessary to ground this theoretical and cognitive/behavior construct as a fiction" (1983, p. 380). He goes on to say that this "fiction" involves any attempt to "'lay aside' ones' views, values, or self" (1983, p. 380). Since this kind of action is impossible, Stewart calls for the practice of "interpretive listening" in order to overcome "the shortcomings of the empathic paradigm" (p. 380).

When one examines Johannesen's writing about dialogue, it becomes clear that he came to reject the empathic aspect of dialogue as unworkable. For instance, in his early writing on dialogue (1971) he says that "a basic element in dialogue is 'seeing the other' or 'experiencing the other side'" (p. 375). This led him, at that time, to state that an essential characteristic of dialogue is "empathic understanding" (p. 376). However, in later writing (as early as *Ethics* in 1983), he removed "empathic understanding" and eventually substituted "Inclusion" (1983, p. 48; 2001, p. 59). When discussing the more recent concept, "inclusion," Johannesen submits that "one attempts to 'see the other' and "'to experience the other side.'" But this differs from actually feeling or experiencing what others experience; rather, it involves trying "'to imagine the real,'" and attempting to understand "the reality of the other's viewpoint." The distinction he makes between empathy and inclusion includes the idea that the speaker or listener does not give up his or her self but attempts to "imagine an event or feeling from the side of the other" (Johannesen, 2002, p. 59).

Another way to deal with the problem of empathy is to consider Kenneth Burke's concept of identification, or consubstantiality, as an alternative. Burke's concept allows for a coming together of persons and, hence, a unity of people without denying the inherent, undeniable differences and separateness of all humans. As Burke (1969) writes in *A Rhetoric of Motives*, "substance, in the old philosophies, was an *act*; and a way of life is an *acting together*; and in acting together, men have common sensations, concepts, images, ideas, attitudes that make them *consubstantial*" (p. 21).

Thus, through identification, people may understand that we can be "both joined and separate, at once a distinct substance and consubstantial with another" (Burke, 1969, p. 21). In a practical sense, when listening to another person speak of experiences, beliefs, values, attitudes, etc., a dialogic *attitude* or *approach* to communication enables one to capitalize on the commonality of humans' feelings and experiences (including language) without any necessity to achieve a merging of persons. The separateness of the individuals is not denied. As Burke (1941) says:

> Situations do overlap, if only because men now have the same neural and muscular structure as men who have left their records from past ages. We and they are in much the same biological situation. Furthermore, even the concrete details of social texture have a great measure of overlap. And the nature of the human mind itself, with the function of abstraction rooted in the nature of language, also provides us with levels of generalization by which situations greatly different in their particulars may be felt to belong in the same class to have a common substance or essence (p. 2).

Thus it seems reasonable to consider dialogic communication – from Burke's identification/consubstantiality and Johannesen's inclusion – to consist, essentially, of the idea of "separate people seeking to come together without denying their separateness" (Floyd, 1984, p. 6). In this way the problem of the impossibility of empathy, of taking the place of or experiencing what another experiences, can be avoided.

The problem of evaluation

Another potential problem that may occur in efforts to listen dialogically is that the listener may encounter dissonance resulting from a strong desire to value the other, to avoid judgment, to accept the other as an equal and to view the other positively rather than negatively. In this case the danger is too readily equating dialogic listening with being agreeable and accepting. To disagree, to reject the speaker's ideas or to become skeptical would cause her or him to degenerate into monologue. Here, we turn to Wolvin and Coakley's (1996) important assertion that listening does not mean "agreement or obedience." Instead, they contend, effective listening can lead to obeying or to disobeying; to agreement or disagreement (pp. 30–1).

Kenneth Burke also appears to counter the necessity of agreement and obedience when he writes that "only in an emancipated society, whose members' autonomy and responsibility have been realized" could "communication have developed into the non-authoritarian and universally practiced dialogue from which both our modes of reciprocally constituted ego identity and our idea of consensus are always implicitly derived" (1969, p. 314). While Burke agrees that human communication "has its peaceful moments," and "at times its endless competition can add up to a transcending of itself," in actuality we assert our identification (our oneness) with others "precisely because there is division." He goes on to say that "if men were not apart from one another, there would be no need for the rhetorician to proclaim their unity." Indeed, "if men where wholly and truly of one substance, absolute communication would be of man's very essence" (1969, pp. 22, 23). This strongly suggests that human communication, even at its best, involves struggle and conflict. Attempting to listen dialogically does not mean, then, that the goal is agreement or lack of argument. Rather than to think in terms of agreement or disagreement, one might attempt to distinguish among types of what Jurgen Habermas refers to as "expressives." This relates to the speaker's expressions of "intentions, attitudes, and experiences." Habermas (2001) presents examples such as "to reveal, disclose, to betray, to confess, to express, to hide, to conceal, to pretend, to obscure, to keep secret, to suppress, to deny …" (p. 83). These examples point to the distinction between monologue and dialogue, regardless of agreement or disagreement between or among communicators.

Brown and Keller appear to support this view of dialogue when they write that "dialogue is not some ideal that belongs to a nonexistent peaceful world." Instead, dialogic communication "goes directly and honestly to the differences between 'me and thee,' and this requires an immense toughness of self – for it does combat without going on the defensive." Finally, they make a crucial distinction between what they call "the struggle of dialogue" and "confrontation." When conflict occurs between people in dialogue, the "other person is confirmed," and "even downright rejection of a view can still stay within the framework of dialogue" (Brown and Keller, 1979, p. 304).

The problem of deception

Another major challenge to the practice of dialogic listening consists of what I shall illustrate under the rubric, the problem of evil. To understand this problem, it may help to return to Johannesen's adjectives that distinguish monologue from dialogue. We can recall, then, that dialogue is honest, without pretense, nonmanipulative, etc. (2002, p. 57). On the other hand, monologue involves pretense, using, seduction, domination, and manipulation (2002, p. 60).

To understand the application of the metaphor, the problem of evil, we consider two ways that evil makes its appearance in the world. On one hand we can observe evil as depicted in various films about devil possession and exorcism. When a small child or some other innocent person becomes demon possessed, the ugliness and grotesqueness of evil is difficult to miss. The child or adult so possessed may shout obscenities, spew vomit, make objects fly about the room, produce a stench, make the room turn cold, distort the face and voice, and so forth. Hardly anyone would have difficulty perceiving such acts as evil and undesirable. Likewise, when a terrible event occurs, such as terrorists flying airplanes into the World Trade Center, leading to the deaths of thousands of people, it is not difficult to identify such behavior as evil.

On the other hand, evil may far more frequently present itself in the form of disguises and attractive, alluring promises. Pushers of illegal drugs are less likely to present them as addictive and capable of totally controlling and ruining a person's life than to emphasize the extreme pleasure and enjoyment that one will experience from using these drugs. Few con artists will tell their victims that they are going to employ trickery and deceit in order to obtain their money or possessions. Instead, they will probably make it appear that one will get something for nothing or for less than normally expected. The promises are positive and attractive. We know that cigarettes were not advertised as a major health hazard, the leading cause of premature death. They were promoted instead as glamorous, sophisticated, macho, and sexy.

As a college student I once participated in a training program for selling encyclopedias. All trainees were required to memorize a sales spiel that was based upon deception and manipulation, making it appear that the consumer would receive a free set of encyclopedias, a set of children's classics, and an attractive bookcase. To allay any suspicions, the customer was told that there were indeed conditions, since the entire marketing strategy was intended to pave the way for a sales push in his/her area "next year." So, the customer had to promise to display the books prominently – so that friends and neighbors could see how nice they looked, etc. Also, the customer had to sign an agreement granting permission for her/his name to be used in the company's national advertising. Finally, all one had to do was show enough appreciation for the free offer by agreeing to keep it up to date. This meant buying just one year book annually, which was "no more than buying a coke and candy bar each day." If the customer fell for the pitch, "keeping it up to date" actually cost the value of the encyclopedias, children's classics, and the bookcase combined.

This approach reflects most of the characteristics of monologic speaking. It is deceptive, manipulative, inauthentic, dishonest, controlling, and exploitative. Notice, however, the speaker presents him or herself so as to come across as highly dialogic. In the encyclopedia example, the speaker stresses the need for typical families to display these books. The speaker appears to appreciate the customer's intelligence and good judgment by agreeing that there are conditions that must be met in order to receive these gifts. Repeatedly the speaker emphasizes how much it will help the children in the family to succeed in school. In no way does the salesperson use anything but what seem like characteristics of dialogue in a presentation that overwhelmingly qualifies as monologue.

Somehow, the dialogic listener must be able to apply effective critical and evaluative listening behaviors without losing sight of or abandoning the practice of dialogue. Brown and Keller offer important ideas as to what one can do in order to scrutinize, evaluate, argue and, at the same time, listen dialogically. They point out, for example that the judgment and evaluation in dialogue differ from a desire to humiliate or destroy the other. One must, therefore, be willing to "reject ideas or behavior in another while confirming him or her as a person." This, as they point out, is "difficult" and requires a deep faith in self. Ultimately it represents "the true test of one's ability to carry on dialogue" (Brown and Keller, 1979, p. 304).

The idealistic, philosophical nature of dialogue requires the development of attitudes and behaviors that demand much of the listener. Ideally, Brown and Keller argue, we cannot actually "test the ability to carry on dialogue if the talk has no threat in it," and we need to keep in mind that "one actually does not know the deepest level of dialogue" unless "one is comfortably related to a person from whom one differs greatly." Finally, they assert, "the ultimate in *self-confrontation* ... takes place when one trusts one's enemy" (1979, p. 305). This view closely resembles the teaching of Martin Luther King, Jr. who told us that "when the opportunity presents itself for you to defeat your enemy, that is the time which you must not do it." His idea of loving one's enemies allows such judgments as "I don't like what they do to me," or "I don't like what they say about me" or "I don't like their attitudes,"or "I don't like some of the things they are doing," or "I don't like them," all suggesting that one can love people in spite of what they do (King, 1998, pp. 46–7, 49).

Self-protection versus acceptance

The challenges to dialogic listening are thus two-fold: One must listen critically for the purpose of self-protection. But, at the same time, one must be able to detect, identify, and reject undesirable and deceptive communication without rejecting the speaker as a person of worth and value. While it goes beyond the scope of this chapter to discuss critical/ evaluative listening in detail, I would posit specific suggestions that dialogic listeners can use. They include: (1) extensive use of feedback; (2) the ability to identify unspoken, implied, premises and assumptions; (3) the ability to listen for adequate support, including the quality and relevance of that support; (4) an ability to identify and to evaluate reasoning; (5) a good understanding of topics and issues being discussed; (6) a development of general interests and knowledge; (7) the ability to envision the potential consequences of a speaker's ideas; (8) the ability to analyze a person's actions without assuming that they are suspect; (9) the capability to detect delivery, style, and personality as covers for purpose or as substitutes for substance, again without having preconceived conclusions; and (10) the ability to differentiate between emotional appeal that circumvents reason and emotional appeal that has a rational basis (See Haiman, 1958, pp. 99–114).

Conclusion

As suggested, and specifically discussed, throughout this chapter, a dialogic approach to communication constitutes a philosophical and idealistic approach to communication. Brown and Keller expressed it well when they wrote that "the great moments in dialogue are hard to come by" (1979, p. 305). At the same time, I would assert that such moments are nonetheless worth striving for in human efforts to achieve understanding and unity. For in spite of the idealistic nature of the characteristics of dialogue, the denial, avoidance or refusal of such ideals have generally led to the worst in human behavior. While I envision no easy answers to the challenges inherent in dialogic listening, it does seem reasonable to be aware of those challenges and difficulties, striving to find ways to overcome them without giving up on the value of dialogue as a desirable attitude toward and approach to effective listening.

QUESTIONS FOR DISCUSSION

1   Do you think the ideas presented in this chapter are too idealistic? Why or why not?
2   Can a person actually listen critically and, at the same time, dialogically?
3   What do you think it means to engage in mental and verbal combat without being defensive? Provide examples.
4   What kinds of listening situations do you think present the greatest challenges for one wanting to listen dialogically?
5   Are there situations in which dialogue may not be necessary or even desirable? Try to describe such situations.
6   In what ways does dialogic listening move us *beyond* debating, arguing and persuading?
7   Have you ever experienced situations in which someone pretended an interest and/ or concern for you that turned out to be a pretense designed to gain your confidence or to throw you off guard. Describe any such situations.
8   Do you agree or disagree with the idea that one can never experience what another person experiences? Defend your response.
9   Can you recall situations in which you have had a productive, even enjoyable, conversation or discussion with someone you strongly disagree with? Describe that experience.
10   Do you think dialogic listening is ethical while monologic listening is not?
11   If concepts such as "inclusion," "confirming," and "mutual equality" are rejected as unrealistic, what are the alternatives?
12   How do such terms as "attitude toward," "approaches to" and "sprits of" communication differ from prescriptions or rules for communicating?

References

Arnett, R.C., and Nakagawa, G. (1983). The assumptive roots of empathic listening: A Critique. *Communication Education*, 32, 368–78.
Brockriede, W.E. (1968). Dimensions of the concept of rhetoric. *Quarterly Journal of Speech*, 54, 1–12.

Brown, C.T., and P.W. Keller. (1979). *Monologue to dialogue: An exploration of interpersonal communication*, 2nd edn. Englewood Cliffs, NJ: Prentice-Hall.

Buber, M. (1958). *I and thou*, 2nd edn.(R.G. Smith, Trans.). New York: Scribners.

Burke, K. (1941). *The philosophy of literary form*. Baton Rouge: Louisiana University Press.

Burke, K. (1969). *A rhetoric of motives*. Berkeley: University of California Press.

Floyd, J.J. (1984). *Dialogic listening*. Paper presented at International Listening Association Convention, Scottsdale, AR.

Habermas, J. (2001). *On the pragmatics of social interaction*, (B. Fuller, Trans.). Cambridge, MA: MIT Press.

Haiman, F.S. (1958). Democratic ethics and the hidden persuaders. *Quarterly Journal of Speech*. 44, 385–92.

Johannesen, R.L. (1983). *Ethics in human communication*, 2nd edn. Prospect Heights, IL: Waveland Press.

Johannesen, R.L. (2002). *Ethics in human communication*, 5th edn. Prospect Heights, IL: Waveland Press.

Johannesen, R.L. (1971). The Emerging concept of communication as dialogue. *Quarterly Journal of Speech*, 58, 373–82.

King, M.L. (1998). "Loving Your Enemies," in C. Carson and P. Holloran (Eds.). *A knock at midnight: Inspirations from the great sermons of Martin Luther King, Jr.*, pp. 37–40. New York: Warner Books.

Larson, C.U. (2007). *Persuasion: Reception and responsibility*, 11th edn. Belmont, CA: Thompson Wadsworth.

Nichols, R.G. (1987). Manipulation versus persuasion. *Journal of the International Listening Association*, 1, 15–28.

Ogden, C.K., and Richards, I.A. (1956). *The meaning of meaning*. New York: Harcourt, Brace and Company.

Stewart, J. (1983). Interpretive listening: An Alternative to empathy. *Communication Education*, 32, 379–91.

Weaver, R.M. (1985). *The ethics of rhetoric*. Davis, CA: Hermagorus Press.

Wolvin, A.D., and Coakley, C.G.(1996). *Listening*, 5th edn. Madison: Brown & Benchmark.

6

The Skills of Listening-Centered Communication

Judi Brownell

The discipline of Communication has traditionally focused on the speaker and on message creation rather than on the listener and the skills of reception. Brownell argues that this approach needs to be revisited, and that listening must become the central focus if individuals are to become effective communicators. Her listening-centered approach to communication is presented and discussed in the following chapter.

Taking a symbolic approach to understanding the communication process, Brownell proposes that only through effective listening can individuals share meanings and align their behavior to accomplish goals. Communication, she suggests, is "listener-defined"; a message means whatever the receiver thinks it does. This view contrasts with the standard practice of highlighting the speaker's task. Brownell believes that unless speakers first listen to understand their partner's perspective, they cannot hope to design effective messages. Listening becomes particularly vital as individuals travel more frequently and as organizations become more global and diverse.

Brownell's HURIER model is presented as an aid to developing effective listening skills. The listening process is viewed as a cluster of interrelated components that can be identified, assessed, and improved. Speaking is the *outcome* of effective listening — it is how the listener responds after he or she has heard, understood, interpreted, and evaluated the other person's ideas.

Finally, Brownell presents the rationale for and challenges of a skills approach to listening. She identifies several issues and questions that arise from taking a skills approach to listening improvement and instruction, and addresses each in turn. She concludes by looking to the future, reemphasizing the need for effective listening as individuals strive to share meanings and build relationships with those from other backgrounds and cultures. In a rapidly changing world, the skills of effective listening are vital to individuals' professional success and personal well being.

What is most central to human interaction? Is it the ability to express thoughts clearly, to gain recognition for ourselves and our ideas? Or, is it our ability to understand, to empathize, to appreciate and focus on the "other"? If the goal of effective communication is to create shared meanings, all of these functions play a role. But where do we begin? This paper argues that our choice of a starting place is significant as it not only defines our approach to communication, but also influences the nature of our relationships, expresses our values, and reflects our world view.

First, a listening-centered approach to communication is presented and discussed. Then, the skills-based HURIER model is described as an example of a behavioral approach to listening. Its six interrelated components are defined, and the challenges of a skills-based approach to listening-centered communication are reviewed. The chapter ends by emphasizing the need for listening development to be viewed within a larger social framework.

Listening-Centered Communication

The complex, multi-faceted process we call communication has been studied from numerous perspectives depending upon the researcher's discipline, purpose, and methods. Our earliest models recognized distinct functions related to the roles of "sending" and "receiving." As new theoretical frameworks evolved, a majority of communication scholars came to agree that relational approaches most accurately describe the dynamic, nonrepetitive, and continuous nature of human interaction. Scholars concluded that sending (speaking) and receiving (listening) do not occur in a sequential, linear fashion; rather, individuals continuously receive and respond to stimuli, processing and creating meaning from cues as they speak. What was once explained by a stimulus – response model came to be viewed as transactional (Clampitt, 1991). The question, "How much time do you spend each day listening?" becomes irrelevant. If you are engaged in human communication, listening never stops.

If we apply a symbolic lens to examine human communication, we recognize even more vividly how central listening is to the process by which meanings are created and shared. Through listening, individuals learn how to behave; they work to align their actions within a particular communication context and to distinguish appropriate from inappropriate responses. Whether visiting in-laws or entering a new organization, the ability to align behavior and recognize situational norms has much to do with our ability to listen.

From this perspective, communicative activity becomes listener-defined; a message "means" whatever the listener believes it means. Speakers are at the mercy of listeners who interpret what they hear and act on that basis. Individuals as listeners actively participate in a creative process, controlling the type and amount of information received and then processing it according to their unique cognitive structures, schemata, interests, needs, and other individual influences. These individual variables suggest that potentially important verbal and nonverbal cues are often missed entirely. On other occasions, meanings may be elicited where messages were never intended. Speakers, from this perspective, are truly at the mercy of the listeners who – literally – have the last word.

The more an individual understands the listening process, the more likely she is to achieve the goal of shared meanings. Those who discount perceptual differences or who ignore important nonverbal cues cannot hope to coordinate actions or achieve goals, as their interpretations of their partner's meanings are likely to be inaccurate. Even when individuals have similar backgrounds and a common body of experience, sharing meanings is difficult. When cultural diversity increases, listeners must work even harder to account for perceptual filters, assumptions, and value orientations. An American woman visiting friends in Paris, for instance, is likely to imagine an "early dinner" at five o'clock, only to discover that early in France is closer to seven o'clock.

While recognizing that the best you can do is to approximate your partner's intentions, learning to attend to, understand, interpret, and evaluate the communicative cues in your environment increases the likelihood that meaningful communication will occur. It should be evident that communication effectiveness requires that these processes take place *before* an individual speaks, and that the extent to which meanings are shared has much to do with the quality of participants' listening.

Even at the macro level, receiver-centered approaches are essential to making wise strategic communication choices. Organizational leaders who are flexible and who adapt to the unique needs of their workforce by considering employees' perceptual filters, beliefs, and assumptions as they design organizational communication strategies have a distinct competitive advantage. Research in this arena makes clear that senior managers' assumptions about how employees receive and process information are often inaccurate. This lack of congruence may result in costly misunderstandings, lack of commitment, and low morale (Brownell and Jameson, 1996).

In listening-centered communication, then, listening is positioned as the primary process influencing communication outcomes. This framing has implications for a variety of other decisions. Communicative activity *begins* with the multi-stage process of listening – a process which concludes with a response (often verbal) that is most often identified as "speaking." It is the quality of the listening that determines the effectiveness of the interaction. It is therefore the listening process and its role in human interaction that deserves our primary and full attention.

A Skills-Based Model of Listening-Centered Communication

It may be useful to review one of the growing number of theoretical frameworks scholars have used to understand listening behavior better. The HURIER model is presented as an example of a behavioral approach that understands listening as the central communication function. In this framework, listening-centered communication is conceived as a cluster of interrelated, overlapping components. Figure 6.1 presents the HURIER model of the listening process which illustrates the relationships among six skill clusters.

As you can see, the listener's response is the final component of the listening process and is influenced by the five processes that precede it. Speaking is viewed as the *outcome* of listening. The effectiveness of the speaker's message or response relates directly to how well the individual listens. The assumption is that only *after* listening has taken place can a communicator speak effectively. With this in mind, each component of the HURIER model is briefly described below. Later we will examine how the situational dimensions of purpose and context also affect the listener's response.

Component 1: Hearing

The HURIER model begins with an individual making decisions about what to focus attention on within the context of an environment filled with stimulus options. As we well know, this component – what is called *hearing* in the model – is influenced by the individual's cultural orientation, past experiences, interests, attitudes, beliefs, and a range of other personal variables and filters that account for individual and cultural differences. You will notice that the HURIER model suggests that these filters continue to influence every component of the listening process.

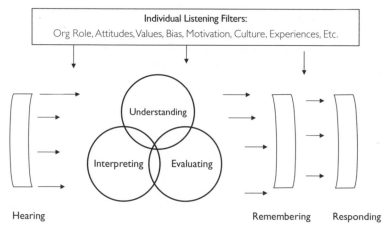

Figure 6.1 The HURIER Listening Model

Component 2: Understanding

Having attended to and "received" the particular stimulus, the next stage in the listening process is understanding. This information processing phase corresponds to reading comprehension and addresses the literal meaning of the words or signs received. Obviously, such factors as the individual's familiarity with the language affect the accuracy and extent of listening comprehension.

Component 3: Remembering

While memory is a separate mental process, it functions within the context of listening-centered communication because the usefulness of information is dependent upon the communicator's ability to act on what is received, either immediately or at some later point in time. Memory, then, is directly related to an individual's ability to formulate an appropriate response.

Component 4: Interpreting

Nonverbal cues play a particularly significant role in the next stage of the process, what we call "interpreting." Glenn, in her 1989 review of listening definitions, concluded that the process of interpreting was common to almost all listening definitions. While use of the term varies, most scholars agree that interpreting messages requires that both verbal and nonverbal cues be considered in assigning meaning. This richer context allows for literal meanings to be modified by such things as tone of voice, posture, facial expression, and contextual knowledge. An effective listening-centered communicator would observe his or her partner's appearance and other variables of the communication context before assigning meaning to the message conveyed; she would, as some researchers suggest, "define the situation" (Weick, 1995).

Component 5: Evaluating

The component of evaluation in listening-centered communication refers to the process by which an individual makes a judgment about the accuracy and validity of the information received. This is the stage at which effective communicators assess what they have heard by weighing evidence and reasoning, recognizing emotional appeals, and drawing other conclusions that will affect their subsequent listening response. Emphasis is placed on the need to understand a message before judging its value.

Component 6: Responding

The outcome of effective listening, then, will be an appropriate response. The communicator's "message" may be verbal or nonverbal, and constitutes the final stage of an integrated, multi-faceted system. This response is influenced by all that has come before it and, since listening is continuous, the communicator continues to process new information as he or she is speaking. This implies that continuous listening enables a speaker to modify messages as he observes his partner's facial expressions, hears his tone of voice, and adjusts to his interpretations of whether the message he is sending is eliciting the anticipated outcomes.

Translating Cognitive Processes to Observable Skills: Educators Bridge the Gap

While educators cannot change the covert nature of mental activity, what they have done is to translate the unobservable listening process into corresponding skill sets that are then accepted as *indicators that listening is taking place.* ~~Other sets of observable behaviors, such as leaning forward or nodding, have been shown to~~ *facilitate the listening process.* Viewing listening from a behavioral perspective enables educators to develop specific instructional strategies around these concrete components of an often elusive process. While the limitations of such an approach are recognized, behavioral models have made listening instruction accessible to educators at all levels.

While the appropriateness of an individual's speech – demonstrated either in interpersonal or presentational contexts – is the most obvious indicator of listening effectiveness, there are five other components in the process that deserve our attention as well. As previously discussed, the HURIER model suggests the following listening tasks – hearing, understanding, remembering, interpreting, evaluating, and responding. Each of these is described in terms of the skills that either indicate or facilitate each stage.

For example, while we cannot observe the process of hearing or attending, we can teach students to "do" such things as: (a) focus on the speaker; (b) choose an appropriate physical location where distractions are limited; and (c) take notes or engage in an activity to increase involvement. Likewise, while we cannot observe the process of understanding, we have measures to assess listening comprehension and also to "teach" activities that have a high probability of increasing shared meanings. Asking questions, paraphrasing, and discriminating between main points and supporting details, all contribute to the component of understanding. Box 6.1 provides examples of skills associated with each of the listening processes.

Listening-centered Communication: Challenges of a Skills Approach

There are a number of issues and questions that emerge as a result of teaching listening-centered communication from a behavioral approach. Four of the most frequently mentioned topics follow.

Role of motivation in listening behavior

Few other skills are as dependent on motivation as listening. Individuals vary significantly in their listening behavior, yet the causes

Box 6.1   HURIER Listening skill clusters

Component 1: Hearing messages
Improve concentration
Use vocalized listening technique
Prepare to listen

Component 2: Understanding messages
Recognize assumptions
Listen to entire message without interrupting
Distinguish main ideas from evidence
Perception check for accurate comprehension

Component 3: Remembering messages
Understand how memory works
Isolate and practice each memory process
Practice with difficult material

Component 4: Interpreting messages
Understand the nature of empathy
Increase sensitivity to nonverbal cues
Increase sensitivity to vocal cues
Monitor personal nonverbal behaviors

Component 5: Evaluating messages
Assess the speaker's credibility
Recognize your personal bias
Analyze logic and reasoning
Identify emotional appeals

Component 6: Responding to messages
Become familiar with response options
Recognize the impact of each response option
Increase behavioral flexibility

of these differences remain poorly understood. Beyond establishing that intelligence correlates with listening ability, the only thing we know for certain is that there is a strong link between motivation to listen and listening effectiveness. In fact, some researchers have suggested that, if we can assume a threshold level of intelligence, then motivation accounts for up to 70 percent of an individual's listening success.

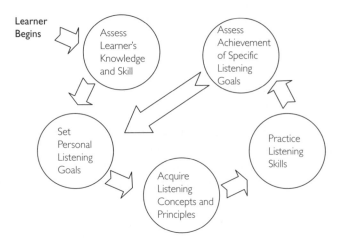

Figure 6.2 The listening assessment cycle

Correspondence between what is taught and what is assessed

Too often there is a lack of correspondence between behaviors being taught and those that are actually assessed. Assessment measures must be selected with consideration for how instructional goals match the dimension evaluated. In this regard, the HURIER model provides one of the clearest blueprints for skill development and testing, as discrete components, related skill sets, and targeted assessments can be developed and aligned. As mentioned previously, cognitive processes cannot be observed directly. Consequently, written and oral indicators must be used to assess behavioral outcomes which are themselves substitutes for the actual listening process.

A self-assessment instrument accompanies the HURIER model and was designed to help learners identify their listening behaviors and to understand the larger skill clusters into which separate skills fit (see Appendix I). An integrated system we call the Listening Assessment Cycle (Figure 6.2) is then readily constructed as learners (a) assess their current performance, (b) set personal goals by identifying the components where improvement is needed, (c) acquire relevant principles and accompanying skills, (d) practice new listening behaviors, and finally (e) take a structured assessment that matches exactly the behaviors that were practiced. When educators and students are clear on listening goals and outcomes, instruction becomes more consistent and is likely to have greater impact. By focusing on observable skills, educators are better able to align individual student needs, instructional strategies, and assessment measures.

The challenge of skill transfer

As in other types of instruction, there also are challenges in skill transfer. Observing students as they demonstrate the target skills in a classroom situation is not a predictor of their likelihood to demonstrate and experience success with these skills outside the classroom. In addition, newly learned skills are not likely to persist in environments that do not support the acquired behavior. Demonstrating skills in a controlled classroom laboratory situation does not ensure that learners will be able to apply these skills appropriately or effectively in out-of-class contexts.

Situational demands on listening

Listening-centered communication can also be influenced by the demands of the particular situation. Situational variables related to the (a) listening purpose and (b) context or setting affect the degree to which each component, or skill cluster, is required for effective listening to occur. For instance, while listening to a friend in trouble might depend heavily on identifying nonverbal cues, listening to directions requires comprehension and memory processes. When listening to someone in a supervisory or higher status role, a formal and unfamiliar office environment may affect concentration and the subsequent response. Figure 6.3 suggests how situational demands – listening purposes and contexts – might affect the listening process.

Looking to the Future: What We Know, What We Need to Know

What we know is that the boundaries of our world will continue to expand throughout the coming decades. We are more likely than ever before to encounter individuals from other countries and other cultures on a daily basis – in our homes, at work, in our schools. Building a global village takes hard work. It requires "reaching out, reaching in"; it requires that individuals as communicators focus their efforts on creating shared

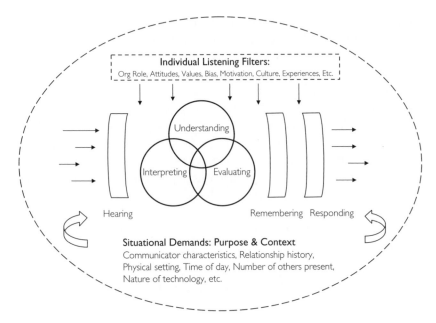

Figure 6.3   The HURIER Listening Model: Situational demands

meanings. The *only* way that we can develop meaningful relationships within our families, communities, and across continents is through effective listening. As we have seen, this requires that every individual shift his or her attention to the task of understanding better the attitudes, values, needs, and orientations of fellow communicators.

We also know that there has never been a greater need for the skills of effective listening than in these times of constant and often revolutionary change. The specific frameworks in which listening skills are taught or the specific definitions applied to desired behaviors are of relatively little consequence. What is imperative is that educators at all levels identify a method by which they can contribute to the future success and well being of their students through listening instruction. A skills approach clearly facilitates this goal. But listening-centered communication begins not with skills in the classroom but with attitudes in the home. It's an orientation that places value on mutual understanding and respect, on recognizing and responding to differences and change. Yesterday's children grew up with "show and tell" – tomorrow's children will be better prepared for the future if this traditional activity becomes "listen and learn."

And what, then, do we need to facilitate listening-centered communication? We need commitment, and we need evidence. Communication scholars, educators, and practitioners must become convinced that listening is central to creating community and advancing knowledge. This can only happen if substantially more research is focused on the core processes involved in creating shared meanings. As it becomes apparent that listening is related to global outcomes such as international conflict and business performance as well as to everyday personal misunderstandings, more urgency will be placed on discovering best practices for teaching listening effectiveness. It is likely that skills-based approaches will provide not only a clear and concrete framework for improving and assessing listening behavior, but will also serve as a means of drawing attention to the role this critical competence plays in helping to realize our brightest future.

QUESTIONS FOR DISCUSSION

1   What is meant by "listening-centered" communication? What are the implications of framing listening rather than speaking as the fundamental communication skill?
2   In what ways does the listener have more influence on communication effectiveness than the speaker when viewed from a meaning-centered perspective?
3   Why is listening so important to effective intercultural communication? Provide a concrete example.
4   Describe each of the six components of the HURIER Listening Model. Which component do you believe is most troublesome for you as a listener? Explain.
5   If you could chose only one component of the HURIER Model to be taught to all children before they leave school, which would it be and why?
6   What do you think is missing from the HURIER Listening Model? What questions are left unanswered?
7   Given the chapter discussion, what do you believe are the key challenges of a behavioral approach to understanding and improving listening?
8   What is meant by "situational demands" on listening? Give an example of two different listening contexts and purposes, and discuss how listening requirements might differ.
9   If you could create the perfect "listening context," what would it be like? Describe features such as communicator characteristics, time of day, physical setting, and so forth.
10   When you "look to the future," in what specific ways do you see listening effectiveness as an important competency?
11   What does the author intend as the underlying fundamental difference between approaching communication as "listen and learn" rather than "show and tell"?

Appendix 6.1: HURIER Listening Assessment Instrument

1. Each of the questions is the listening assessment below corresponds with one of six listening components:
   - Hearing
   - Understanding
   - Remembering
   - Interpreting
   - Evaluating
   - Responding

2. It might be fun, before you go any further, to guess how you will do:

   I think I will score highest on component _____

   I will probably score lowest on component _____

3. When you have completed the questionnaire, process your scores in the following manner:
   - Write the number of points you assigned to each response on the appropriate line below.
   - Add up the points you gave yourself for each of the following sets of questions.
   - Place your total for each set in the "total" space.

Hearing	Understanding	Remembering
4 _____	5 _____	3 _____
15 _____	11 _____	7 _____
16 _____	25 _____	10 _____
20 _____	28 _____	18 _____
24 _____	32 _____	31 _____
Total _____	Total _____	Total _____

Interpreting	Evaluating	Responding
2 _____	1 _____	6 _____
12 _____	8 _____	9 _____
14 _____	22 _____	19 _____
17 _____	23 _____	26 _____
21 _____	29 _____	27 _____
Total _____	Total _____	Total _____

4. What does this information tell you about your self-perceptions of your listening behavior?
5. Rank each of the six components according to the question totals.

	Points total	Rank
Hearing	_____	_____
Understanding	_____	_____
Remembering	_____	_____
Interpreting	_____	_____
Evaluating	_____	_____
Responding	_____	_____

6. In what skill areas are you high?
7. Which one do you see as a potential problem?
8. How did your actual ranking compare with your earlier guess?
9. Use the chart below to assess each skill area:
    - 30–25 points: you see yourself as an excellent listener
    - 25–15 points: you consider your listening skills adequate
    - 10–15 points: you perceive some problems in your listening behavior
10. You might also ask yourself:
    - Is there a particular component with a significantly different total – either higher or much lower than the others?
    - How do you think someone else would rank your listening behaviors?
    - Take the role of one of your team members, your spouse, or some other important person and answer the questionnaire from that person's perspective. How did you do?

Listening Self-Assessment

Respond to each of the following questions concerning your perceptions of your listening behavior.

Use the following key: 5 (always); 4 (usually); 3 (sometimes); 2 (infrequently); 1 (never).

When you respond, keep one specific situation in mind. It might be useful to use your team as a context for your listening behavior.

____ I weigh all evidence before making a decision.
____ I am sensitive to the speaker's feelings in communication situations.
____ I approach tasks creatively.
____ I concentrate on what the speaker is saying.
____ I use clear and appropriate words to express my ideas.
____ I encourage others to express their opinion.
____ I am able to see how different pieces of information or ideas relate to one another.
____ I listen to the entire message when someone speaks, whether I agree with what they have to say or not.
____ I let the speaker know immediately that he or she has been understood.
____ I remember what I am told even in stressful situations.

___ I recognize the main points in a presentation and am not distracted by supporting details.

___ I am sensitive to a speaker's vocal cues in communication situations.

___ I provide sufficient feedback on the job.

___ I consider the speaker's mood in understanding the message being presented.

___ I hear what is said when someone speaks to me.

___ I give an individual my complete attention when he is speaking to me.

___ I take into account situational factors that influence interactions when someone is speaking to me.

___ I can recall the specific information someone gives me several days later.

___ I respond in an appropriate and timely manner to information and requests.

___ I am ready to listen when approached by a speaker.

___ I notice the speaker's facial expressions, body posture, and other nonverbal behaviors.

___ I wait until all the information is presented before drawing any conclusions.

___ I allow for the fact that people and circumstances change over time.

___ I overcome distractions such as the conversations of others, background noises and telephones when someone is speaking to me.

___ I accurately understand what is said to me.

___ I seek information for better understanding of a situation.

___ I communicate clearly and directly.

___ I focus on the main point of a message rather than reacting to details.

___ I am receptive to points of view which differ from my own.

___ I time my communications appropriately.

___ I remember the details of things that happened weeks or months ago.

___ I let the speaker complete his or her message without interrupting.

References and related reading

Barker, R.T., Pearce, C.G., and Johnson, I.W. (1992). An investigation of perceived managerial listening ability. *Journal of Business and Technical Communication*, 6, 438–57.

Bechler, C., and Johnson, S.D. (1995). Leadership and listening: A study of member perception. *Small Group Research*, 26, 77–85.

Bentley, S. (1997). Benchmarking listening behaviors: Is effective listening what the speaker says it is? *International Journal of Listening*, 11, 51–68.

Brownell, J. (1994a). Managerial listening and career development in the hospitality industry. *Journal of the International Listening Association*, 8, 31–49.

Brownell, J. (1994b). Teaching listening: Some thoughts on the behavioral approach. *Business Communication Quarterly*, 57, 4, 19–26.

Brownell, J. (1994c). Creating strong listening environments: A key hospitality management task. *The International Journal of Contemporary Hospitality Management*, 6, 3, 3–10.

Brownell, J. (2002). *Building active listening skills*. Boston: Allyn & Bacon, Publishers.

Brownell, J. (2003). Developing receiver-centered communication in diverse organizations. *The Listening Professional*, 2, 1, 5–7, 22–26.

Brownell, J., and Jameson, D. (1996). Getting quality out on the street: A case of show and tell. *Cornell Hotel and Restaurant Administration Quarterly*, 37, 1, 28–33.

Clampitt, P.G. (1991). *Communicating for managerial effectiveness*. Newbury Park, CA: Sage Publishers.

Ford, W.S.Z., Wolvin, A.D., and Chung, S. (2000). Students' self-perceived listening competencies. *International Journal of Listening*, 14, 1–13.

Glenn, E.C. (1989). A content analysis of fifty definitions of listening. *Journal of the International Listening Association*, 3, 21–31.

Halone, K.K., Cunconan, T.M., Coakley, C.G., and Wolvin, A.D. (1998). Toward the establishment of general dimensions underlying the listening process. *International Journal of Listening*, 12, 12–28.

Hunter, D., Gambell, T., and Randhawa, B. (2005). Gender gaps in group listening and speaking: Issues in social constructivist approaches to teaching and learning. *Educational Review*, 57, 3, 329–41.

Imhof, M. (1998). What makes a good listener? Listening behavior in instructional settings. *International Journal of Listening*, 12, 81–105.

International Listening Association Research Subcommittee (1995). An ILA definition of listening. *The Listening Post*, 53, 1, 4.

Johnson, S.D., and Bechler, C. (1998). Examining the relationship between listening effectiveness and leadership emergence: Perceptions, behaviors, and recall. *Small Group Research*, 29, 452–71.

Maes, J.D., Weldy, T.J., and Icenogle, M.L. (1997). A managerial perspective: Oral communication competency is most important for business students in the workplace. *The Journal of Business Communication*, 34, 67–80.

Pearce, C., Johnson, I., and Barker, R. (1995). Enhancing the student listening skills and environment. *Business Communication Quarterly*, 58, 4, 28–43.

Pecchioni, L.L., and Halone, K.K. (2000). Relational listening II: Form and variation across social interpersonal relationships. *International Journal of Listening*, 14, 69–93.

Spitzberg, B.H. (2000). A model of intercultural communication competence. In L.A. Samovar and R.E. Porter (Eds.). *Intercultural Communication: A Reader*, pp. 375–87. Belmont, CA: Wadsworth.

Villaume, W.A., and Weaver, J.B. III. (1996). A factorial approach to establishing reliable listening measures from the WBLT and the KCLT: Full information factor analysis of dichotomous data. *International Journal of Listening*, 10, 1–20.

Weick, K.E. (1995). *Sensemaking in organizations*. Thousand Oaks, CA: Sage Publications.

Witkin, B.R. (1995). Listening theory and research: The state of the art. *Journal of the International Listening Association*, 4, 7–32.

Witkin, B.R., and Trochim, W.W.K. (1997). Toward a synthesis of listening constructs: A concept map analysis. *International Journal of Listening*, 11, 69–87.

Wolvin, A.D. (1989). Models of the listening process. In C.V. Roberts and K.W. Watson (Eds.). *Intrapersonal Communication Processes*, pp. 508–27. New Orleans: Spectra.

Wolvin, A.D., and Coakley, C.G. (1991). A survey of the status of listening training in some Fortune 500 corporations. *Communication Education*, 40, 2, 152–64.

7

Listening in a Second Language
John Flowerdew and Lindsay Miller

In this contribution Flowerdew and Miller set out what they consider to be the essential features of a pedagogic model of second language listening. The model consists of a set of dimensions derived from a range of theories about listening. These dimensions are eclectic, in so far as they draw on cognitive, social, linguistic, and pedagogic theory. Drawn together, they make possible a unified model of second language listening. The model incorporates previous models of listening: *bottom-up processing*; *top-down processing*; and *interactive processing*, but it also has distinct dimensions of listening which make it more intricate than previous models. The authors explain and provide examples of the following dimensions:

1 individualization;
2 cross-cultural aspects;
3 social features;
4 contextualized dimensions;
5 affective factors;
6 strategic aspects;
7 intertextuality; and
8 critical discourse features.

Introduction

In this chapter we outline some of the major areas of research that have developed in second language listening over the past 30 years. As a result of the increased interest in listening in a second and/or foreign language, a research agenda has developed, and this research has influenced the way teachers view the pedagogy they use. After our review of the literature we sketch out a pedagogical model for the teaching of second language listening based on our understanding of the needs of second language learners in modern-day society. This model is more fully explained and exemplified in Flowerdew and Miller (2005).

It was not until the early 1970s that second language listening research developed its own agenda. Prior to this, there had been concentrated efforts into researching listening in the first language and reading in the first and second language, but not on listening in the second language. The assumption was that listening in the second language was the same as in the learner's native language, and that reading and listening were so similar, both being receptive skills, that what was true for reading must also be true for listening. Without doubt, research into first language listening and first and second language reading has been helpful in understanding some of the issues important to second language listening. Referring to this related research, Faerch and Kasper (1986, p. 263) stated that "[it] has inspired research into L2 comprehension with respect to developing comprehension models, formulating research problems, and selecting suitable methods of investigation." At the same time, however, this research into first language listening and reading also highlighted the need for a research agenda that is specific to second language listening.

There were other reasons which prevented second language listening from having its own research agenda prior to the 1970s. Gilman and Moody (1984) list three reasons: (i) learning a language meant being able to speak the language and so listening was relegated to a secondary position; (ii) listening was considered something which could be "picked-up"; and (iii) language teachers (and researchers) never had lessons in "understanding spoken English" when they attended school so they did not perceive a learner's need for this.

Viewed from another perspective, the relative lack of research into listening seems somewhat strange, given the fact that it is the language skill most often used in everyday life. More than 40 percent of our daily communication time is spent on listening, 35 percent on speaking, 16 percent on reading, and only 9 percent on writing (Burley-Allen, 1995). During school years, listening is the skill teachers focus on most with their students, with some 60 percent of elementary students' time taken up with listening (Brown, 1990). As other modes of communication are learned, the focus on listening decreases until students enter college when once again it becomes a major focus via the lecturing system. It therefore seems strange that listening has been the poor relation in terms of the amount of research time and energy expended on it.

One of the main reasons for this lack of research interest may be that it is easier to conduct experiments on reading skills, for instance, rather than listening skills, given the ephemeral nature of the latter.

Problems Associated with Researching Second Language Listening

As the agenda for researching second language listening became more identified in the 1970s, the complexity of the issue began to be seen. It became obvious that in order to gain a perspective on what was involved in second language listening comprehension, it was necessary to look at both the process and the product (Field, 2000). Listening comprehension also had to be investigated from a number of angles, namely: phonology; lexis; syntax-semantics; schema theory; socio-linguistics; and culture (Dirven and Oakeshott-Taylor, 1984). Each of these levels of comprehension interrelates with each of the others. In addition to this, listening had to be investigated from a variety of competence levels (beginners, intermediate, advanced learners), from a variety of contexts (listening to a radio broadcast, to a movie, as part of a conversation etc.), and from the perspective of the type of listening involved – discriminative listening (distinguishing between fact and opinion), comprehensive listening (understanding the message), critical listening (evaluation of the message), therapeutic listening (using the listener as a sounding board), and appreciative listening (listening for entertainment) (Wolvin and Coakley, 1996).

Along with the number of dimensions that had to be part of an investigation into listening, there was the problem of how to actually go about undertaking research when the information was 'inside-the-head'. Faerch and Kasper (1986), for instance, discuss the difficulties in conducting experimental research of a psycholinguistic/sociolinguistic nature where the researchers had to rely on the ability of the subjects (second language learners) to tell them what was going on inside their heads. In order to do this, learners would need to possess sophisticated knowledge about the second language, knowledge about its socio-cultural context and the ability to interpret it, and knowledge of their strategic competence and the ability to describe this.

One further problem with the early research into second language listening comprehension was that there was no baseline research unless the research into first language listening and second language reading is considered. Instead, researchers (who were often language teachers) had to interpret their research findings on the basis of their perceptions and 'hunches' rather than on the basis of theories and models. As Dirven and Oakeshott-Taylor (1984, p. 443) maintain, issues investigated as part of the second language listening research agenda 'have sprung from logico-deductive speculation, fuelled by professional intuition garnered as a result of years of classroom teaching.' This is not to say that following a hunch or investigating a 'problem' is wrong, it is just that the research agenda for second language listening lacked cohesion to begin with.

In spite of the problematic start to research into second language listening, a research agenda has developed over time. Research into listening can be divided into four main areas, depending on the basis of the research, namely *measurement, analysis, identification* and *perceptions*. These four bases of research have resulted in four different types of study, namely (i) *psychometric* studies measuring aspects of speech or listening, (ii) *discourse analyses* of speech, (iii) the identification of *strategies* conducive to success in listening, and (iv) *ethnographic investigations* observing, describing and interpreting listening in natural conditions.

Psychometric research

Several researchers in applied linguistics have taken a positivist approach to investigating factors involved in listening. Some of the areas which have been examined include speech rate and pausology (Derwing, 1990; Griffiths, 1989; Tauroza and Allison, 1990; White, 1997; Zhao 1997); the effect of syntactic and discourse level modification (Cervantes and Gainer, 1986; Chaudron and Richards, 1986; Chiang and Dunkel, 1992; Dunkel and Davis, 1994; Flowerdew and Tauroza, 1995); lexis (Jackson and Bilton, 1994; Kelly, 1991; Meccartty, 2000); visuals (Ginther, 2002); foreign accents (Derwing and Rossiter, 2003; Munro and Derwing, 1995, 2001); comparisons between first language and second language recall (Klaassen and Snippe, 1998); and comparisons of different types of listening support (Chang and Read, 2006).

Discourse analysis

A second major research approach to second language students' listening is discourse analysis. Discourse analysts examine, in detail, the (spoken) texts which are the object of listening. Work by discourse analysts has focused on lexical phrases (DeCarrico and Nattinger, 1988); propositions (Lehrer, 1994; Rost, 1994); length of texts and silent periods (Klaassen and Snippe, 1999); discourse patterns in talk (Olsen and Huckin, 1990; Thompson, 1994); non-relevant information in talk, for example, asides (Strodt-Lopez, 1991). There is also a considerable literature within the field of second language acquisition, which, while not focusing on listening per se, is clearly relevant to second language listening. For example, research has been conducted on how interlanguage forms evolve in spoken interaction, on the structure of "foreigner talk", and on adjustments to interaction among second language learners (for a review see Larsen-Freeman and Long, 1991).

Identifying what the features of spoken text are might seem like a straightforward approach. However, knowledge about discourse structure does not tell us anything about the listening process. For instance, if we discovered that "lists" occur frequently in lectures, we might consider using lists in our teaching of listening. In academic listening, writers of textbooks on listening often assume that we can discover which linguistic features and factors constitute a coherent lecture, advise lecturers to use these features, and train students to recognize them (cf. Lynch, 2004). However, there are so many features of general lecture presentations and so many idiosyncratic aspects to individual lectures that it is simply not possible to produce a textbook with a definitive list of all the desirable features of a generic lecture which can then be used to train L2 students to comprehend specific lectures. Discourse analysis does add to our understanding of the issues involved in second language listening, but it must be viewed as only one dimension of the research agenda. Investigations into these aspects of listening using a discourse analytical approach are on-going, and further research continues to be undertaken.

Listening strategies

Over the past 25 years extensive work has been carried out into identifying how good second language learners learn. Much of this work began with influential papers by Rubin (1975) and Stern (1975). Their work has resulted in a body of literature focused on learner strategies, and more recently on listening strategies. According to Willing (1988, p. 7), a learning strategy is "a specific mental procedure for gathering, processing, associating, categorizing, rehearsing and retrieving information or patterned skills." The initial work in this area postulated that once the "good" learner strategies had been identified, these could be introduced to weak language learners in order to make them more effective learners. Although this hypothesis still underlies much of the research into learner strategies, the task of identifying what are "good" strategies and how these can be introduced to learners is not as easy as first thought. The main problem is determining what an effective strategy is, and how variables such as age, gender, culture, proficiency level etc. are to be taken into account in assessing the effectiveness of strategies (Oxford, 1989).

In an illuminating study into the large number of strategies that learners make use of O'Malley, Chamot, Stewner-Manzanares, Russo, and Kupper (1985) report that ESL high school students' in the United States used no fewer than 638 strategies in integrated learning tasks (using all four language skills). This wide range of strategies, however, was classified by O'Malley, Chamot, Stewner-Manzanares, Russo, and Kupper (1985) into 20 distinct categories which encapsulated the three main uses of strategies, namely metacognitive, cognitive and socio-affective strategies respectively, see also Brown and Palincsar, (1982). Metacognitive strategy refers to the ways in which learners organize, monitor and evaluate their learning; cognitive strategy to the processes which learners use to acquire the language; and socio-affective strategy to the ways in which learners use others to enhance their learning and the ways in which they encourage themselves to continue learning. Specifically with regard to listening, O'Malley and Chamot (1990) identified a range of effective strategies used by second language listeners, classified according to the three types of *metacognitive* – for example, thinking about the learning process, self monitoring, problem identification; *cognitive* – for example, note-taking, deduction, summarization; and *social and affective* – for example, questioning for clarification, cooperation with other learners.

Vandergrift (1997) states that, although the number of research studies that investigate strategies has increased, the area of listening strategies, despite its importance in language learning, is still rather under-researched: "Listening internalises the rules of language and facilitates the emergence of other language skills." (1997, p. 387). Researchers have attempted to identify the listening strategies which second language learners use and to assess how efficient these strategies are. The most recent studies into listening strategies use a variety of research tools, including the analysis of listening tests and questionnaires (Vogely, 1995;

Chien and Wei, 1998); the analysis of students' listening diaries (Goh, 1997, 1998, 2000); the use of students' talk-aloud procedures (Vandergrift, 1999, 2002, 2003); and strategy instruction session (Carrier, 2003; Goh and Taib, 2006). Through these different tools researchers have identified certain types of learner strategy; the relationships between types of strategy and language proficiency; and some of the learner problems when using listening strategies.

Ethnography

Although qualitative research techniques are now used in second language research, they are still not widely used to investigate listening skills. In particular, ethnographic research into second language listening is lacking. There are several reasons for this, among which are that there are: (i) a variety of research instruments usually used to ensure triangulation of the data, resulting in a complex methodology; (ii) ethnographies often take a long time to complete; and (iii) usually two or more researchers have to be involved to ensure data verification. However, when ethnographic methods are used, they provide us with rich insights into second language listening.

Two main ethnographic studies in recent years into academic listening are reviewed here, one an intensive investigation of one NNS student's experiences in attending university in the United States, the other a long-term investigation of Chinese students attending an English-medium university in Hong Kong.

Benson (1989) reports an ethnographic study of one post-graduate Arab student during one semester at a university in the United States. Various research instruments were used to collect data from the student, namely primary data via participant observations and interviews with the student and his lecturer, and secondary data such as the student's written notes and lecture outlines. Benson (1989, p. 440) summarizes his research findings about this one student's attempt to negotiate his way through an academic course as follows:

- The need to learn content altered the ESL student's approach to the course.
- The ESL student's learning conception (largely reproductive) dominated his activities throughout the course, leading to his extrinsic experience of the classes.

- The presence of the teacher shifted the focus away from content, bringing in a range of affective factors.
- The ESL student's note taking primarily recorded 'main' points at the expense of 'subsidiary' ones.
- Background knowledge formed an important part of the course for the ESL student, often leading to a personal interpretation of the material.
- Classroom interaction was largely disregarded by the ESL student in his note taking.
- Specific teaching gambits produced predictable responses across both L1 and L2 students (as seen by the researcher) in the observed lectures.
- The ESL student needed to be able to participate verbally in the class but did not.

Benson's study was an attempt to investigate how the experiences of one ESL student might offer insights into the listening process of a graduate student and how this information might be used to inform ESL courses in the university. He suggests that the type of listening students engage in while attending content lectures is qualitatively and quantitatively different from what they practice in ESL classes, and that ESL classes should contain some content-based assessment so as to prepare students for this type of listening.

While Benson's study was an in-depth ethnography carried out over one semester and using only one student as its focus, Flowerdew and Miller (1992, 1995, 1996a, 1996b, 1997), Flowerdew, Li and Miller (1998), and Flowerdew, Miller and Li (2000) report on an ethnographic investigation which took place over a period of 9 years and had a large number of informants. The data from these studies can be divided into two main categories, the first category being reported in three articles dealing with the perceptions, problems and strategies used by students and lecturers in receiving and giving lectures in English, and the second category being reported in a series of articles dealing with special features of the lecture event.

In their ethnographic study, Flowerdew and Miller (1992, 1995, 1996a, 1996b) show that students and lecturers share some perceptions about lectures in English, but that there were several gray areas where each group had differing perceptions of the lecturing event; for instance, although most of the lecturers reported that they enjoyed lecturing and that lectures were of central importance to conveying information to the students, the students had minimal experience of attending lectures prior to university and so did not seem to appreciate the importance the lecturers attached to lectures. This mismatch in perceptions can obviously lead to lack of preparation for listening to academic discourse and loss of comprehension on the part of the student. It led to frustration on the part of the lecturer, and a search for ways to present information in a second language that would assist learners more.

The second group of articles by Flowerdew, Miller and Li (1998, 2000) deals with special issues which are generated from the grounded data. Some of these special issues are *cultural*: ethnic culture, local culture, academic culture, and disciplinary culture; *socio-cultural*: purpose of lectures, role of lecturers, styles of lecturing, simplification, listener behavior, and humor; and *features of lectures*: features of spoken language, interpersonal strategies, discourse structuring, and integration with other media. Each of these aspects needs to be taken into account when presenting spoken text and taken together they highlight the complexity of the nature of academic listening in a second language.

A Pedagogical Model for Second Language Listening

As we stated earlier in this chapter, little attention was previously paid to how to teach listening to students either in a first-language or second-language context. Fortunately, as research into this area developed, textbook authors and teachers became more aware of the need to include listening activities in materials and language classes. However, although listening was introduced into the syllabus of most courses, a product model which focused on testing listening rather than a process model with a focus on developing listening skills, was used (Mendelson, 2001). Things are changing, and recent teacher educational publications, such as Helgensen and Brown (2007), encourage teachers to go beyond the testing paradigm in their classroom.

It is with insights into the previous research into second language listening, and the realization that listening skills are complex processes that the present authors developed their own model for listening in a second language. Our pedagogic model of second language listening consists of a set of dimensions which are derived from a range of theories about listening. These dimensions are eclectic, insofar as they draw on cognitive, social, linguistic and pedagogic theory. Drawn together, they make possible a unified model of second language listening.

Process Models of Listening

Over the past 40 years or so, there have been three approaches to explain the processes of listening: bottom-up; top-down; and interactive.

Bottom-up processing

The first model of listening to be developed was the so-called bottom-up model. It was developed by researchers working in the 1940s and 1950s. According to the bottom-up model, listeners build understanding by starting with the smallest units of the acoustic message, individual sounds, or phonemes. These are then combined into words, which, in turn, together make up phrases, clauses and sentences. Finally, individual sentences combine together to create ideas and concepts and relationships between them.

Top-down processing

Developed after bottom-up models, top-down models emphasize the use of previous knowledge in processing a text rather than relying upon the individual sounds and words. The top-down model was developed when researchers considered the fact that experimental subjects are unable to identify truncated words in isolation from the words of which they form a part, while, on the other hand, they are quite able to identify these same truncated words so long as they are presented with the surrounding context.

Interactive processing

If listening involves both bottom-up and top-down processing, it follows that some sort of model which synthesizes the two is required. This we have in the so-called interactive model, as developed, most notably, by Rumelhart and his associates (for example, Rumelhart and McClelland, 1982). According to Rumelhart, language is processed simultaneously at different levels. In this *parallel processing*, phonological, syntactic, semantic and pragmatic information interact with each other.

Dimensions of Listening

The above three models have been used extensively over the past decades to develop materials for teaching second language listening. However, they do not cater for all the complexities of the listening process, a process which also encompasses affective, individual, strategic, contextual, social, cultural, critical and intertextual dimensions (Flowerdew and Miller 2005). When we include such other dimensions into teaching listening, we are able to demonstrate how a pedagogical model of second language listening might be conceptualized.

In this section, after a brief explanation of each dimension, we illustrate the dimension with the type of listening exercise which helps learners develop this dimension of their listening. The exercises are based on an extended listening task of an interview with a famous singer. This type of listening task would normally be presented to learners who would be required to listen intensively and then asked questions based only on the information in the interview – for instance, When did the singer leave Cuba to come to the US? What was the singer's mother's name? What does the singer think about her life in the US? When questions like these are presented after an extended stretch of spoken discourse they function as a memory test, and do not aid the learners in developing their listening skills, as we outline above.

An affective dimension

Most models of listening basically try to explain comprehension. However, comprehension can take place only if individuals are motivated to listen. There are many influences on listeners which may affect the way they listen to something and either increase or decrease their effectiveness as listeners. Mathewson (1985) suggested a four dimensional model for *reading* in a second language which includes attitude, motivation, affect, and physical feelings. Such a model can be easily adapted to a listening context. A pedagogic model of listening needs an affective dimension which accounts for the decision to listen and to maintain appropriate levels of concentration.

In our interview listening lesson, as a pre-listening exercise, the teacher could ask the learners about their favorite singers, why they like these particular singers, if there are any singers the learners do not particularly enjoy listening to. This type of exercise engages learners in the lesson, motivates them to want to be a part of the lesson, and offers them the opportunity to interact with the teacher and each other in a realistic fashion – chatting about popular singers.

Individual variation

An important advantage of the interactive model over hierarchical models, whether they be bottom-up or top-down, is that it allows for the possibility of individual variation in linguistic processing. From the pedagogic point of view, this opens up the possibility of a model which is sensitive to individual learning styles and strategies, on the one hand, and the needs of particular groups, on the other.

As a follow on to asking learners about their musical preferences, the teacher could then introduce the singer about to be interviewed, in this case Gloria Estefan. Many learners may not have heard of this singer before, so the teacher could play a short exert of one of her songs. Then learners may be asked to comment on the type of song they had just heard, whether they liked it or not, and why. The teacher could also at this point elicit any information the learners knew about the singer or the type of music. Learners are encouraged to have differing opinions about the singer and her music and are provided with the opportunity to listen using their preferred style.

A strategic dimension

Any second language model of listening needs to incorporate specific features of the second language listening process. The learning dimension of a second language model of listening must identify the specific learning strategies which are beneficial to the acquisition of the listening skill. These can then be considered in the development of pedagogic materials, as is increasingly becoming the case. See for example the *Tapestry* series of course books on listening and speaking with Rebecca Oxford as series editor and Benz and Dworak, (2000).

In a third pre-listening activity, learners could be encouraged to activate their vocabulary about the four areas which the singer will talk about in her interview: work; family; personality; and childhood. The teacher could write up words on the board given by the learners as a way of activating their schemata on each of the categories so that when they listen to the interview they will not be 'listening in the dark', so to speak. Predicting what you will hear is a well-known listening strategy.

A contextualized dimension

In our own ethnographic work on academic listening (cited above), one of the most striking of the findings has been the close integration of listening with other processes and activities. In the lecture context, students are not only required to listen to what the lecturer says. They probably also have to read a handout and look at visual aids. They probably need to take notes. Before the lecture they may have been expected to do some preparatory reading. And following the lecture they may be required to participate in a tutorial and/or complete a written assignment. Later, they may have to sit an exam. All of these activities which accompany the listening process are likely to affect the way an individual actually listens.

Having motivated the learners to take part in the singer's interview lesson, invited learners' personal comments about the type of music of the singer interviewed, and asked them to brainstorm vocabulary associated with the type of listening topics they will hear, the teacher can then move onto a while-listening exercise. In this case, we may ask the learners to draw a simple table and write down any information they hear during the interview under each category on the table: work; family; personality; and childhood. The learners will then have a record of what they heard, or what they thought they heard from the interview, and they will have been provided with a meaningful context within which to listen.

A social dimension

Bottom-up models of listening have been developed within the context of the processing of individual sounds, words, or sentences. Top-down and interactive models have used more extended text. Both have been limited to monologue, however. Neither type of research has considered interactive dialogue. While there are practical reasons for this (it is much simpler to conduct experiments using single sounds, words, sentences or monologic texts), it is unfortunate insofar as the most pervasive context within which listening occurs in the real world is dialogue. Listening, in the context of conversation, is not just a psycho-perceptual process, as the models outlined above might lead one to believe. It is also a very social activity, in which both speaker and hearer affect the nature of the message, on the one hand, and how it is to be interpreted, on the other. Grice's maxims (Grice, 1975), for example, are based upon the assumption of such mutual cooperation in conversation. Any comprehensive model of listening needs, therefore, to take conversation into account.

The social dimension of the lesson has already been introduced in the individual dimension stage where learners were encouraged to chat about the singer they would hear in the interview. We can now take this dimension further and ask the learners to work in pairs to share the information they have recorded on their table with each other. In this way, learners will engage in more than simple information transfer and will probably use many of the social features of spoken texts in talking with each other about the information they collected.

A cross-cultural dimension

If we consider the role of schemata and background knowledge in the listening process, this leads us to the question of different cultural interpretations. Different cultures are likely to give rise to different schemata and consequently different expectations and interpretations of a given (spoken or written) text.

As a post-listening activity to our lesson, we might consider asking the learners to compare some of the information that was mentioned in the tape. For instance, the singer came from Cuba and so learners might be asked to talk about the differences she mentioned between working in Cuba and in the US. The learners also may be asked to compare any other information about the four categories she was interviewed about and extend their discussion to their personal experiences of differences between their own cultures and that of the US.

A critical dimension

In considering intertextuality from the point of view of listening, we are concerned with how the spoken message we hear is related to other texts. Texts, of course, are social artifacts, produced by individuals situated within particular societies, at particular times, and in particular places. If texts are social in nature, they can be said to represent society. At the same time, however, society, to some extent, is constituted by texts, by what people say; our conception of reality is necessarily mediated through language. If we consider texts in this way, then listening becomes a political activity, because what we hear is imbued with the assumptions, or ideologies, which are shared by the society from which the texts emanate. Given the inequalities in power between members of contemporary society and the potential for exploitation of the less powerful by the more powerful, the possibility arises of a critical approach to listening, an approach which seeks to interpret language critically in the light of unequal distribution of power.

As a further extension to the cultural dimension, we might consider introducing a critical dimension to the lesson by asking learners to critically analyze the position of women in the workplace or elderly in society as a way of extending the topics from the interview. In this way, we encourage our learners to go beyond the listening for information task of the interview and develop their own personal opinions on topics.

An intertextual dimension

The comparatively recent resurgence of interest in the work of the Soviet linguist Bakhtin (see, for example, Holquist, 1990) has drawn attention to the pervasive *intertextual* nature of language, how any utterance is likely to reflect the past linguistic experience of the speaker and hearer. The contextualized view of listening outlined in the previous section is concerned with one type of intertextuality, in the terminology of some scholars. We prefer to distinguish the broader type of textual relation, which is concerned with conceptual knowledge rather than actual language forms, from the more overtly linguistic relations which for us constitute intertextuality.

This sort of intertextuality can be found in advertising. In a television advertisement for Thai International Airlines, a voice whispers the words "smooth as silk." This phrase is a commonly used idiom in English, but when used in this particular context it takes on a new meaning; smoothness does not refer to a surface here, but to the smooth ride one has with this particular airline and the smooth service, a distinctive feature of certain South-East Asian airlines. As well as advertisers adapting everyday language and attaching new meanings in specific contexts, everyday conversation often draws on advertising language for its own uses

Intertextuality is thus pervasive in many forms of language, including casual conversation. It is an aspect of comprehension which demands a high level of familiarity with the target culture over and above knowledge of the basic language system. Whatever the challenges, given its pervasiveness, a model of L2 listening needs to incorporate intertextuality at some level.

One way of dealing with the intertextual dimension of the model could be to introduce to the learners the fictitious task of helping Gloria Estefan prepare titles for a new CD based on her family and her life. We then would encourage our learners to re-interpret language they have into a new form; song titles.

Conclusion

The selected review of the research into listening presented in this chapter clearly shows the complexity of the issues involved. In spite of the seemingly chaotic start to research into L2 listening, a research agenda has developed over time. In our literature review of the types of research into listening we have divided the research into four main parts, depending on the basis of the research, namely *measurement, analysis, identification of strategies* and *perceptions*. Any one of these approaches constitutes a major research area in its own right. Taken together, these four areas highlight the complexity of the issues involved in researching second language listening. Although the approaches to researching listening overlap to some extent – and some overlap considerably – a researcher may prefer to use one approach over another when investigating listening. Regardless of any one approach taken, though, research following the other approaches also needs to be considered in order to frame the research within the current overall listening research agenda.

Research which has been undertaken in the past 30 years of so into second language listening allows us to appreciate the complexity of the listening skill. In light of this body of research, we now need to re-conceptualize how we teach listening to second language learners. In this chapter we have shown how previous models which were used to develop listening pedagogy did not go far enough to include essential dimensions which listeners face in contemporary society. Therefore, we have proposed a new pedagogical model which we have briefly explained here. Once textbook writers and teachers take the dimensions we suggest into account we believe that not only will second language learners develop better listening skills, but that listening lessons will become more enjoyable also.

References

Benson, M.J. (1989). The academic listening task: A case study. *TESOL Quarterly*, 23, 3, 421–45.

Benz, C., and Dworak, K. (2000). *Tapestry: Listening and speaking 1*. Boston, MA. Heinle and Heinle.

Brown, A.L., and Palincsar, A.S. (1982). Inducing strategic learning from texts by means of informed, self-control training. *Topics in Learning and Learning Disabilities*, 2, 1, 1–17.

Brown, G. (1990). *Listening to spoken English*. Harlow: Longman.

Burley-Allen, M. (1995). *Listening: The forgotten skill*. New York: John Wiley & Sons, Inc.

Carrier, K. A. (2003). Improving high school English language learners' second language listening through strategy instruction. *Bilingual Research Journal*, 27, 383–408.

Cervantes, R., and Gainer, G. (1986). The effects of syntactic simplification and repetition on listening comprehension. *TESOL Quarterly*, 26, 4, 767–74.

Chang, A. C.-S., and Read, J. (2006). The effects of listening support on the listening performance of EFL learners. *TESOL Quarterly*, 40, 2, 375–97.

Chaudron, C., and Richards, J.C. (1986). The effect of discourse markers on the comprehension of lectures. *Applied Linguistics*, 7, 2, 113–27.

Chiang, C.S., and Dunkel, P. (1992). The effect of speech modification, prior knowledge, and listening proficiency on EFL lecture learning. *TESOL Quarterly*, 26, 2, 345–74.

Chien, C.N., and Wei, L. (1998). The strategy use in listening comprehension for EFL learners in Taiwan. *RELC Journal*, 29, 1, 66–91.

DeCarrico, J., and Nattinger, J.R. (1988). Lexical phrases for the comprehension of academic lectures. *English for Specific Purposes*, 7, 91–102.

Derwing, T.M. (1990). Speaker role is no simple matter. *SSLA*, 12.

Derwing, T.M., and Rossiter, M.J. (2003). The effects of pronunciation instruction on the accuracy, fluency and complexity of L2 accented speech. *Applied Language Learning*, 13, 1, 1–17.

Dirven, R., and Oakeshott-Taylor, J. (1984). State of the art: Listening comprehension, Part I. *Language Teaching*, 17, 326–42.

Dunkel, P.A., and Davis, J.M. (1994). The effects of rhetorical signalling cues on the recall of English lecture information by ESL and ENL listeners. In J. Flowerdew (Ed.). *Academic listening: Research perspectives*, pp. 55–74. Cambridge: Cambridge University Press.

Faerch, C., and Kasper, G. (1986). The role of comprehension in second-language learning. *Applied Linguistics*, 7, 3, 155–274.

Field, J. (2000). Not waving but drowning: A reply to Tony Ridgway. *ELT Journal*, 54, 2, 186–97.

Flowerdew, J., and Miller, L. (1992). Student perceptions, problems and strategies in second language lecture comprehension. *RELC Journal*, 23,2, 60–80.

Flowerdew, J., and Miller, L. (1995). On the notion of culture in L2 lectures. *TESOL Quarterly*, 29, 2, 345–73.

Flowerdew, J., and Miller, L. (1996a). Lectures in a second language: Notes towards a cultural grammar. *English for Specific Purposes*, 15, 2, 121–40.

Flowerdew, J., and Miller, L. (1996b). Lecturer perceptions, problems and strategies in second language lectures. *RELC Journal*, 21, 1, 23–60.

Flowerdew, J., and Miller, L. (1997). The teaching of academic listening comprehension and the question of authenticity. *English for Specific Purposes*, 16, 1, 27–46.

Flowerdew, J., and Miller, L. (2005) *Second language listening: Theory and practice.* Cambridge: Cambridge University Press

Flowerdew, J., and Tauroza, S. (1995). The effect of discourse markers on second language lecture comprehension. *Discourse Markers in L2 Lecture Comprehension*, 17, 435–58.

Flowerdew, J., Li, D., and Miller, L. (1998). Attitudes towards English and Cantonese among Hong Kong Chinese university lecturers. *TESOL Quarterly*, 32, 2, 201–31.

Flowerdew, J., Miller, L., and Li, D. (2000). Chinese lectures' perceptions, problems and strategies in lecturing in English to Chinese-speaking students. *RELC Journal*, 31, 1, 116–37.

Gilman, R.A., and Moody, L.M. (1984). What practitioners say about listening: Research implications for the classroom. *Foreign Language Annuals*, 17, 4, 331–3.

Ginther, A. (2002). Context and content visuals and performance on listening comprehension stimuli. *Language Testing*, 19, 133–67.

Goh, C. (1997). Metacognitive awareness and second language listeners. *ELT Journal*, 41, 4, 361–9.

Goh, C. (1998). Emerging environments of English for academic purposes and the implications for learning materials. *RELC Journal*, 29, 1, 20–33.

Goh, C. (2000). A cognitive perspective on language learners' listening comprehension problems. *System*, 28, 55–75.

Goh, C., and Taib, Y. (2006). Metacognitive instruction in listening for young learners. *ELT Journal*, 60, 3, 222–32.

Grice, H.P. (1975). Logic and conversation. In P. Cole and J.L. Morgan (Eds.). *Syntax and semantics 3: Speech acts*, pp. 41–58. New York: Academic Press.

Griffiths, R. (1989). Facilitating listening comprehension through rate-control. *RELC Journal*, 21, 1, 55–65.

Helgensen, M., and Brown, S. (2007). *Listening*. New York: McGraw-Hill.

Holquist, M. (1990). *Dialogism: Bhaktin and his world*. London: Routledge.

Jackson, J., and Bilton, L. (1994). Stylish variables in science lectures: Teaching vocabulary. *ESP Journal*, 13,1, 61–80.

Kelly, P. (1991). Lexical ignorance: The main obstacle to listening comprehension with advanced foreign language learners. *IRAL*, 29, 2, 135–50.

Klaassen, R.G., and Snippe, J. (1998). *Effectiveness of university teaching in a second language; an experimental study on students' learning from a lecture*. Paper presented at the 1998 IUT Conference, Dublin, July, 1–12.

Klaassen, R.G., and Snippe, J. (1998). *Effective learning behaviour in English-medium instruction: A pilot study*. Delft: Delft University Press.

Larsen Freeman, D., and Long, M.H. (1991). *An introduction to second language acquisition research*. London: Longman.

Lehrer, A. (1994). Understanding classroom lectures. *Discourse Processes*, 17, 2, 259–81.

Lynch, T. (2004). *Study Listening: Understanding Lectures and Talk in English*, 2nd edn. Cambridge: Cambridge University Press.

Maccartty, F. (2000). Lexical and grammatical knowledge in reading and listening comprehension. *Foreign Language Annals*, 34, 439–45.

Mathewson, G. C. (1985). Toward a comprehension model of affect in the reading process. In H. Singer and R.B. Ruddell (Eds.). *Theoretical models and processes of reading*, 3rd edn. pp. 841–56. New York, Delaware: International Reading Association.

Mendelson, D. (2001). Listening comprehension: We've come a long way, but.... *Contact*, 27, 33–40.

Munro, M.J., and Derwing, T.M. (1995). Foreign accent, comprehensibility, and intelligibility in the speech of second language learners. *Language Learning*, 45, 73–97.

Munro M. J., and Derwing, T.M. (2001). Modeling perceptions of accentedness and comprehensibility of L2 speech. *Studies in Second Language Acquisition*, 23, 451–68.

O'Malley, J.M., and Chamot, A.U. (1990). *Learning strategies in second language acquisition*. Cambridge: Cambridge University Press.

O'Malley, J.M., Chamot, A.U., Stewner-Manzanares, G., Russo, R.P., and Kupper, L. (1985). Learning strategies applications with students of English as a second language. *TESOL Quarterly*, 19, 3, 557–84.

Olsen, L.A., and Huckin, T.N. (1990). Point-driven understanding in engineering lecture comprehension. *English for Specific Purposes*, 9, 33–47.

Oxford, R.L. (1989). Use of Language learning strategies: a synthesis of studies with implications for strategy training. *System*, 17, 2, 235–47.

Rost, M. (1994). *Introducing listening*. London: Penguin English Applied Linguistics.

Rubin, J. (1975). What the "Good Language Learner" can teach us. *TESOL Quarterly*, 9, 1, 41–51.

Rumelhart, D.E., and McClelland, J.L. (1982). An interactive activation model of context effects in letter perception: Part 2. The contextual enhancement effect and some tests and extensions of the model. *Psychological Review*, 89, 60–94.

Stern, H.H. (1975). What can we learn from the good language learner? *Canadian Modern Language Review*, 31, 304–18.

Strodt-Lopez, B. (1991). Tying it all in: Asides in university lectures. *Applied Linguistics*, 12, 2, 117–40.

Tauroza, S., and Allison, D. (1990). Speech rates in British English. *Applied Linguistics*, 11, 1, 90–105.

Thompson, S. (1994). Aspects of cohesion in monologue. *Applied Linguistics*, 15, 1, 58–75.

Vandergrift, L. (1997). The Cinderella of communication strategies: Reception strategies in interactive listening. *Modern Language Journal*, 81, iv, 494–505.

Vandergrift, L. (1999). Facilitating second language listening comprehension: Acquiring successful strategies. *ELT Journal*, 53, 3, 168–76.

Vandergrift, L. (2002). 'It was nice to see that our predictions were rights': Developing metacognition in L2 listening comprehension. *Canadian Modern Language Review*, 58, 4, 555–76.

Vandergrift, L. (2003). Orchestrating strategy use: Towards a model of the skilled second language listener. *Language Learning*, 53, 3, 463–96.

Vogely, A. (1995). Perceived strategy use during performance on three authentic listening comprehension tasks. *The Modern Language Journal*, 79, 1, 41–56.

White, R. (1997). Back channeling, repair, pausing, and private speech. *Applied Linguistics*, 18, 3, 314–44.

Willing, K. (1988). *Learning styles in adult migrant education*. Adelaide: National Curriculum Resource Centre for Adult Migrant Education Program.

Wolvin, A.D., and Coakley, C.G. (1996). *Listening*, 5th edn. Dubuque, IA: Brown.

Zhao, Y. (1997). The effects of listeners' control of speech rate on second language comprehension. *Applied Linguistics*, 18, 49–68.

Part IV

Listening in Contexts

8

Listening Practices: Are We Getting Any Better?

Sheila C. Bentley

In this chapter, Bentley explores how businesses are moving towards a performance improvement approach for enhancing listening skills and listening performance. Some of the difficulties encountered, however, lie in identifying which specific behaviors impact the listening performance and can be directly tied to improved outcomes and a return on the investment for developing or encouraging these behaviors. In other words, which listening behaviors affect outcomes and profits in a business setting, and how can those behaviors be taught, measured, and reinforced?

This chapter seeks to determine whether measurable gains are being made in listening effectiveness in the business world. If gains are being made, how are the gains being measured – specifically what behaviors are being observed, counted or measured, and related to listening improvement. Finally, if there are measurable improvements, are these improvements related to the business goals of the organization? In short, this chapter examines whether we are getting any better at listening, and if so, is it making any difference to the business?

In her address to the 2003 ASTD Annual Convention, Tina Sung, the president of ASTD (the American Society for Training and Development), stated that the two most important trends in training today are:

1   linking learning to the business strategy of the organization; and
2   performance consulting.

Sung (2003) also emphasized that those in the training and development field need new measurements that show the value of learning to the organization. She said, "We should be asking: How is training tied to your organization's business strategies? What is the problem you are trying to solve?" Consequently, if we are trying to improve listening effectiveness, the skills we teach should be tied to the organization's business strategies, and we should be providing measures that show not only that there are measurable changes, but also that the changes are producing the desired impact on the organization.

Tying Performance to Business Goals

Truly, the demand has increased for tying employee performance and training and development to business outcomes, and the emphasis has shifted from training as the answer to all performance problems to training as one possible strategy out of many for improving performance (Blanchard, Robinson, and Robinson, 2002; Robinson and Robinson, 1998; Rummler and Brache, 1995). In fact, in many cases, businesses are no longer offering training in soft skills or employee development areas unless it can be shown that these skills relate to the bottom line or the company's strategic goals. Kaplan and Norton (2001) present a model that traces an effective organization's mission down through core values, the vision, strategic initiatives, and finally to what an individual worker should be doing (p. 73). Training, while delivered to the individual worker, is generally expected to be focused up through the organization at the mission, vision, and strategic goals.

Consequently, in listening training, the need to show a relationship between improved listening skills and factors that affect the bottom line has increased. Showing this relationship is perhaps the greatest challenge facing listening experts. While intuitively we feel that if you listen better, you get more information and have a better relationship with the speaker, we now are being challenged to prove that specific behaviors will increase sales or decrease costs or improve customer satisfaction or employee morale. In a performance improvement environment, we are even required to count or measure the behaviors and then show correlations to achieving the organization's business goals. Thus, if we propose that customer service agents who spend less time talking (theoretically listening to the customer) will do a better job of satisfying the customer, we would need to measure the time spent listening (or not talking) and then measure changes in per-customer sales or customer retention. (Of course, since there could be other factors, such as reduced prices, that could be impacting the increase in sales, it can be a complicated connection to make.) Still, in the training arena, the pressure is on to connect training and performance with business outcomes.

Identifying Desired Outcomes and Related Behaviors

In business, the adage is to "start with the end in mind." What do you want to get better at? Typical measures of outcomes related to business goals include:

- reduced costs;
- increased revenue;
- increased profits;
- increased efficiency;
- increased effectiveness;
- reduced customer turnover;
- improved safety;
- improved employee morale; and
- reduced employee turnover.

Once the business or organizational goals are identified, an assessment phase should follow, where performance models are developed, performance gaps are identified, and cause analyses are conducted. For instance, if a business wanted to reduce customer turnover, what would be the ideal listening behaviors that would decrease the customer turnover, what are customer service representatives (CSRs) doing now, what performance gaps exist, what causes these gaps (perhaps not enough time to listen, or the CSR has a script to follow that doesn't build in listening time), and how will the new behaviors be taught, measured, and supported. Finally, if these behaviors are implemented, is there a resultant decrease in customer turnover? Does the behavior change produce the desired business result? One other question of importance in business is does the cost of making the change produce a sufficient financial benefit, or what is the return on the investment (ROI)? (If we give CSRs more time to listen and customers are more satisfied, do they buy more or do they just talk to the CSRs more?)

After the business or organizational goals are set, the next step would be to tie listening performance to those business goals. Robinson and Robinson (1998) developed a Five-Phase Model for evaluating performance improvement projects. The five phases are:

Phase 1 – Goal setting;
Phase 2 – Performance analysis;
Phase 3 – Design for improvement;
Phase 4 – Implementation; and
Phase 5 – Impact.

This model serves as a good starting point, but because listening effectiveness can vary so much from one situation to another, expanding the model could provide better guidance to listening improvement. The steps in the process might be as follows:

Listening Improvement Process Model

Phase 1 – Establish business goals.

Phase 2 – Assess performance factors for the specific situation (that is, environmental factors, speaker or customer expectations, processes, equipment, job performer, available time).

Phase 3 – Identify outstanding performers (Who does the job well?).

Phase 4 – Identify desirable behaviors (What do the outstanding performers do?).

Phase 5 – Measure current performance and determine performance gaps in underperforming individuals.

Phase 6 – Conduct a cause or gap analysis.

Phase 7 – Train, coach, or provide support for new behaviors.

Phase 8 – Measure performance.

Phase 9 – Provide feedback and retrain as needed.

Phase 10 – Measure impact on business goals.

In a performance improvement model, there are three "levels of performance" (Robinson and Robinson, 1998):

Level 1 – The organizational level;
Level 2 – The process level; and
Level 3 – The job/performer level.

Training and development may focus on Level 3, the job/performer level, but performance is still tied to the process level and the organizational level. For example, an effective listener in a bad process or in a failing business will still not be successful. Consequently, training may be only one piece of the performance improvement approach.

Furthermore, in a performance improvement approach, training is no longer considered to be the automatic answer to all performance problems. In the past, once a need was identified, training often was ordered for the affected employees. However, the return on the investment (ROI) from the training was often disappointing – the training was costly, and the results were disappointing. As a result, the trend has been to examine what the factors are that affect performance and then address those factors, and sometimes these factors may have nothing to do with training. (For instance, many people feel they could be better listeners if they had more time and weren't expected to multi-task while listening.) Or if the first contact with a customer is through a lengthy voice mail menu, it might be difficult for listening training to overcome the irritation of a frustrated customer who had to listen to voice mail options rather than a live voice. Instead of a training solution, changing the process or hiring additional customer service representatives might lead to better performance. Or it may be the reward system or productivity measures that cause the problem, such as rewarding the number of calls taken, rather than the quality or satisfaction of the customer. For example, physicians aren't reimbursed for time spent listening to patients; consequently, less time is built into the appointment time for listening to the patient. Thus, training the physicians in listening skills might not improve their listening effectiveness.

Another result of the emphasis on performance improvement and return on investment is the development of long-term partnerships between management and trainers or coaches that focus on performance and a resulting improvement in ROI or financial benefit. So listening training is moving away from the one-day seminar to longer-term partnerships where business goals are established, processes are developed, behaviors that support these processes are identified, measured, coached or taught, remeasured, and outcomes assessed. The next challenge to address becomes what specific listening behaviors will produce the desired results, are they observable and measurable, and are we measuring them to determine if progress is being made?

Identifying and Measuring Listening Behaviors

One report on customer service (Report on Customer Relationship Management, 2003) concludes that customer service representatives are still measured on efficiency rather than value – the number of calls handled, rather than the quality or outcome. Arussy reports, "Agents are still paid bonuses for hanging up quicker ... there are no processes for them (customers) to voice their opinions." This report also concludes that call center metrics are still lagging behind the goals they are meant to support. "Fifteen percent, probably less, have the religion to measure effectiveness, customer satisfaction, or lifetime customer value." (p. 8) Andre Harris, director of reservation training and quality assurance at Continental Airlines says: "At Continental, we've tossed out the per-call time goals for more big-picture targets. It's still a balance, but today it's customer service first, sales second, and efficiency third" (p. 8). This report also states that the top customer service trend in 2003 is to put greater emphasis on key performance indicators (KPIs) that guarantee success. So, it would seem that some companies are making progress toward measuring effectiveness.

However, this same report asserts that customer relationship management initiatives fail because functional ROI-driven efforts add little customer value. Executives want to retain and gain customers while increasing overall satisfaction, but they use ROI-focused metrics which produce only improved operational efficiency. There may be more achieved by attracting new, high-value customers and by training and supporting a reputation for customer service, which would more than likely require effective listening, which would hopefully translate to customer loyalty. Furthermore, businesses in general are not yet identifying specific listening behaviors that relate directly even to operational efficiency. Consequently, while progress is being made in identifying effectiveness, we may not be up to measuring the ROI of the improved effectiveness or the specific listening behaviors that make listeners more effective in the targeted situation.

Measuring Individual Listening Performance

At the level of the individual job performer, behaviors are described very specifically and measurable behavioral goals are set that include a quantity, quality, and manner of performance. Thus, just saying that someone will spend 50 percent of their communication time listening to a customer is not a specific enough goal. This goal should specify such behaviors as sincerely empathizing with the customer by saying things such as "I can see that you are upset." Manner of performance might include a description of the tone of voice or the use of polite or respectful words or behaviors (thanking the customer for calling, apologizing for the problem, using the customer's name, smiling, using a sympathetic tone of voice, etc.)

Katzenbach (2000) describes five paths to peak performance, one of which is the "Process and Metrics" path. Katzenbach acknowledges that all good companies use a process and metrics approach at least to some degree. The Process and Metrics path is based on principles of accountability and consequence management. Clear measures and standards for performance are established, a set of integrated processes for delivering value to customers is established, and people know and can see how they and others are performing. Performance goals are set, and revenue, cost, and profitability measures are established, tracked, and compared. Competitive position and market share are reported frequently. Examples of companies that use a Process and Metrics approach include KFC, Marriott, and Avon.

If an organization were using a Process and Metrics path, establishing what listening behaviors are observable, quantifiable, and can be shown to have an impact on performance would be a requirement. Clearly one difficulty in improving listening effectiveness is the task of finding observable behaviors that in fact measure listening effectiveness. For example does making eye contact mean that you are a more effective listener? Of course, many of the listening behaviors that we can observe differ by culture, by age, by gender, by situation and environment, by region of the country, and by the technology being used during listening. Furthermore, the behaviors that are appropriate and effective in one situation or type of business are not necessarily those that produce better results in another type of business. An additional difficulty is that the most popularly used listening assessment tools, such as the Watson-Barker Listening Styles Profile, measure general patterns rather than the behaviors actually used in a certain situation.

According to Johnson, Pearce, Tuten, and Sinclair (2003), "listening training has been limited to lectures on the process of listening and to experiential exercises designed to provide for listening practice and to assist in recognizing a person's own beneficial and detrimental listening behaviors" (p. 23). However, these researchers reported on a pilot study that showed that periods of self-imposed silence greatly improved the awareness of the listener's own listening behaviors and those of others. The study does not, however, relate the periods of silence to any measured outcome (for example, did the listeners gather more information, did they create a more positive relationship with the speaker). Silence would be an observable, measurable behavior, but it would be difficult to observe or measure what the listener was doing mentally during the silence. It could be possible to measure outcomes following the silence, though.

Another difficulty in identifying the listening behaviors for training is that we don't yet have a clear formula for what effective listening is and what will produce the types of results or business outcomes that people want in specific situations. (Does being silent increase sales or customer satisfaction?)

Gunn (2001) stated that good listening is an essential skill for those that achieve outstanding performance, and noted that there are experts who can describe what someone who listens well does, including mentally. He then asks, however, "if their techniques are so good, then why do we waste so much time repeating ourselves?" (p. 12). He continues, "Few people realize that the art of listening has everything to do with a kind of feeling and little to do with the mental gymnastics of trying to concentrate on the words themselves" (p. 12). Gunn admits that it was difficult for him to accept that he could do a better job of listening by focusing on listening for the feeling, rather than the content. He even admitted that he had focused in the past on the content to the point that he took notes while others were talking, rather than just listening. But, he also found himself asking people to repeat themselves. He said that he wanted to be seen as someone with important things to say, that he was often just waiting for the other person to stop talking, and that he wanted to be right, so he often listened for only those statements that he agreed with. "What became clear was the more I thought – the greater my own mental activity – the less insight and understanding I gained and the harder it was to remember what had been said!" (p. 12).

Gunn suggests trying an experiment: When you meet someone, take time to build rapport before conducting any business. Make a connection with the other person first. Then turn your back on your own thoughts – quit thinking about what you are thinking. Let yourself be drawn into the other person's world. Finally, notice your own feelings. He says that being present doesn't mean that you have to join in. "Listen for the deeper feeling that comes from a more mindful and spiritual place, and then act on that thought" (p. 12). While all of this may lead to positive outcomes, it will still be necessary to identify those behaviors that reflect listening for feeling.

A medical center that was losing $2 million per month turned their performance around to an operating gain of $3.9 million or 2.1 percent in 2001 and a gain of $5.7 million or 2.6 percent in 2002 (Conemaugh, 2002), and in-patient satisfaction scores reached as high as the 92nd percentile, and the facility earned the 100 Top Hospitals designation in orthopedics and cardiology. They achieved this by rethinking their bottom-line goals and instead gave clinical excellence and service excellence equal weight alongside cost-effectiveness. They "listened" to the patients who told them "to be nice; to include them in decision making; to make some facility changes; to talk to their families; to not let them wait too long; to explain things" (p. 26). While this medical center relates listening to a business goal, one could ask if it was really "listening" that produced the results, and if so, what where the specific listening behaviors.

At the Time Warner call center in Memphis, Tennessee, where customer service representatives handle 5,000 calls per day, Customer Service Representatives (CSRs) have a performance goal of handling 70 calls per day and spending 7 hours per day on the phone. Their calls are monitored and can be recorded while simultaneously capturing the screens that the CSR is viewing and entering data on during the call. In addition, the CSRs have quality standards that specify processes and behaviors. These include:

1 Listen.
2 Empathize. Recognize the customer's emotional state. Use phrases such as "I can see that you are upset by …."
3 Gather facts. Use open-ended and closed-ended questions.
4 Act quickly and appropriately to solve the problem. Have answers at hand.;
5 Commit to follow up, even if the customer is satisfied (call back within 24–36 hours).
6 You own the interaction.

The CSRs do have performance goals that are measured, and they are monitored and evaluated against a perfect call model. Average call times are examined with the assumption that high talk time may indicate too much "chit chat" and low talk time may indicate that the CSR is not taking the customer seriously enough. Supervisors look for training opportunities and monitor soft skills. The calls are scored, and these scores are used to give feedback and for evaluation purposes. Time Warner has the technology to measure a number of aspects of the calls, but they currently are not measuring correlations between the specific behaviors (such as showing empathy) and customer satisfaction, retention, and/or sales or profitability, but these measures are targeted for the near future (Savko, 2003). Thus, at least one company is identifying and measuring specific behaviors related to listening. As yet, the effectiveness and the ROI, however, are not yet being measured.

Once the business goals have been set and the listening behaviors identified for the specific situation, the next phase involves training, coaching, or providing the support for the desired behavior. While it appears that we are making headway in refining the process, there is still much research to be done in identifying specific listening behaviors that produce the desired business outcomes. And while certain behaviors may work in some situations, those same behaviors may be counter-productive in others. (For example, writing down what someone is saying while they are speaking is usually seen as a positive listening behavior, but when doctors take notes while the patient is speaking, some patients are confused about whether the doctor is listening or not.) Thus, it becomes more important for those involved in listening training to ensure that the behaviors being trained work in that environment and produce the desired business outcomes.

Conclusions

What is better listening for a physician is not necessarily the same as for a customer service representative, a 911 operator, or an individual in a business. Thus, before determining whether we are getting better at listening, we must determine what the desired outcomes are (what are we going to get better at?) and then determine which listening behaviors will produce that outcome, and determine how those behaviors can be encouraged and measured. Many businesses and organizations are focused in the direction of performance improvement, but as of yet, they are only beginning to identify and train specific listening behaviors.

Few are at the point of actually measuring listening behaviors and of tying those behaviors back to the business's strategic goals. Because the listening behaviors that would produce greater listening effectiveness vary from business to business and situation to situation, it will be difficult for businesses to just adopt what someone else is doing. Finally, it will take listening experts to be able to identify specific behaviors that are likely to produce the results, and because measuring the behaviors would have to occur in the actual listening environment to determine the effectiveness, the complexity of the process will be compounded. In spite of the challenges of improving listening effectiveness in a business setting, the rewards could prove invaluable in terms of increasing customer satisfaction, reducing the costs of having to redo work, or in improving the profitability of the business.

QUESTIONS FOR DISCUSSION

1 What are some of the deficits in listening skills or listening behaviors that cause people to be poor listeners on the job?
2 What are some of the environmental factors on the job that cause people to be ineffective or less effective listeners?
3 What listening behaviors would enhance an employee's listening effectiveness in a typical business meeting? Could these behaviors be measured? How could the impact of these behaviors on the success of the meeting be measured?
4 Select a business situation that you have been in recently in which you were dissatisfied with the way the person representing the company listened to you. What listening behaviors should the employee have exhibited in order to satisfy you as a customer? How could these behaviors be measured? How could the company's employees be trained to use these behaviors in similar situations?
5 Select a different business from the previous question. How might the listening behaviors of the employees of this company need to be different? Again, how could the company measure whether the employees are exhibiting these behaviors? And how could this company's employees be trained to use these behaviors?
6 Create a case that would encourage a business to give its employees more time to dedicate to listening, whether it is to other co-workers or customers or clients. How could you demonstrate that this increase in time might actually save the company money rather than being an increase in expenses?
7 If an organization or business wanted to decrease its costs by having employees spend less time listening to customers (in other words, reduce the length of call time on the phone), what behaviors could be encouraged and rewarded? Would these behaviors, if implemented, have an impact on the quality of the communication interaction? If so, how could this impact be minimized or mitigated?

8   Select a business goal, such as increasing sales, decreasing costs, or improving customer satisfaction. Describe how a company could identify listening behaviors that would impact this goal. Then explore how these behaviors and the impact they have on the business goal could be measured.

9   Select a business situation and describe how the *quality* of listening could be measured (as opposed to measuring the quantity of listening).

10   Select an industry or a specific job title. How could the return on the investment (ROI) for improved listening skills be measured?

11   Since the speaker determines whether the listener is a "good listener" or not, how could the speaker's assessment of the listener be measured for work-related listening?

12   How could listeners do a better job of identifying what the speaker needs from the listener, so that listening performance could be adjusted to fit that speaker's current needs?

References

Blanchard, K., Robinson, D.G., and Robinson, J.C. (2002). *Zap the gaps: Target higher performance and achieve it!* New York: William Morrow.

Conemaugh (2002, December 23) "Listening to patients improves bottom line; Spirit of Excellence Award for Service – Winner" *Modern Healthcare*. Retrieved on November 19, 2003, from: http://exlibris.lib.memphis.edu.2056/universe/document.

Gunn, B. (2001, Feb.). Listening as a feeling. *Strategic Finance*, 82, 8, 12.

Johnson, I.W., Pearce, C.G., Tuten, T.L., and Sinclair, L. (2003, June). Self-imposed silence and perceived listening effectiveness. *Business Communication Quarterly*, 66, 2, 23.

Kaplan, R.S., and Norton, D.P. (2001). *The strategy-focused organization*. Boston, MA: Harvard Business School Press.

Katzenbach, F.R. (2000). *Peak performance*. Boston: Harvard Business School Press.

Report on Customer Relationship Management, IOMA. (2003, February 8). Retrieved on November 19, 2003, from: http://exlibris.lib.memphis.edu.2056/universe/document?

Robinson, D.G., and Robinson, J.C. (Eds.). (1998). *Moving from training to performance*. San Francisco, CA: Berrett-Koehler Publishers, Inc.

Rummler, G.A., and Brache, A.P. (1995). *Improving performance: How to manage the white space on the organizational chart*. San Francisco, CA: Jossey-Bass.

Savko, P. (2003) Manager, personal communication. *Training and Development*, Time Warner, Memphis, TN, November 18.

Sung, T. (2003) Opening address at ASTD Annual Convention, May 18, San Diego, CA.

9

Listening Pedagogy: Where Do We Go from Here?

Laura A. Janusik

In this chapter, Janusik first reviews listening pedagogy from the early 1900s through 2007. She then argues that much of what is believed to be known about listening is not supported by research, and some of which is supported by research is actually supported by outdated research. Thus, we need to refocus our attention not on how to teach listening, but rather to make certain that what we teach about listening is based on supported studies. Janusik offers a theoretically grounded approach to teaching listening – the listening quad.

Historically, a person listens more than he speaks (Barker, Edwards, Gaines, Gladney, and Holley, 1980; Davis, 2001; Rankin, 1930; Werner, 1975), but communication educators have spent a disproportionate amount of time on teaching speaking as opposed to teaching listening (Janusik and Wolvin, 2002, Perkins, 1994). Listening instruction is not required at most universities (Wacker and Hawkins, 1995), and, on average, students who are required to take a basic communication course receive approximately 7 percent of the semester's time focused on listening instruction (Janusik and Wolvin, 2002; Perkins, 1994). The lack of time spent on listening instruction is unfortunate, as 64 percent of a university students' instruction is delivered through lecture and discussion formats that require listening (Taylor, 1964).

Not only is listening comprehension viewed as critical to college success (Boyer, 1987), but listening ability has also been linked to greater academic success (McDevitt, Sheenan, and McMenamin, 1991) as well as an increased likelihood that a student will continue in education (Conaway, 1982). Further, the ability to listen effectively is still one of the top three skills sought in job applicants and one of the top skills that determine promotions (AICPA, 2005; Goby and

Lewis, 2000; Hynes, and Bhatia, 1996; James, 1992; Maes, Weldy, and Icenogle, 1997; Waner, 1995; Willmington, 1992; Winsor, Curtis, and Stephens, 1997).

Students readily admit that they do not listen to their ability because they do not have a clear concept of what listening is and how they can improve and control their own listening process (Ford and Wolvin, 1993; Imhof, 1998). Instructors resist teaching listening because they feel they are not properly trained, it would take too much time, and there are not enough materials (Steil, 1984).

Finally, a new debate involves whether the focus of listening should be on teaching listening or research to develop a solid listening construct (Wolvin, 2003). More mature disciplines and fields, like psychology and the hard sciences, focus their energy on further refining their constructs as opposed to figuring out how to teach them.

Purpose

Little is known about why listening is not positioned centrally in the university curriculum; however, contributions to its placement include limited scholarly classroom materials, a lack of agreement as to the construct of listening, and inadequate research to keep the field recent. This chapter first will provide a synopsis about what is known about teaching listening as the university level. It will then explain and counter the three contributions to the status of listening in the university classroom. Finally, the chapter concludes with a brief introduction of the listening quad (Janusik, 2007b), a research-based approach to teaching listening.

Recent Research on Listening Pedagogy

The most recent comprehensive work on listening pedagogy utilized articles and books from 1930 through early 2002 (Janusik, 2002a). Materials for the analysis were selected due to their primary focus on the teaching of listening at the university level. Articles were not restricted to communication publications or journals, but they were restricted to academic work, research publications, and textbooks. What follows is a brief review of the findings.

Publications prior to 1980

Publications prior to 1980 laid the groundwork for what is known about the teaching of listening. The literature primarily consisted of materials used to teach and assess listening, as well as the effects of instructional methods. Though Rankin's (1930) study brought attention to listening, it was not until the 1946–1947 academic year that Nichols headed the instruction of listening at the university level (Brown, 1987). Concurrently, a communication course at Florida State University included a graded listening assignment with every speaking assignment (Edney, 1949). A survey of the member schools of the American Association of Colleges for Teacher Education concluded that three schools offered specialized courses in listening, and an additional 33 percent offered listening as a separate unit in another course (Markgraf, 1962).

Materials used to teach listening prior to 1980 included a compilation of readings (Brown, 1987; Drake, 1951) and two annotated bibliographies (Duker, 1968; Toussant, 1960). The first two undergraduate listening texts were introduced in the early 1970s (Barker, 1971; Weaver, 1972). A Theory and Research Into Practice (TRIP) booklet assisted university instructors in developing listening units and courses (Wolvin and Coakley, 1979).

In addition to "how to" publications, listening tests were developed to measure comprehension and listening skills. These included the Brown-Carlsen Listening Comprehension Test (Brown and Carlsen, 1955) and The Sequential Tests of Educational Progress (STEP) Test, developed by the Educational Testing Service (1955, 1979). Many studies on the success of teaching listening showed mixed results (Duker, 1968). Specifically, three studies using the Brown-Carlsen Listening Test found that listening training significantly impacted listening effectiveness, while two using the same instrument found no significant differences (Janusik, 2002a).

Thus, research on listening instruction prior to the 1980s focused on developing materials that could be used to teach and assess listening in the classroom.

Publications during the 1980s

Publications of the 1980s offered new materials to teach and assess listening, numerous journal articles, many of them focused on teaching listening (Rhodes, 1985), and a continued attempt to identify effective instructional strategies.

Many new university-level textbooks for use in undergraduate listening courses were developed (Wolff, Marsnik, Tracey, and Nichols, 1983; Wolvin and Coakley, 1982) as well as cross-over texts for both the classroom and business training (Burley-Allen, 1982; Maidment, 1984; Steil, Summerfield and de Mare, 1983; Steil, Barker and Watson, 1983).

Two new listening tests were developed – the Kentucky Comprehensive Listening Test (Bostrom and Waldhart, 1980) and the Watson-Barker Listening Test (Watson and Barker, 1984). These two tests, in addition to the Brown-Carlsen Listening Test (Brown and Carlsen, 1955) and the STEP Test (Educational Testing Service, 1979) quickly came under attack for lack of validity (Bostrom 1990a; Fitch-Hauser and Hughes, 1987; Roberts, 1988; Weaver, 1972). Another listening test, the Northern Illinois University Listening Exam, was introduced toward the end of the decade (Cooper, 1988). Its reliability was slightly lower than statistically sound (.557 to .764); however, the exam fared statistically better than the other standardized listening tests.

Many journal publications focused on listening instruction and assessment; however, the most popular approach to teaching listening remained fairly consistent, which was the lecture–discussion–practice test sequence (Rhodes, 1985). Written instruction on how to teach listening that was published in communication journals remained constant as well, using the approach developed by Nichols and Stevens (1957) that identified negative listening habits and then implemented the 10 guides to effective listening.

Therefore, as with the previous period, the 1980s focused on developing a greater foundation in terms of listening texts and corporate publications. More listening tests were developed to assess effectiveness; however, none of the tests met standards of validity and reliability.

Publications from 1990 to 2001

The listening community held a strong belief that listening could be taught, and this was evidenced in the number of publications about teaching listening. The topic of listening instruction was the fourth most prominent discourse in the first 20 years of the *Journal of the International Listening Association/International Journal of Listening* (Wolvin, Halone, and Coakley, 1999). What we know about listening during the decade from 1990 to 2001 primarily comes from listening instruction surveys, materials used to teach and assess listening, and studies.

A review of listening instruction during the decade prior to 1990 was summarized by Coakley and Wolvin (1990). They were neither encouraged nor discouraged. They documented many advances in listening curriculum development and corporate training, yet heeded the call for researchers to assess the impact of technology on listening. In addition, they summarized and moved forward the discussion on listening competency (Wolvin and Coakley, 1994).

Listening was more likely to be taught in conjunction with another course, such as a basic communication course, rather than as a stand-alone course (Wacker and Hawkins, 1995; Wolvin, Coakley, and Disburg, 1991, 1992), and most basic courses did include a unit on listening (Morreale, Hanna, Berko, and Gibson, 1999). The communication course was generally at the 100 or 200 level; it was offered for 3 credits, and the primary instructional methods were lecture and discussion (Wolvin, Coakley, and Disburg, 1992). The focus was closely divided between teaching an overview of the five types of listening in Wolvin and Coakley's taxonomy (54 percent) versus teaching critical listening (44 percent) (Perkins, 1994). One-third of the instructors preferred to teach listening as a separate unit, while another third chose to integrate listening instruction throughout the basic course. Instruction primarily focused on skills developed through lectures.

While listening instruction was moving forward, the materials used to teach listening were often outdated and atheoretical. Most of the widely used basic communication textbooks had a separate chapter devoted to listening, but the chapter focused more on tips and techniques – recipes for how to listen (Janusik and Wolvin, 2002). Most authors described listening as a process, but the process model varied by text and rarely was grounded in research. As in the 1980s, the formulaic approach to listening instruction was similar to Nichols' original approach: the chapter explained listening as a process, identified the most common listening barriers, and then provided strategies to improve listening. Few texts cited current listening scholarship, and many texts provided information that was not based on listening scholarship at all.

When listening was taught as a stand-alone course, the average class size was 26.19 (Wacker and Hawkins, 1995), and it was taught either at the 100–200 level (Wolvin, Coakley, and Disburg, 1991, 1992) and later in the decade at the 300–400 level (Wacker and Hawkins). The course was typically a 3-credit course in a lecture/discussion format. The listening course was rarely required for communication majors, and it was offered most often as an elective. The topics frequently covered included the different types of listening, a commitment to listening, setting goals to listen, and practicing listening skills. Also important were the concepts of listening as an integral part of the communication process, and visual listening through non-verbal cues.

Brownell introduced her listening text for the university classroom in 1996, and updated versions were released in 2002 and 2006. The text built on the HURIER model, the behavioral approach to teaching listening (Brownell, 1985). Wolvin and Coakley (1996a) released their fifth edition of their listening text complete with instructors' manual (1996b), and Wolff and Marsnik (1992) offered an update of the Wolff, Marsnik, Tracey, and Nichols' (1983) text. All three texts assumed an independent listening course.

Listening tests

The 1984 Watson-Barker Listening Test was revised, and the authors addressed validity concerns and produced a statistically significant instrument (Watson and Barker, 2000) yet no research was provided to support or deny the claim. An additional test, the Steinbrecher-Willmington Listening Test, was introduced in 1993 and revised in 1997 to correct validity concerns (Steinbrecher and Willmington, 1997).

Research studies in listening instruction

Almost all of the empirical studies published about listening were perceptual studies that asked one to rate oneself or others on effective listening. University students perceived themselves to be better listeners and better students, particularly after listening instruction (Imhof, 1998; Wolvin and Coakley, 1992; Wolvin, Coakley, and Halone, 1995). Even though university students perceived themselves to be better listeners than all other age groups, they also had a stronger desire to improve their listening effectiveness (Wolvin, Coakley and Halone, 1995). In terms of students listening to lectures, students admitted that they generally did not prepare for a lecture or self-monitor while in the lecture, and this resulted in them having difficulty concentrating during the lecture (Imhof, 1998). Most students admitted being unaware of listening as a process, but they expressed a greater desire to become better listeners (Wolvin Coakley and Halone, 1995). However, after listening instruction, students rated themselves as less competent than prior to instruction (Ford, Wolvin, and Chung, 2000). The decline in self perception is attributed to students recognizing how complex it is to be an effective listener, so their post-instruction perceptions were probably a more realistic indicator of their competency level.

The only empirical study on listening instruction that was not perception based addressed the effects of listening instruction. Students who received listening training for approximately 2.5 hours scored higher in 4 out of the 5 areas of the Watson-Barker Test than students who had no training. However, only one of those areas, *understanding and remembering* lectures, was statistically significant (Schramm and Wayne, 1993).

Theoretical approaches to teaching listening were offered (Bentley, 1997; Brownell, 1992; Coakley and Wolvin, 1997; Wolvin and Coakley, 1999); however, none of the approaches provided testable theories.

Therefore, compared to the 1980s, listening pedagogy publications and studies decreased. Listening instruction was delivered primarily through a section in the basic communication course as opposed to a stand-alone course. Studies mainly focused on perceptions of self and others as a listener.

Overview of listening education through 2001

The notion that listening could be taught has been popular for decades; however, there exists a lack of consensus on what should be taught and how it should be taught. An underlying assumption of the literature suggests that automatic transfer always has been in full force. That is, if students know how the listening process works, and if they know the verbal and nonverbal behaviors perceived to be an effective listener, then students automatically will become good listeners. However, anyone who has ever taught knows that knowledge alone does not change behavior; behavioral change, and subsequent competence, requires the correct attitudes, too (Wolvin and Coakley, 1994). Still, the importance of attitudes in listening instruction has not been underpinned with research. Additionally, even the tests to measure what a good listener is have come under fire as measuring constructs such as intelligence (Fitch-Hauser and Hughes, 1988) or memory (Bostrom, 1990b), but not listening.

Listening education 2001–2007

Little research on listening in the classroom has been conducted since 2001. What we do know about listening pedagogy consists of the placement of listening instruction in communication across the curriculum – the Integrative Listening Model – and a brief update of listening course pedagogy at the university level, which was compiled from three unpublished conference papers.

Oral Communication across the Curriculum (OCXC) programs began approximately 25 years ago (Cronin, Grice, and Palmerton, 2000) as a way to assist students with being communicatively competent upon graduation so that they could perform their jobs more effectively (Helsel and Hogg, 2006). An overriding belief was that students should be practicing and improving their communication competence in every course they took, not just on their communication course. Because university course instructors in non-communication courses did not feel qualified to teach oral communication, communication centers were developed, mostly through grants. In a study of speaking center directors, the results indicated that, "Listening instruction was clearly lacking in speaking centers, as it was not mentioned in any of the data from the nationwide survey" (Helsel and Hogg, 2006, p. 47). Further, directors indicated that listening instruction would be provided if it was requested; however, requests were rare to nonexistent. This suggests that many faculty members and students are not aware that listening effectiveness can be improved through instruction and training (McCracken, 2006). After all, a faculty member can see or hear when a student has difficulty relaying his thoughts or being anxious to speak, but an instructor cannot use those same powers to assess whether a student is having difficulty listening.

Even more specific than communication across the curriculum is listening across the curriculum. Alverno College has developed the Integrative Listening Model (ILM) (Thompson, Leintz, Nevers, and Witkowski, 2004). The ILM incorporates the three basic components of the ILA definition of listening, which are: (1) receiving; 2) constructing meaning from; and 3) responding to verbal and nonverbal messages. The ILM is a framework to teach and assess these components of listening in all classes across the college. The impetus for this model was that faculty already assumed that listening effectively was a prerequisite for their discipline, but many of their assumptions about students' abilities were questionable. For example, faculty members assumed that students entered college with basic listening skills, were open minded when listening to opposing ideas, and had the ability to remain focused during the entire class period. Upon entering the college, students are taught the ILM initial systematic framework and are not only expected to use the steps in class, but they also are assessed as to how effectively they use the steps. The four step model includes: (1) preparing for the listening event; (2) applying the listening process model; (3) assessing listening effectiveness; and (4) establishing future listening goals. The model has been used successfully at Alverno College, and is now available for public use (Thompson, Leintz, Nevers, and Witkowski, 2007).

To understand the current situation in classroom instruction better, a convenience sample of 36 universities was surveyed to learn more about their listening courses (Janusik, 2005b). While a majority of schools did not require listening instruction for all students, 14 schools did require a listening course for some majors, particularly communication and professional development majors. One school, Marylhurst, reported that a listening course was part of the core curriculum and therefore required for every student. The trend appeared to be listening classes that were driven by a strong individual who believed in the importance of listening as opposed to a move strongly supported by the administration. Thus, it was a bottom up approach rather than a top down approach. Class sizes ranged from 10 to 45 students, with an average of 24 students. Results were bi-modal, and most classes were either capped at 20 or 30 students. These classes primarily used the texts by Brownell (2006) or Wolvin and Coakley (1996a).

In a concurrent study, Fitch-Hauser (2005) focused on the textbook used for the listening course and the relationship of the concepts of the textbook to the listening standards identified by the National Communication Association in 2004. A convenience sample of 20 was generated; however, only 9 of them had a stand alone listening course, so only those responses were used. Results indicated that assigned textbooks included Barker and Watson (2000), Brownell (2006), Nichols (1995), Purdy and Borisoff (1997), and Wolvin and Coakley (1996a). When matched with the NCA competencies, Wolvin and Coakley's text covered more than the other texts. This is not surprising, as Wolvin and Coakley began their work on listening competency earlier (1994). Competencies included recognizing main ideas and supporting details, recognizing relationships, recalling main ideas and details, as well as critical competencies, such as attending with an open mind, detecting bias, and identifying incongruencies between verbal and nonverbal behaviors.

In a final study of listening syllabi (Worthington, 2005), the sample was the same as the review of the listening text study (Fitch-Hauser, 2005). Consistent with Janusik (2005b), the course was generally an elective course with an average class size of 30 students. Worthington also found that the course was primarily taught at the junior or senior level, similar to the latter trend that began a decade earlier (Wacker and Hawkins, 1995). Four objectives were consistent in a majority of the sample, including understanding the listening process and models, improving personal skills, recognizing and managing different listening situations, and assessing one's own listening behaviors. Though assignments were varied, the majority of classes did require an individual or group research project. The trend that listening instruction has moved to an upper level course in the last decade is disturbing, as students are not gaining the instruction that will help them during their college careers. In addition, the trend conflicts with instructor's assumptions that students enter college with a high degree of listening effectiveness.

Thus, there have been minor changes since the comprehensive overview of teaching listening at the university level (Janusik, 2002a). A review of the literature suggests that what is noticeably missing is decisive instruction on *how* to teach listening so that students could not only comprehend, but also apply effective listening skills. What research has not provided yet is an instructional method that will ensure that both the cognitive and behavioral components of listening are comprehended, practiced, and assessed effectively. However, this is a challenge of all skills-based courses, and it is not unique to listening instruction.

These are pedagogical challenges, and it could be that the pedagogical challenges will not be solved until the greater challenges of listening research are addressed. One greater pedagogical challenge is identifying the purpose of a college textbook. One side argues that "textbooks must still participate in the production of knowledge in the field" (Alred and Thelen, 1993, p. 471). The other side counters that the textbook's role is to reflect the proven truths of the discipline (Connors, 1986). With either of these stances, implicit is that that what is included in the text, and subsequently taught, is true. However, a comprehensive review of what is being taught in the listening chapters of basic course textbooks indicates that most of the information has not been supported through research (Janusik and Wolvin, 2002). A smaller follow-up study supported this study, and found that even less time is being devoted to listening instruction (Engleberg, 2009). Many instructors, though, believe that information included in textbooks is solid, or it would not have been published. Clearly this is not the case, but most instructors do not take the time to read the research cited in the text.

The most serious pedagogical challenge is that the foundation of the listening models in the two listening course textbooks (Brownell, 2006; Wolvin and Coakley, 1996a) is grounded in psychological research that has not been supported for over 40 years (Janusik, 2004). Thus, as a field, we have approached a crossroads because much of what we have believed to be true about listening is not supported, and without supported knowledge, new knowledge cannot be created. It is time for us to step back from worrying about how to best teach listening and look at the larger picture: What do we have to teach? We need to move in the direction of the mature disciplines that spend their energies researching the constructs of the discipline, not worrying about how to teach the discipline (Wolvin, 2003). Listening research must progress in this direction.

Listening Research Challenges

It could be argued that listening is not included in the communication curriculum because it has not earned its rightful place in the curriculum. Listening lacks legitimacy due to its limited current scholarly classroom materials, a lack of agreement as to the construct of listening, and inadequate research to keep the field current. Until listening scholars solve these challenges, then there is little to teach.

Limited current scholarly materials to teach listening

As was indicated in the comprehensive overview of listening pedagogy (Janusik, 2002a), there are many materials with which to teach listening. However, the challenge is that there are not many scholarly materials from which to teach listening. The textbooks still in print all provide a good overview of the field in its infancy (Brownell, 2002; Wolff and Marsnik, 1992; Wolvin and Coakley, 1996a). Industrious instructors also can pull material from other academic and nonacademic books (Barker and Watson, 2000; Bostrom, 1990a; Purdy and Borisoff, 1997; Wolvin and Coakley, 1993) and the *International Journal of Listening*. This is not to suggest that any of these sources are not appropriate to teach listening, as they are very useful for reflecting where the field has been and where it currently is. However, these sources still are not complete, as they reflect two integral problems in the field. First, there is a lack of agreement as to the construct of listening, and current research does not reflect scholarship from the most recent advances in attention and memory research; the foundation of most listening research.

The construct of listening

A major challenge to listening research, and subsequently, listening pedagogy, is that there is not a generally accepted agreement of what listening is. The construct of listening and listening models have not changed considerably since the inception of listening research in the 1970s. Definitions and models have been iterations of previous definitions and models, and the models that do withstand scientific research still have challenges due to their methods of validation.

Listening definitions

A generally accepted listening definition does not exist among communication scholars; however, there are consistent elements that many agree should be included in a definition of listening. A content analysis of 50 definitions of listening found that the five most used elements were perception, attention, interpretation, remembering, and response (Glenn, 1989). Those five components have been a part of listening definitions for more than 60 years. Consider some of the following definitions:

> an attachment of meaning to oral symbols (Nichols, 1948)

> the complete process by which oral language communicated by some source is received, critically and purposefully attended to, recognized, and interpreted (or comprehended) in terms of past experiences and future expectancies (Petrie, 1964).

The selective process of attending to, hearing, understanding, and remembering aural symbols (Barker, 1971, p. 17).

When a human organism receives verbal information aurally and selects and structures the information to remember it (Weaver, 1972).

The process of receiving, constructing meaning from, and responding to spoken and/or nonverbal messages (An ILA Definition of Listening, 1995, p. 4).

The process of receiving, attending to, and assigning meaning to aural and visual stimuli (Wolvin and Coakley, 1996a, p. 69).

Listening is hearing, understanding, remembering, interpreting, evaluating, and responding (Brownell, 2002).

The listening act really consists of four connected activities – sensing, interpreting, evaluating and responding (Steil et al., 1983a, p. 21).

The dynamic, interactive process of integrating appropriate listening attitudes, knowledge, and behaviors to achieve the selected goal(s) of a listening event" (Thompson, Leintz, Nevers, and Witkowski, 2004, pp. 229–230).

The similarity in definitions is both of concern and not of concern. Communication scholars do not agree on a definition of communication (Dance, 1970), and it is unfair to hold listening scholars to a higher standard. Moreover, it is unlikely that a single definition will be sufficient, as there are differences in conversational listening and linear listening that need to be investigated. For example, when placed within the context of a conversation, a listener always provides a response (Janusik, 2004, 2007a). If meaning is made in the receiver, no response is interpreted as some type of response, so it is preferable to provide a conscious and intentional response. Conversely, in linear listening situations, such as listening to the television, no response is necessary. Thus, it is likely that the cognitive processing involved in listening in a face-to-face interaction is different than the cognitive processing involved in listening in a passive linear context, such as watching television. However, this is information that is not yet known through listening research, but is available to be known because of the sophisticated instrumentation that is available today as well as the rich research in the cognitive psychology field.

Listening Models

Precisely because there is no standard definition of listening, no standard model to depict the listening process currently exists, though a model introduced by Bodie, Worthington, Imhof, and Cooper (2008) shows promise. Listening has both cognitive *and* behavioral components (Witkin, 1990), and both must be viewed *within* the context of communication to establish a line of research that is distinct from cognitive processing, because it is the overt response that differentiates listening from cognitive processing (Janusik, 2004, 2005a, 2007a). Listening models that include the cognitive and behavioral models do exist, but they are not adequate for research or teaching for two reasons. First, as with the listening definition, there is not an agreed model. Second, and more importantly, with one exception, the models have not been supported through research.

Cognitive listening models

Current listening models can be described as cognitive or behavioral (Janusik, 2004, 2005a). Many cognitive listening models exist (Bostrom, 1990a; Goss, 1982; Lundsteen, 1979; Taylor, 1964; Wolff, Marsnik, Tracey, and Nichols, 1983)[1] and they are similar in that they address what goes on inside the listener at the time of listening. Most of the models share similar components, and almost all are consistent with the five most used elements in listening definitions: perception; attention; interpretation; remembering; and response (Glenn, 1989). This is not coincidental, Glenn (1989) performed a content analysis of 50 listening definitions, and many researchers who had created their own listening definition created their own listening process model that was based on their definition.

Despite its origin or author, all cognitive listening models share two serious drawbacks. First, only one of the models (Bostrom, 1990a) has been empirically validated. Without testing, models carry little respect in the scientific community. Second, none of the models has successfully distinguished listening from cognitive processing. Disciplinary boundaries often are permeable, but they must be staked to include

---

[1]   For a more thorough review of individual models, see Wolvin (1989), for a criticism of the models, see Janusik (2004).

items that are solely studied in the discipline. What makes the study of listening within the context of face-to-face communication unique is the overt response from the listener. In fact, it is only in the overt response in which listening competency can be assessed (Rhodes, Watson, and Barker, 1990; Ridge, 1984; Wolvin and Coakley, 1994). Thus, if these models did measure anything, they would measure cognitive processing, not listening.

Behavioral listening models

Behavioral listening models can be viewed as cognitive models with the additional component of response. Behavioral models include Barker, 1971; Brownell, 1985, 2002; Maidment, 1984; Steil, et al., 1983a; and Wolvin, 2002.[2] Most of the models are heavily weighted towards the cognitive components. Behavioral models have a major drawback similar to the cognitive models in that only one of the models (Brownell, 1985, 1996, 2002) has undergone testing. However, three validated models – the cognitive (Bostrom, 1990a), the behavioral (Brownell, 1985, 1996, 2002) and the relational (Halone and Pecchioni, 1999; Pecchioni and Halone, 2000) – deserve a closer inspection.

Validated listening models

The first validated listening model, a cognitive model, was created by Bostrom and colleagues, who based their listening model on linear memory models (Bostrom, 1990a; Bostrom and Bryant, 1980; Bostrom and Waldhart, 1980). Their five step model (signal acquisition, selection, literal processing, retention, comprehension) was built upon four different theorists (Barker, Goss, Nichols, and Weaver), and Bostrom and colleagues were the first to fully explicate the psychological foundations in their model. The primary criticism of this model is that it represents cognitive processing as opposed to listening, as it does not involve the component of response.

The second validated model was Brownell's (1985) HURIER (Hearing, Understanding, Remembering, Interpreting, Evaluating, and Responding) behavioral model of listening. Brownell validated

---

[2] See Wolvin (1989) for an explanation of the models and Janusik (2004) for a criticism of them.

this model with an exploratory factor analysis and then a confirmatory factor analysis with over 1,000 subjects. The HURIER model is one of the most solid listening models for communication scholars today; however, it does have some weaknesses. First, the HURIER model is presented largely as a behavioral model, even though four of the six elements (Understanding, Interpreting, Evaluation, and Remembering) of the model are cognitive. Second, it is not surprising that the names of the elements mirror the ideas in the 60 years of listening definitions, as the elements comprised for the factor analysis came from the literature. Brownell's research consisted of both an exploratory and confirmatory factor analysis (Brownell, pers. com. November 2002), and the method involved individuals responding to how they *perceived* the listening process to work. Thus, using the base from the literature and a factor analysis, it is probable that Brownell would produce a validated model. Finally, Brownell (2002, Ch. 2) does explicate the communication framework and relational perspective upon which her model is based, yet it is the attention and memory terms that dominate her model; however, research to support these portions is limited or outdated.

The final model that was shown to be valid was developed by Pecchioni and Halone (2000). It differs from the previous models in that it is a model for relational listening developed through grounded theory. Their model details the macro and micro level cognitive, behavioral, and affective processes of relational listening. Like Brownell's model, this is a sound theoretical model developed through a qualitative method. However, the means exist to validate models such as these through more sophisticated methods, and until that is done, these should be considered perceptual models of the listening process. What all of the models lack is theoretically grounded and empirically supported attention and memory research.

Attention and memory research

The final criticism of listening research in general, and the definitions and models of listening in particular, is that no listening research exists that is grounded in current attention and memory research. All definitions and models, if grounded, are grounded in outdated linear attention and memory research.

The foundation of listening research rests in attention and memory research. Communication assesses patterns of behavior, and because listening is primarily a cognitive process that is perceived behaviorally, listening researchers have had to cross disciplines to establish a foundation for the cognitive aspects of listening. Cognitive listening definitions and models that do explicate their psychological foundations cite Broadbent (1971), Kahneman (1973) and Treisman (1960) (Janusik, 2002c). Those that do not explicate psychological foundations generally cite former listening models and theorists who cite the aforementioned psychological researchers (Janusik, 2002b, 2004).

Broadbent (1971), Kahneman (1973) and Treisman (1960, 1964) grounded their work in linear attention and memory models consistent with Sensory Register – Short Term Memory – Long Term Memory. This theoretical model was popular in cognitive psychology until the mid to late 1960s when more sophisticated measurement techniques did not find support for the model (Janusik, 2002c). The field experienced a state of flux until the notion of a dynamic model of attention and memory was introduced (Baddeley and Hitch, 1974). This model was called Working Memory (WM), and WM has been the dominant paradigm of attention and memory research since the early 1980s (Miyake and Shah, 1999). Its acceptance is largely based on its elegance and ability to withstand rigorous testing, something that the linear models never did. WM has dominated cognitive psychology research for over 35 years, and revisions to the model through rigorous testing have been minimal (Baddeley, 1986, 1992, 2000, 2001, 2003).

In a social scientific sense, the strength of our field rests in our ability to produce sound research, and in the sense of constructs, this means validating models and converging definitions. However, none of the three validated listening models are grounded in WM theory. The two that do cite psychological research (Bostrom, 1990a, 1990b; Brownell, 2002) cite the linear theorists. Thus, the foundations of their models are based on outdated attention and memory research, and conclusions drawn from them are circumspect.

Because communication theories must be consistent with known neurobiological processes (Beatty and McCroskey, 2001), the field of listening can be faulted with not staying abreast of and integrating current attention and memory research. Advancements in listening research are predicated on advancements in psychological research, and we will not progress as a field of study until our research reflects the foundational changes.

Therefore, it is clear that the study of listening lacks legitimacy in research, which makes it challenging to develop innovative and effective ways to teach listening. The importance of listening is apparent at an intuitive level, but to justify its inclusion in the curriculum, we need solid empirical evidence that listening is critical to academic and professional success. Until now, there has not been a consolidation of solid empirical research to support listening. The introduction of the Listening Quad (Janusik, 2007b) offers instructors the ability to customize their teaching of listening by offering empirically supported literature.

The Listening Quad

The listening quad is a theoretical and research-based foundation from which to teach listening, and it can be customized for individual sections of any communication course or for an entire listening course (Janusik, 2007b). As the name implies, it approaches listening from four perspectives: affective; cognitive; behavioral; and relational, and it is grounded in the general dimensions that underlie the listening process (Halone, Cunconan, Coakley, and Wolvin, 1998). Although their research identified five general dimensions: cognitive; affective; behavioral/verbal; behavioral/nonverbal; and behavioral/interactive (Halone, Cunconan, Coakley, and Wolvin, 1998), upon reviewing the literature that could support each dimension, the decision was made to collapse the behavioral/verbal and behavioral/nonverbal dimensions into one perspective entitled behavioral (see Figure 9.1).

The explanation of each dimension includes a definition of the dimension and then different ways to approach the teaching of the dimension by providing references and brief explanations of research literature. The listening quad is an approach to teaching listening rather than a prescribed roadway of how to teaching listening. It puts the power back in the instructor's hand, as the instructor is responsible for reviewing the research and incorporating it into the classroom.

For example, in the listening as affective section, affective is defined as how one feels about listening and how one feels when listening. The importance of feeling and motivation to listening competence are outlined. In addition, various instruments, such as the Willingness to Listen Scale (Roberts and Vinson, 1998), Receiver Apprehension Test (Wheeless, 1975), Listening Preference Profile (Barker and Watson, 2000), and Self-Monitoring Scale (Brownell, 2002; Snyder, 1974) are offered as ideas to

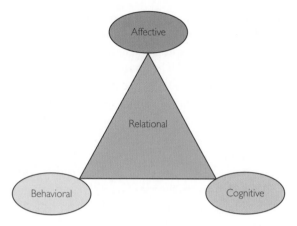

Figure 9.1 The listening quad

help students better understand their motivation to listen, their schema for listening, and their fears about listening.

The second dimension, listening as cognitive, includes how one thinks about listening and how one thinks while listening. This section can include much of the scientific brain research in which students are very interested. This section begins with an introduction to the cognitive listening models (Bostrom, 1990a, Wolff, Marsnik, Tracey, and Nichols 1983) and an explanation of the outdated attention and memory research that most listening models are built upon, which is Broadbent's (1971) model of sensory register/short-term memory/long-term memory. Then the concept of working memory theory is introduced (Baddeley, 2000, 2001, 2003; Baddeley and Hitch, 1974). Of particular interest is that in linear listening tasks, Miller's $+/- 7$ (1956) often holds up. That is, when one is asked to memorize a list of items, one generally can recall from 5 to 9 of them. However, in an interactive task, like a conversation, then the number of items that one can hold active and respond to in the conversation is approximately 2.9 (Janusik, 2004, 2007a). This is important, as the conversational listening process utilizes working memory, not just long-term memory.

This listening-as-cognitive section also includes how various cultures conceptualize listening differently. For example, German university students perceive listening primarily as a relationship building activity, while US American students perceive listening as an integrating and organizing task (Imhof and Janusik, 2006). The question, then, is that if one thinks about listening in a certain way, is it processed in a way that is different from another person who thinks about listening differently?

Also of interest in the listening as cognitive section are the activities and studies that have to do with brain research. For example, the Stroop Test (Experience Dynamics, 2004) is an exercise to demonstrate how the left and right brain hemispheres do not always work in synchronization. The test is a series of words that can be projected electronically. Each word is the name of a color, but the name of the color and the actual color do not match. For example, the word blue might be written in red ink. The goal is to say the color of the word, as opposed to the word. When done in unison, the class quickly understands how their brain gets stuck, which helps students understand how listening is an automatic process and a conscious process.

Additional studies to use in the listening as cognitive section include how men and women listen differently in terms of which side of the brain hemisphere is activated in a listening task (Frost, Binder, Springer, et al., 1999; Phillip, Lowe, Lurito, Dzemidzic, and Matthews, 2001; Sousa, 2001), as well as the structural differences in the brains of men and women (Gur, Turetsky, Matsui, et al., 1999; Rabinowicz, Dean, Petetot, and de Courten-Myers, 1999). Though the gender research in terms of listening is rather scarce and inconsistent, students' experiences provide rich examples for classroom discussion.

Next, the listening as behavioral section focuses on the nonverbal and verbal behaviors that indicate that one is or is not listening. Listening is primarily a cognitive activity that is perceived behaviorally (Witkin, 1990), and cognitions and behaviors are not always in synchronization. Thus, it is critical for students to understand that others perceive them as listeners by how they act.

This section begins with an introduction of the behavioral listening models (Brownell, 2006; Steil, et al., 1983a), and then addresses what is known about listening and nonverbal behaviors based on limited studies (Alexander, Penley, Jernigan, 1992; O'Heren and Arnold, 1991; Ostermeier, 1993; Thomas and Levine, 1994; Timm and Schroeder, 2000). Though limited, the studies do suggest that there is a relationship between nonverbal behaviors and listening comprehension.

In this section, students also can identify their ability to decode others' nonverbal behavior by using the Profile of Nonverbal Sensitivity (PONS) Test (Rosenthal, Hall, DiMatteo, Rogers, and Archer, 1979).The session ends with an explanation of the effective verbal and nonverbal listening behaviors and how they are contextual, which transitions to the final dimension, listening as relational, as all relationships take place within a context.

This section incorporates the other parts of the listening quad into the human communication process. The section addresses the idea that the sum is greater than its parts in that one's thoughts, feelings, and behaviors can combine in both positive and negative ways in human interaction. There is one relational listening model (Pecchioni and Halone, 2000), established through grounded theory, which is a model of assumptions of what is important in the listening act with differing partners.

The model investigates the macro level of listening, or the time of the interaction (before, during, after) as well as the micro level, or what happens during each of those parts and how it can be characterized as cognitive, behavioral, verbal, nonverbal, or interactive. The model and study confirms that we listen differently with different people.

Another area to address in listening as relational is the rather new area of communication research that addresses comforting messages and providing support (Bodie and Burleson, 2008; Burleson and Feng, 2005; Burleson, Holmstrom, Bodie, and Rack, 2007; Burleson, Holmstrom, Bodie, et al., 2005) as well as listening and empathy (Bommelje, Houston, and Smither, 2003; Brownell, 1992; Purdy, 1991; Walker, 1997). And, although Gibb's (1961) supportive and defensive climates is well dated, it has withstood the test of time in helping students understand how to create a positive listening context.

Also of interest in the listening as relational sections are the studies that have been performed in specific contexts. For example, how listening changes across the lifespan (Coakley, Halone, and Wolvin, 1996; Halone, Wolvin, and Coakley, 1997), listening in the classroom (Ford, Wolvin and Chung, 2000; Imhof, 1998, 2001, 2002) listening in the workplace (Brownell, 1985, 1994; Cooper and Husband, 1993; Gilchrist and Van Hoeven, 1994; Lobdell, Sonoda, and Arnold, 1993; Stine, Thompson, and Cusella, 1995), and listening in marriage (Doohan, 2007).

Thus, any of the dimensions of the listening quad can be used to supplement a class, or to customize an entire listening section or listening course.

The listening quad approaches the listening curriculum as a cultural construction (Grundy, 1987). In this approach, meaning is not provided to the students by the instructor, rather it is built through interaction (Eisner, 1982). This notion is consistent with the Social Construction of

Reality (Berger and Luckmann, 1966). The instructor acts as midwife who assists with the birth of knowledge, but the midwife is clear that the "baby" belongs to the learner (Belenky, Clinchy, Goldberger, and Tarule, 1997). In the applied sense, the instructor is responsible for utilizing the research-based materials in class in a way that students can create meaning about the multifaceted nature of listening.

Thus, the listening quad temporarily solves the challenge of outdated listening research. However, it does not diminish the need for researchers to continue to investigate the construct of listening to learn more about this construct that we so firmly believe is important to teach.

Conclusion

Therefore, the development of listening pedagogy is at a standstill. While it is important to teach listening, it is the instructor's responsibility to make certain that content being taught is supported through research. Little of what passes as listening information in communication textbooks is supported. It is hopeful that we will develop new definitions, models, and theories, grounded in current conceptualizations, and rigorously tested, so that we will have something new and solid to teach our students. Until then, the listening quad offers a customizable approach to teach listening that is theoretically grounded and empirically supported.

QUESTIONS FOR DISCUSSION

1   Why is it easier to teach or learn speaking than listening?
2   Is it more important to teach listening cognitions or listening behaviors? Justify your answer.
3   Some say that it is impossible to teach listening because it is a covert activity. What other covert activities have been successfully taught at the university level? How could listening instructors apply what is known from the other covert activities that are taught?
4   Compare and contrast what is known about teaching listening within the periods presented. Has the field progressed in a logical method? Explain.
5   Janusik makes a strong claim that "Listening is not included in the communication curriculum because it has not earned its rightful place in the curriculum." Do you agree or disagree with her? Explain.
6   Does a compilation of materials make something worth teaching? If there is no compilation, does that mean that the topic is not worth teaching? Explain.

7 Select the definition of listening (pp. 204–5) that you most endorse. On what criteria did you select it?

8 Are multiple definitions and models for the same construct a benefit or a drawback to a field?

9 Is the *listening quad* a theoretically sound way to teach listening? If you were going to use it for your class, identify and explain which part(s) of the listening quad would be most appropriate to use.

10 Is it the teacher's job to make sure the content included in a textbook is accepted fact? If the content in the textbook is not factual, how does it end up in a textbook? How do textbook readers know what to believe?

References

AICPA (2005). *Highlighted responses from the Association for Accounting marketing survey. Creating the future agenda for the profession – managing partner perspective.* Retrieved on April 8, 2005, from: http://www.aicpa.org/pubs/tpcpa/feb2001/hilight.htm

Alexander III, E.R., Penley, L.E.U., and Jernigan, I.E. (1992). The relationship of basic decoding skills to managerial effectiveness. *Management Communication Quarterly*, 6, 1, 58–73.

Alred, G.J., and Thelen, E.A. (1993). Are textbooks contributions to scholarship? *College Composition and Communication*, 44, 4, 466–77.

An ILA definition of listening. (1995, April). *Listening Post*, 53, 4.

Baddeley, A.D. (1986). *Working memory.* New York: Oxford University Press.

Baddeley, A.D. (1992). Working memory. *Science*, 255, 556–9.

Baddeley, A.D. (2000). The episodic buffer: A new component of working memory? *Trends in Cognitive Sciences*, 4, 11, 417–23.

Baddeley, A.D. (2001). Is working memory still working? *American Psychologist*, 56, 11, 851–7.

Baddeley, A.D. (2003). Working memory and language: An overview. *Journal of Communication Disorders*, 36, 3, 189–208.

Baddeley, A.D., and Hitch, G.J. (1974). Working memory. In G Bower (Ed.). *The psychology of learning and motivation*, Vol. 8, pp. 47–90. New York: Academic Press.

Barker, L.L. (1971). *Listening behavior.* Englewood Cliffs, NJ: Prentice-Hall.

Barker, L., and Watson, K. (2000). *Listen up.* New York: St. Martin's Press.

Barker, L, Edwards, R., Gaines, C., Gladney, K., and Holley, F. (1980). An investigation of proportional time spent in various communication activities by college students. *Journal of Applied Communication Research*, 8, 101–9.

Beatty, M.J., and McCroskey, J.C., (with Valenci, K.M.). (2001). *The biology of communication: A communibiological perspective.* Cresskill, NJ: Hampton Press, Inc.

Belenky, M.F., Clinchy, M.B., Goldberger, N.R., and Tarule, J.M. (1986). *Women's ways of knowing*. New York: HarperCollins

Bentley, S.C. (1997). Benchmarking listening behaviors: Is effective listening what the speaker says it is? *International Journal of Listening*, 11, 51–68.

Berger, P.L., and Luckmann, T. (1966). *The social construction of reality: A treatise in the sociology of knowledge*. Garden City, NY: Anchor Books.

Bodie, G.D., and Burleson, B.R. (2008). Explaining variations in the effects of supportive messages: A dual-process framework. In C. Beck (Ed.), *Communication yearbook 32*, pp. 354–98. New York: Routledge.

Bodie, G.D., Worthington, D.L., Imhof, M., and Cooper, L. (2008). What would a unified field of listening look like? A proposal linking past perspectives and future endeavors. *International Journal of Listening*, 22, 2, 103–22.

Bommelje, R., Houston, J.M., and Smither, R. (2003). Personality characteristics of effective listeners: A five factor perspective. *International Journal of Listening*, 27, 32–46.

Bostrom, R.N. (Ed.). (1990a). *Listening behavior: Measurement and application*. New York: Guilford.

Bostrom, R.N. (1990b). Listening, communicative skill, and attitudes about communication. In R.N. Bostrom (Ed.). *Listening behavior: Measurement and application*, pp. 42–56. New York: Guilford.

Bostrom, R.N. and Bryant, C.L. (1980). Factors in the retention of information presented orally: The role of short-term listening. *Western Journal of Speech Communication*, 44, 137–45.

Bostrom, R.N., and Waldhart, E. (1980). *The Kentucky Comprehensive Listening Test*. Lexington, KY: Kentucky Listening Research Center.

Boyer, E.L. (1987). *College: The undergraduate experience to America*. New York: Harper and Row.

Broadbent, D.E. (1971). *Decision and stress*. London: Academic Press.

Brown, J.I. (1987). Listening – ubiquitous – yet obscure. *Journal of the International Listening Association*, 1, 3–14.

Brown, J.I., and Carlsen, G.R. (1955). *Brown-Carlsen Listening Comprehension Test*. New York: Harcourt, Brace and World, Inc.

Brownell, J. (1985). A model for listening instruction: Management applications. *ABC Bulletin*, 48, 3, 39–44.

Brownell, J. (1992). Preparing students for multicultural environments: Listening as a key management competency. *Journal of Management Education*, 16, 81–93.

Brownell, J. (1994). Managerial listening and career development in the hospitality industry. *Journal of the International Listening Association*, 8, 31–49.

Brownell, J. (1996). *Listening: Attitudes, principles, and skills*. Boston, MA: Allyn and Bacon.

Brownell, J. (2002). *Listening: Attitudes, principles, and skills*, 2nd edn. Boston, MA: Allyn and Bacon.

Brownell, J. (2006). *Listening: Attitudes, principles, and skills*, 3rd edn. Boston, MA: Allyn and Bacon.

Burleson, B., and Feng, B. (2005, May). *A critical review of research on cultural similarities and differences in emotional support: Implications and future directions*. Paper presented at the annual conference of the International Communication Association, in New York.

Burleson, B.R., Holmstrom, A.H., Bodie, G.D., and Rack, J.J. (2007, March). *What counts as effective emotional support? Three studies exploring individual and situational differences.* Paper presented to the Interpersonal Communication Division of the Central States Communication Association, Minneapolis, MN.

Burleson, B., Samter, W., Jones, S.M., Kunkel, A., Holmstrom, A.J., Mortenson, S.T., and MacGeorge, E.L. (2005). Which comforting messages really work best? A different perspective on Lemieux and Tighe's "receiver perspective". *Communication Research Reports*, 22, 2, 87–100.

Burley-Allen, M. (1982). *Listening: The forgotten skill*. New York: John Wiley and Sons, Inc.

Coakley, C.G., and Wolvin, A.D. (1990). Listening pedagogy and andragogy: The state of the art. *Journal of the International Listening Association*, 4, 33–61.

Coakley, C., and Wolvin, A. (1997). Listening in the educational environment. In M. Purdy and D. Borisoff (Eds.). *Listening in everyday life: A personal and professional approach*, 2nd edn, pp. 179–212, Lanham, MD: University Press of America.

Coakley, C.G., Halone, K.K., and Wolvin, A.D. (1996). Perceptions of listening ability across the life-span: Implications for understanding listening competence. *International Journal of Listening*, 10, 21–48.

Conaway, M.S. (1982). Listening: Learning tool and retention agent. In A.S. Algier and K.W. Algier (Eds.). *Improving reading and study skills*, pp. 51–63. San Francisco, CA: Jossey-Bass.

Connors, R.J. (1986). Textbooks and the evolution of the discipline. *College Composition and Communication*, 37, 2, 178–94.

Cooper, L., and Husband, R. (1993). Developing a model of organizational listening competency. *Journal of the International Listening Association*, 7, 6–34.

Cooper, M. (1988). NIU listening exam: Assessing college level listening skills. *Journal of the International Listening Association*, 2, 53–74.

Cronin, M., Grice, G. and Palmerton, P. (2000). Oral communication across the curriculum: The state of the art after twenty-five years of experience. *Journal of the Association for Communication Administration*, 29, 66–87.

Dance, F. (1970). The "concept" of communication. *Journal of Communication*, 20, 201–10.

Davis, D.F. (2001). Two ears and one mouth: Two eyes and one hand. *The Listening Post*, 77, 10–13.

Doohan, E. (2007). Listening behaviors of married couples: An exploration of nonverbal presentation to a relational outsider. *International Journal of Listening*, 21, 1, 24–41.

Drake, F.E. (1951, May). How do you teach listening? *Southern Speech Journal*, 16, 268–71.

Duker, S. (1968). *Listening bibliography*, 2nd edn. Metuchen, NJ: Scarecrow Press.

Educational Testing Service. (1955). *Sequential tests of educational progress: Listening*. Princeton, NJ: ETS.

Educational Testing Service (1979). *STEP III Manual and Technical Report*. Menlo Park, CA: Addison-Wesley Publishing Co.

Eisner, E.W. (1982). *Cognition and curriculum: A basis for deciding what to teach*. New York: Longman.

Engleberg, I.N. (2009). Changing the way we teach listening. Paper presented at the National Communication Association conference on November, 13 2009, Chicago, IL.

Experience Dynamics. (2004). Cognitive science: Understanding the science behind the findings. Retrieved on May 27, 2005, from: http://www.experiencedynamics.com/science_of_usability/cognitive_science/index.php

Fitch-Hauser, M. (2005, November). *State of listening education: Current textbooks*. Paper presented to the National Communication Association conference, Boston, MA.

Fitch-Hauser, M., and Hughes, M.A. (1987) A factor analytic study of four listening tests. *Journal of the International Listening Association*, 1, 129–47.

Fitch-Hauser, M., and Hughes, M.A. (1988). Defining the cognitive process of listening: A dream or reality? *The Journal of the International Listening Association*, 2, 75–88.

Ford, W.S.Z., and Wolvin, A.D. (1993). The differential impact of a basic communication course on perceived communication competencies in class, work, and social contexts. *Communication Education*, 42, 3, 215–23.

Ford, W.Z, Wolvin, A.D., and Chung, S. (2000). Students' self-perceived listening competencies. *International Journal of Listening*, 14, 1–13.

Frost, J.A., Binder, J.R., Springer, J.A., Hammeke, T.A., Bellgowan, P.S.F., Rao, S.M., and Cox. R.W. (1999, February). Language processing is strongly left lateralized in both sexes. *Brain: A Journal of Neurology*, 122, 2, 199–208.

Gibb, J.R. (1961). Defensive communication. *Journal of Communication*, 11, 3, 141–8.

Gilchrist, J.A., and Van Hoeven, S.A. (1994). Listening as an organizational construct. *Journal of the International Listening Association*, 8, 6–32.

Glenn, E. (1989). A content analysis of fifty definitions of listening. *Journal of the International Listening Association*, 3, 21–31.

Goby, V.P., and Lewis, J.H. (2000, June). The key role of listening in business: A study of the Singapore insurance industry. *Business Communication Quarterly*, 63, 2, 41–51.

Goss, B. (1982). Listening as information processing. *Communication Quarterly*, 30, 4, 304–6.

Grundy, S. (1987). *Curriculum: Product or Praxis.* London: The Falmer Press.

Gur, R., Turetsky, B., Matsui, M., Yan, M., Bilker, W., Hughett, P., and Gur, R.E. (1999, May 15). Sex differences in brain gray and white matter in healthy young adults: Correlations with cognitive performance. *The Journal of Neuroscience*, 19, 4065–72.

Halone, K.K., and Pecchioni, L.L. (1999, November). *Everyday listening expectations in relational communication: A grounded theoretical model.* Paper presented at the National Communication Association Convention, Chicago, IL.

Halone, K.K., Cunconan, T.M., Coakley, C.G., and Wolvin, A.D. (1998). Toward the establishment of general dimension underlying the listing process. *International Journal of Listening*, 12, 12–28.

Halone, K.K., Wolvin, A.D., and Coakley, C.G. (1997). Accounts of effective listening across the life-span: Expectations and experiences associated with competent listening practices. *International Journal of Listening*, 11, 15–38.

Helsel, C.R., and Hogg, M.C. (2006). Assessing communication proficiency in higher education. Speaking labs offer possibilities. *International Journal of Listening*, 20, 29–54.

Hynes, G. E., and Bhatia, V. (1996). Graduate business students' preferences for the managerial communication course curriculum. *Business Communication Quarterly*, 59, 2, 45–55.

Imhof, M. (1998). What makes a good listener? Listening behavior in instructional settings. *International Journal of Listening*, 12, 81–105.

Imhof, M. (2001). How to listen more efficiently: Self-monitoring strategies in listening. *International Journal of Listening*, 15, 2–19.

Imhof, M. (2002). In the eye of the beholder: Children's perceptions of good and poor listening behavior. *International Journal of Listening*, 16, 40–56.

Imhof, M., and Janusik, L.A. (2006). Development and validation of the Imhof-Janusik listening concepts inventory to measure listening conceptualization differences between cultures. *Journal of Intercultural Communication Research*, 35, 2, 79–98.

James, M. (1992). Essential topics and subtopics of business communication: Are we teaching what employers want? *Business Education Forum*, 46, 4, 8–10.

Janusik, L.A. (2002a). Teaching listening: What so we do? What should we do? *International Journal of Listening*, 16, 5–39.

Janusik. L.A. (2002b, November). *Listening and cognitive processing: Is there a difference?* Paper presented at the meeting of the National Communication Association, New Orleans, LA.

Janusik, L.A. (2002c, November 15). *Reconceptualizing listening through working memory*. Colloquium presented at the University of Maryland at College Park.

Janusik, L.A. (2004). Researching listening from the inside out: The relationship between conversational listening span and perceived communicative competence. UMI Proquest: Digital dissertations. Available at : http://www.lib.umi.com/dissertations

Janusik, L.A. (2005a). Conversational listening span: A proposed measure of conversational listening. *International Journal of Listening, 19,* 12–30.

Janusik, L.A. (2005b, November). *Undergraduate listening education: Current trends and future directions*. Paper presented to the National Communication Association conference, Boston, MA.

Janusik, L.A. (June 2007a). Building listening theory: The validation of the conversational listening span. *Communication Studies, 58, 2,* 1–18.

Janusik, L.A. (2007b). Teaching listening: A research based approach. Unpublished manuscript.

Janusik, L.A., and Wolvin, A.D. (2002). Listening treatment in the basic communication course text. In D. Sellnow, (Ed.). *Basic communication course annual,* 14, pp. 164–210. Boston, MA: American Press.

Kahneman, D. (1973). *Attention and effort*. Englewood Cliffs, NJ: Prentice Hall.

Lobdell, C.L., Sonoda, K.T., and Arnold, W.E. (1993). The influence of perceived supervisor listening behavior on employee commitment. *Journal of the International Listening Association, 7,* 92–110.

Lundsteen, S.W. (1979). *Listening: Its impact on reading and the other language arts*. Urbana, IL: National Council of Teachers of English.

Maes, J.D., Weldy, T.G., and Icenogle, M.L. (1997). A managerial perspective: Oral communication competency is most important for business students in the workplace. *The Journal of Business Communication, 34, 1,* 67–80.

Maidment, R. (1984). *Tuning In: A guide to effective listening*. Gretna, LO: Pelican Publishing.

Markgraf, B. (1962, March). Listening pedagogy in teacher-training institutions. *Journal of Communication, 12,* 33–5.

McCracken, S.R. (2006). Listening and new approaches to the creation of communication centers. *International Journal of Listening, 20,* 60–1.

McDevitt, T.M., Sheenan, E.P., and McMenamin, N. (1991). Self-reports of academic listening activities by traditional and non-traditional college students. *College Student Journal, 25,* 478–86.

Miller, G.A. (1956). The magical number seven, plus or minus two: Some limits of our capacity for processing information. *Psychological Review, 63,* 81–97.

Miyake, A.and Shah, P. (Ed.). (1999). *Models of working memory: Mechanisms of active maintenance and executive control*. New York: Cambridge University Press.

Morreale, S.P., Hanna, M.S., Berko, R.M., and Gibson, J.W. (1999). *The basic communication course at U.S. colleges and universities: VI Basic communication course annual 1999*. Boston: American Press.

Nichols, M. (1995). The *lost art of listening*, New York: Guilford Press.

Nichols, R.G. (1948). Factors in listening comprehension. *Speech Monographs*, 15, 154.

Nichols, R.G., and Stevens, L.A. (1957). *Are you listening?* New York: McGraw-Hill.

O'Heren, L., and Arnold, W.E. (1991). Nonverbal attentive behavior and listening comprehension. *International Journal of Listening*, 5, 86–92.

Ostermeier, T. H. (1993). Perception of nonverbal cues in dialogic listening in intercultural interview. *International Journal of Listening, Special Edition*, 64–75.

Pecchioni, L.L., and Halone, K.K. (2000). Relational listening II: Form and variation across social and interpersonal relationships. *International Journal of Listening*, 14, 69–94.

Perkins, T.M. (1994). A survey of listening instruction in the basic speech course. *Journal of the International Listening Association*, 8, 80–97.

Petrie, C. R. (1964). What we don't know about listening. *Journal of Communication*, 14, 248.

Phillips M., Lowe M., Lurito J. T., Dzemidzic M., and Matthews V. (2001). Temporal lobe activation demonstrates sex-based differences during passive listening. *Radiology*, 220, 202–7.

Purdy, M. (1991). Intrapersonal/Interpersonal listening? In D. Borisoff and M. Purdy (Eds.). *Listening in everyday life: A personal and professional approach*, pp. 21–58, Lanham, MD: University Press of America.

Purdy, M., and Borisoff, D. (1997). *Listening in everyday life. A personal and professional approach*, 2nd edn. Lanham, MD: University Press of America.

Rabinowicz, T., Dean, D., Petetot, J., and de Courten-Myers, G. (1999, February). Gender differences in the human cerebral cortex: More neurons in males; more processes in females. *Journal of Child Neurology*, 14, 98–107.

Rankin, P.T. (1930). Listening ability: Its importance, measurement, and development. *Chicago School Journal*, 12, 177–9.

Rhodes, S.C. (1985). What the communication journals tell us about teaching listening. *Central States Speech Journal*, 36, 24–32.

Rhodes, S.C., Watson, K.W., and Barker, L.L. (1990). Listening assessment trends and influencing factors in the 1980s. *Journal of the International Listening Association*, 4, 62–82.

Ridge, A. (1984, July). *Assessing listening skills*. Paper presented at the International Listening Convention, July 12–13, St. Paul, MN.

Roberts, C.V. (1988). The validation of listening tests: Cutting the Gordian knot. *International Journal of Listening*, 2, 1–19.

Roberts, C.V., and Vinson, L. (1998). Relationship among willingness to listen, receiver apprehension, communication apprehension, communication competence, and dogmatism. *International Journal of Listening*, 12, 40–56.

Rosenthal, R., Hall, J.A., DiMatteo, M.R., Rogers, P.L., and Archer, D. (1979). *Sensitivity to nonverbal communication: The PONS Test*. Baltimore, MD: Johns Hopkins University Press.

Schramm, R.M., and Wayne, F.S. (1993). Can listening skills be taught in business communication classes? *NABTE Review*, 20, 25–32.

Snyder, M. (1974). The self-monitoring of expressive behavior. *Journal of Personality and Social Psychology*, 30, 526–37.

Sousa, D.A. (2001). *How the brain learns. A classroom teacher's guide*, 2nd edn. Thousand Oaks, CA: Corwin Press.

Steil, L.K. (1984, March). *The ILA and certification of teachers and trainers*. Paper presented at the International Listening Association Convention, Scottsdale, AZ.

Steil, L.K., Barker, L.L., and Watson, K.W. (1983a). *Effective listening: Key to your success*. Reading, MA: Addison-Wesley.

Steil, L.K., Summerfield, J., and de Mare, G. (1983b). *Listening: It can change your life*. New York: John Wiley and Sons.

Steinbrecher, M.M., and Willmington, S.C. (1993). *The Steinbrecher-Willmington Listening Test*. Oshkosh, WI: University of Wisconsin.

Steinbrecher, M.M., and Willmington, S.C. (1997). *The Steinbrecher-Willmington Listening Test*, 2nd edn. Oshkosh, WI: University of Wisconsin.

Taylor, S. (1964). *Listening: What research says to the teacher*. Washington, DC: National Education Association.

Thomas, L.T., and Levine, T.R. (1994). Disentangling listening and verbal recall. *Human Communication Research*, 21, 1, 103–29.

Thompson, K., Leintz, P., Nevers, B., and Witkowski, S. (2004). The integrative listening model: an approach to teaching and learning listening. *The Journal of General Education*, 53, 3–4, 225–46.

Timm, S., and Schroeder, B.L. (2000). Listening/nonverbal communication training. *International Journal of Listening*, 14, 109–28.

Toussant, I.H. (1960). A classified summary of listening 1950–1959. *The Journal of Communication*, 10, 3, 124–34.

Treisman, A.M. (1960). Contextual cues in selective listening. *Quarterly Journal of Experimental Psychology*, 12, 242–8.

Treisman, A.M. (1964). Selective attention in man. *British Medical Bulletin*, 20, 12–16.

Wacker, K.G., and Hawkins, K. (1995). Curricula comparison for classes in listening. *International Journal of Listening*, 9, 14–28.

Walker, K.L. (1997). Do you ever listen? Discovering the theoretical underpinnings of empathic listening. *International Journal of Listening*, 11, 127–37.

Waner, K.K. (1995, December). Business communication competencies needed by employees as perceived by business faculty and business professionals. *Business Communication Quarterly*, 58, 4, 51–6.

Watson, K.W., and Barker, L.L. (1984). *Watson/Barker Listening Test*. New Orleans, LA: Spectra, Inc.

Watson, K.W., and Barker, L.L. (2000). *Watson/Barker Listening Test*, 2nd edn. New Orleans, LA: Spectra, Inc.

Weaver, C.H. (1972). *Human listening: Processes and behavior*. Indianapolis, IN: Bobbs-Merrill.

Werner, E.K. (1975). A study of communication time. Unpublished master's thesis, University of Maryland at College Park.

Wheeless, L.R. (1975). An investigation of receiver apprehension and social context dimension of communication apprehension. *The Speech Teacher*, 24, 261–5.

Willmington, S.C. (1992). Oral communication skills necessary for successful teaching. *Educational Research Quarterly*, 16, 2, 5–17.

Winsor, J.L., Curtis, D.B., and Stephens, R.D. (1997, September). National preferences in business and communication education: A survey update. *JACA*, 3, 170–9.

Witkin, B.R. (1990). Listening theory and research: The state of the art. *Journal of the International Listening Association*, 4, 7–32.

Wolff, F.L., and Marsnik, N.C. (1992). *Perceptive listening*, 2nd edn. Fort Worth, TX: Harcourt Brace Jovanovich.

Wolff, F.L., Marsnik, N.C., Tracey, W.S., and Nichols, R.G. (1983). *Perceptive listening*. New York: Holt, Rinehart and Winston.

Wolvin, A.D. (1989). Models of the listening process. In C.V. Roberts and K.W. Watson (Eds.). *Intrapersonal communication processes: Original essays*, pp. 508–27. New Orleans, LA: Spectra, Inc.

Wolvin, A.D. (2002, March). *Understanding listening: The evolution of a process model*. Paper presented at the International Listening Association, Scottsdale, AZ.

Wolvin, A.D. (2003). Listening Legend – Dr. Andrew D. Wolvin. *ILA Listening Post*, 85, 3.

Wolvin, A.D., and Coakley, C.G. (1979). *Listening instruction. Theory and research into practice*. Falls Church, VA: Speech Communication Association.

Wolvin, A.D. and Coakley, C.G. (1982). *Listening*. Dubuque, IA: W.C. Brown Co. Publishers.

Wolvin, A.D., and Coakley, C.G. (1992). A listening course in higher education: initial response – A case study. *ACA Bulletin*, 80, 39–45.

Wolvin, A.D., and Coakley, C.G. (Eds.). (1993). *Perspectives on listening*. College Park, MD: Ablex Publishing.

Wolvin, A.D., and Coakley, C.G., (1994). Listening competency. *Journal of the International Listening Association*, 8, 148–60.

Wolvin, A.D., and Coakley, C.G. (1996a). *Listening*, 5th edn. Dubuque, IA: Brown and Benchmark.

Wolvin, A.D., and Coakley, C.G. (1996b). *Listening: Instructors' manual*, 5th edn. Dubuque, IA: Times Mirror Higher Education Group.

Wolvin, A.D., and Coakley, C.G. (1999, November). *Listening education.* Paper presented at the meeting of the National Communication Association, Chicago, IL.

Wolvin, A.D., Coakley, C.G., and Disburg, J.E. (1991). An exploratory study of listening instruction in selected colleges and universities. *Journal of the International Listening Association*, 5, 68–92.

Wolvin, A.D., Coakley, C.G., and Disburg, J.E. (1992). Listening instruction in selected colleges and universities. *Journal of the International Listening Association*, 6, 59–65.

Wolvin, A.D., Coakley, C.G., and Halone, K.K. (1995). A preliminary look at listening development across the life-span. *International Journal of Listening*, 62–83.

Wolvin, A.D., Halone, K.K., and Coakley, C.G. (1999). An assessment of the "intellectual discussion" on listening theory and research. *International Journal of Listening*, 13, 111–29.

Worthington, D.L. (2005, November). *Listening education: A review of listening syllabi.* Paper presented to the National Communication Association conference, Boston, MA.

10

Perspectives on Intercultural Listening

Melissa L. Beall

In this chapter, Beall provides a review of intercultural listening literature, identifying some of the characteristics of good listeners and of intercultural listening within different cultures. She also identifies guidelines to help people be better intercultural listeners, and posits some concerns for needed research in this area.

Perspectives on Intercultural Listening

In a world increasingly fraught with tension, dissension, and outright conflict, it would seem that more academicians, policy-makers, diplomats and others would take the time to learn more about those who inhabit this planet. Despite some 30 years of intercultural research and thousands of articles, there are often insufficient intercultural findings and applications disseminated to the appropriate parties to "make a difference" in global relations. And, even when it is disseminated, there is inadequate application of intercultural communication competence to create a difference in the world. Added to this is the problem that there has not been enough practical research undertaken or disseminated, despite the numerous consultants and business persons who spend a considerable amount of time helping employers and employees learn more about listening.

While listening researchers have conducted considerable research in intercultural listening in the past two decades, a review of the literature makes it apparent that much more needs to be completed in order to make a difference in this global society. Our technologically advanced world has allowed us to become much more aware of cultural practices. Intercultural awareness and sensitivity is usually viewed as both a positive characteristic and a necessity in today's global society. In many elementary and secondary classrooms around the world, "multiculturalism" is a required part of the curriculum and many colleges require a course in multiculturalism or, more specifically, in intercultural communication. College and university general education or liberal arts core requirements encourage the study of various cultures. Many US colleges mandate at least one course in non-western culture as a part of core requirements.

While many courses focus on differences, there are, in fact, many similarities between and among various cultures that we often ignore. What is apparent, however, is that unless the interactants in diverse communication events are aware of both similarities and differences, problems may occur. And, listening researchers in particular have determined that awareness of the role of listening in communication events between and among people of different cultures is critical to success. Culture is the basis for the ways people think, talk, and act. Culture, however, is not contained within ethnic or national boundaries. There are many layers of cultures within any given country or society. Thus, while it may be easy to refer to "cultural perspectives," it is not always easy to define what we mean by the term. Culture pervades everything people do and varies from country to country, workplace to workplace, and group to group. Despite the awareness of the need to know more about other cultures, unless there's an employer mandate, or another significant reason to learn more about others and their culture, little or no emphasis is placed on listening in general, let alone on intercultural listening. And, despite the prevalence of the need for effective listening, listening is often not included in the training provided by employers for personnel sent on global assignments. Furthermore, the concept of intercultural listening also almost defies categorization. Thomlison (1997, p. 91) asserts, "Western cultures as a whole, place much greater emphasis on speaking than on listening ... Western cultures take listening for granted .... In contrast, many non-Western cultures emphasize listening rather than speaking." Thus, it would seem that trainers and educators should expend greater effort to raise people's awareness of the importance of listening, in general, and intercultural listening, specifically.

Gudykunst (2005, p. viii) suggests that culture is one of the many group memberships that influence communication. He further states that numerous intercultural communication theories have been generated in the past 20 years. This growth of theories and the development and expansion of intercultural communication theory will undoubtedly also affect listening research and theory building. Anthropologists Kroeber and Kluckhorn (1993) examined 300 different definitions of "culture." Scholars in a variety of disciplines suggest that there are some fundamental characteristics of culture.

Trenholm and Jensen, (2000) indicate that culture is the set of values and beliefs, norms and customs, and rules and codes that socially defines a group of people, binds them to one another and gives a sense of commonality. Neuliep (2003) says that intercultural communication occurs whenever a minimum of two persons from different cultures or microcultures come together and exchange verbal and nonverbal symbols. Cooper, Calloway-Thomas and Simonds (2007) propose that both intercultural communication and intercultural listening are contextual; that is, a combination of factors such as setting, situation, circumstances, the people involved, and the relationship of those people must be considered.

In this chapter, we will explore what we already "know" about intercultural listening, identify some of the characteristics of intercultural listening within different cultures, identify guidelines to help people be better intercultural listeners, and posit some concerns for needed research in the area.

A Review of the Literature

Clinard (1985, p. 39) suggests that listening may be the best tool for understanding the people with whom we work. Wolvin and Coakley (1996, p. 124) offer "ten factors influencing the listening process." Significantly, the first factor is culture and the authors suggest that "Communication scholars have come to recognize that culture is a primary determinant of all communication behaviors – including listening – because one's culture essentially serves to define who one is and how one will communicate through one's perceptual filter." Wolvin and Coakley (1996, p. 125) further suggest that [cultures and] subcultures within the United States illustrate differences that require adaptation for the listener to understand and to respond appropriately. They also state, "communication between blacks and whites is shaped by cultural influences." Intercultural communication scholars, Samovar and Porter (1994, p. 19), describe the profound impact of culture on listening behavior as follows: "The ways in which we communicate, the circumstances of our communication, the language and language style we use, and our nonverbal behaviors are all a response to and a function of our culture. And, as cultures differ from one another, the communication practices and behaviors of individuals reared in those cultures will also be different." Thomlison (1997) indicates that just as communication and culture are inseparable, so too, are listening and culture. He also suggests that, "the ultimate goal of the cross cultural listener is to reduce uncertainty in the communication process" and what may be "effective listening in one culture is totally inappropriate or misunderstood in another culture." In a series of research reports with a focus on nonverbal effects on intercultural listening, Ostermeier (1987, 1989, 1992, 1993, 1995, 1996, 1997a, 1997b, 1999) suggests, "intercultural listening is a challenging arena for participants to enter. Factors other than language such as cultural values and nonverbal cues take on significant importance."

Wolvin (1987), in a study of perceptions of listening behavior found that international students perceived Americans to be less willing and less patient as listeners than they perceived listeners in African, South American, or European cultures. The respondents in Wolvin's study indicated, "good listeners in any culture are those who care about their relationships with others." Wolvin and Coakley (1996, p. 126) cite Chan-Herur, who recommends that when Americans conduct business internationally, they should: "1. Observe. 2. Listen. 3. Speak." These recommendations are the direct opposite of the usual pattern for people in the United States. Chan-Herur's suggestions should also be considered whenever US citizens interact with anyone, but especially when interacting with people from other cultures or co-cultures.

Anthropologist Edward T. Hall (1959) identified cultures as either high context or low context. The United States and Canada are both low context cultures; this means that communicators expect to gain most of the information in communication events in the words of the messages. The high context perspective, found in many parts of Asia and the Middle East, is a situation where more information is contained in the communication setting and in the communicators themselves than is contained in the words uttered. In the high-context culture, then, according to Hall, messages tend to be shorter, more general, and faster. Speakers and listeners in high-context cultures rely on a common understanding of values and rules. So, in the (low context) United States, speakers believe that it is their responsibility to

help their listeners understand their messages, whereas people in high context cultures believe it is the responsibility of the listener to understand. For this reason, when some Asian students, for example, interact with others, whether it is in a class or in an interpersonal communication event, they expect to understand what is being said, and if they do not, they usually will not express their lack of understanding because in their own cultures, it is their duty to understand without asking questions or making their lack of knowledge or understanding known to others. Americans who believe that it is their responsibility to "make people understand" may be seen as overbearing, patronizing, and even pompous when they explain and repeat things in an effort to help the listener, especially if the listener is from a high context culture.

Chen and Starosta (1998) list three issues that affect our ability to listen interculturally: (1) listening across emotions; (2) fusing horizons; and, (3) selective listening. According to Chen and Starosta, we all have our own worldviews. If we become locked in those worldviews, it becomes difficult to listen to someone from another culture. Thus, we can see that effective communication may be difficult to attain unless all listeners are aware of the both similarities and differences and able to work around them.

In other research, Purdy and Newman (1999) identified good and poor listener differences according to gender and compared their findings to earlier studies. Purdy and Newman found that there were several characteristics that respondents identified as characteristics of good listeners, no matter which gender: eye contact; willingness to listen; shows interest; asks for clarity; gives feedback; and offers advice when wanted. Purdy and Newman claim that people today are more aware of listening and the discipline required in being a good listener.

Imhof (2001b) investigated "specific variations in the assessment of good and poor listening behavior across different areas of communication (personal conversation, professional communication), perceived listener status, and cultural backgrounds. She found that "participants' accounts for good and poor listening behavior were subject to significant inter- and intra-cultural variation due to relevant situational factors which determine the character of a listening episode." Imhof focused on good listener characteristics and found similar results to Purdy and Newman. Furthermore, she found that different communication contexts call for different listener characteristics.

Imhof and Janusik (2006) look at listening as a cognitive construct. Their work is promising for all listening research and especially for intercultural listening. Imhof and Janusik suggest four factors need to be taken into account as listening concepts are mapped and analyzed.

The Effect of Specific Behaviors on Intercultural Listening

Ostermeier (1995) provides an excellent overview of the effects of nonverbal behavior on intercultural listening. He reports that American students, who interviewed international students from Africa, Asia, Europe, Latin America, and the Middle East, indicated that five nonverbal behaviors affected the Americans' perception of listening: use of voice; conversational space; eye behavior; facial expressions; and hand gestures. Ostermeier's (1995) conclusions can help us understand intercultural listening contexts.

- Differences in meanings of voice and conversational space made it more likely that it would be difficult to listen to the international speaker.
- Differences in the meanings of facial expressions and hand gestures made it more likely that it would be easier to listen.
- Differences in meanings of eye behavior were no more likely to be a help or a hindrance to listening.
- The adverse impact on listening due to differences in nonverbal cue meanings may be in the perception of the listener that something negative is being directed at them personally or it may be the perception that something negative is being directed at what they are saying.
- The differences in meanings for nonverbal cues appear more likely to make it easier or more difficult to listen depending on the cultural area of the world of the international person.
- Differences in meanings would seem more likely to make it more difficult to listen to persons from the Middle East and Latin America.
- Differences in these cues seem to make it easier to listen to Africans.
- Nonverbal differences appear to be as likely a help as a hindrance in listening to Asians and Europeans.

- It is apparent that persons from one country within a particular cultural group may very well exhibit behaviors differently than persons from another country within the same cultural group.
- One always must be cautioned to be prepared to adapt to a particular country within a particular cultural area, and, to that particular individual. (Ostermeier, 1995, p. 33)

Ostermeier's (1995) research promotes the idea that listening to the nonverbal communication in intercultural situations may be a key element in achieving intercultural listening competence.

A Study on the Role of Intercultural Listening

A number of essays and research reports suggest that collectivist cultures (for example, Eastern cultures) place a higher value on listening than do individualistic cultures (for example, the US and Canada). Native Americans tend to be more collectivist and are similar to people from Asia in their views of storytelling as means of preserving and maintaining the traditions of the culture. Ostermeier's (1995) findings suggest that we should all be aware of the role of intercultural listening in our exchanges with others. Given the relative currency of intercultural listening research, and the relative paucity of information on intercultural listening, this author interviewed people from different world areas to determine the role of listening in various countries and cultures. There are some interesting generalizations that would seem to corroborate what previous researchers have found.

Students from Western Europe were surprised that anyone would be interested in the study of listening. The students from Scandinavia indicated that little time is spent on communication in their educational systems, and listening is something that is taken for granted – you listen because you have to in order to understand messages. Scandinavian businesspersons stated similar ideas: "What can you study about listening? You just do it!" In conversations with people throughout Sweden and Denmark, interviewees were also surprised that anyone would research or teach listening. After conversing with them for a bit, they conceded, "there is something to this idea of listening." Native-speaking German Professors in the Modern Language department at this writer's home institution responded to questions about the role of listening in their own country and culture with these statements: "Well, of course, we are interested in listening! We teach language." "One cannot teach or learn language without listening. But, in our home country, it is just expected that people will listen and understand." German research and the teaching of listening, however, are increasing. Imhof and Weinhard (2004) found that elementary school children are expected to listen about 2/3 of the time. In an earlier German study, Imhof (1998) found that students do not have a clear concept of listening as an active process that they can control. In a more recent study, Imhof (2001a) found that students report greater listening comprehension when they use metacognitive strategies such as asking questions prior to listening, managing interest in the subject, and using elaboration strategies to apply the information. Listening has also been the focus for determining sensitivity to multicultural issues. Timm and Schroeder (2000) found that combining listening and nonverbal communication training significantly increases multicultural sensitivity. From these studies, it is apparent that greater listening competence creates better students, with a greater understanding of what it means to live in a multicultural world. In addition to this research, the German Listening Society is conducting annual workshops to help teachers teach listening.

World Perspectives on Listening

Asians, and South Americans, however, indicate different perspectives on listening. Interviews were conducted with students from Argentina, Brazil, China, Ecuador, Japan, Korea, Malaysia, Taiwan, and Thailand. Three major questions were provided to the interviewees prior to the interview in order to give them time to think about and formulate their answers and to facilitate the process:

1 Tell me about listening in your culture. What is the role of listening in your culture?
2 In your culture, what is a "good listener"?
3 Are there differences in listening between your country/culture and the United States?

In interviews with Asian students attending a small Midwestern university in the United States of America, there were similar responses to

Figure 10.1   The word "to listen" in Chinese

all three questions. Students indicated that they do not have classroom instruction in "listening" *per se*, but they learn early that they *must* be good listeners. Family members demand respect from children, and respect is displayed in one's listening to others. In the classroom, the expectation is that one will listen and think and not talk, not ask questions, and not cause the speaker to lose face, unless the class is one where interaction and asking questions is specifically identified as appropriate behavior. One of the students suggested that listening continues long after the classroom experience ends, because one must truly reflect on what was said and the meaning. Each Asian student indicated that listening is lengthy, and something that Americans do not seem to comprehend. "Americans are always in such a hurry. They don't take the time to listen properly. They are always rushing on to the next thing before they understand what is being said." The students from China and Taiwan, especially, referred to the Chinese characters "ting" (see Figure 10.1) and how those characters define and explain listening well.

The characters in "ting" represent the eyes, the ears, the heart, (the total being) and undivided attention. These aspects of listening capture the essence of what they learn about the role of listening in their own cultures. Listening requires the whole being to be involved when trying to understand what is being communicated. And, the concept of undivided attention is crucial. Several interviewees suggested that one "must listen between the lines. You have to listen to what is said and what is not said, and then you have to think about all of it. It takes time to think about everything that is said, but it takes more time to think about what was not said, but is a vital part of the message." Listening in their classrooms means that one listens with the whole being. Eyes are focused on the teacher/professor and one works hard to avoid all distractions. Students from South America identified similar kinds of attitudes and behaviors in their cultures.

Discussion

Each country, culture, or microculture has a somewhat different and unique perspective of listening, with Western and Eastern ways distinctly different from each other. We have much to learn about intercultural listening, but research can provide additional information about what we need to know and what we need to study in the future. The stories about listening from the Chinese women in the research provide guidelines for how to understand others.

Responses to the interview questions indicate that previous research findings suggesting that people in Asian cultures view listening as a much stronger and much more valuable skill or trait. While these students say they are not *directly* taught to be good listeners, Chinese cultural traditions create expectations that listening is much more valuable than any other attribute. And, everything in the culture provides implications for appropriate behaviors. The four themes pervading the interviews were: (1) Listening is important; (2) Listening is expected; (3) Listening is learned by example and by expectation; and (4) One must listen for what is *not* said. All Asian interviewees indicated that listening is very important in their own cultures, and they were surprised that it was less so in the United States. In their own cultures, they indicate that there are punishments for failure to listen, especially to one's parents or teachers. While they were hesitant to state that they were taught to listen, they were quite descriptive about the ways that good, careful listening is expected, and that parents, elders, and teachers expect to say something only once, and that the listener will receive, comprehend and comply with the message. Students provided numerous examples of how one must listen to not just the words, but to the meaning intended. This listening with the mind also includes listening with the heart, the eyes, and the ears. "We must listen to what is not said," was a common phrase they offered about listening. Many of their examples of good listening also included instances of listening to more than the words, and with more than the ears. It was clear in these interviews that in their culture, listening can indeed be defined as it has been delimited by the International Listening Association (1995): Listening: The process of receiving, constructing meaning from, and responding to spoken and/or nonverbal messages (p. 1).

The informal interviews with the western European students and faculty, and the lengthy interviews with the Chinese women suggest that we can learn a great deal about another's culture, and the world's view of intercultural listening if we will take the time to learn about the culture and, especially, to learn to listen with the ears, eyes, mind and heart.

We have much to learn about culture and listening if we are to successfully interact in this global community. Visitors to other countries need to learn about the people, their culture, their language, and their views on listening. Only through an awareness of and sensitivity to the cultural practices and traditions of others, will we be able to effectively communicate with the people around us. Harris (2002) provides several strategies for listening interculturally:

1 Listen for your own cultural/individual values.
2 When you are introduced to someone from another culture, listen for his/her cultural/individual values.
3 Expand your knowledge of the cultural norms of other peoples.
4 Listen with your eyes open and an open mind.

Harris further describes a global listener as one who has: knowledge; attitude; and skills. She says we have to begin with understanding our cultures, our values, and ourselves before we can gain and use knowledge of others' cultures. Once we know our own values, strengths, and weaknesses, we can develop attitudes that will help us in intercultural encounters. Finally, we need to develop the skills that will allow us to approach each intercultural encounter as a unique experience.

This writer also developed some guidelines for effective intercultural listening.

1 Be prepared to listen.
2 Learn to control internal and external distractions.

3   Behave as a good listener. Stop talking; let others have a chance. Don't interrupt. Concentrate on what is said, not who is saying it, or what the speaker is doing.
4   Good listeners maintain eye contact with speakers, if it is a part of their culture.
5   Good listeners learn the "rules" of the culture!
6   Good listeners ask questions at appropriate times and maintain flexibility as they carefully listen to the speaker's views.
7   Remember that dialects, accents, and "different" vocal dynamics can but should not distract. Learn to focus on the message.
8   Learn to ask appropriate questions.
9   Remember that all cultures and co-cultures have both similarities and differences. We should not focus on differences!
10   Enjoy the journey!

Future Research

This chapter and the review of literature contained in it provide ample justification for needed research in the area of intercultural communication. Those whose business or personal travels to other lands and cultures have undoubtedly already learned that "good" listening depends on a number of variables, including the situation, the status, and the cultural variables themselves. We need to learn more about other cultures before visiting. And, research needs to be completed to help us find the answers to "what is good listening?" in the various cultures of the world.

QUESTIONS FOR DISCUSSION

1   What is culture? How can we define intercultural communication? Is intercultural listening defined differently than intercultural communication? How so? If not, should it be?
2   Describe the relationship between culture and listening.
3   How is intercultural listening affected by nonverbal communication?
4   What are the major differences between listeners in high context and low context cultures?
5   How is listening perceived in Scandinavian countries?
6   How can you apply Harris's strategies and your author's guidelines for effective intercultural listening to your own lives.

7 If you were planning to visit another country, what kinds of things would you wish to learn about the culture before you travel?

References

Chen, G., and Starosta, W.J. (1998). *Foundations of intercultural communication.* Boston: Allyn and Bacon Publishers.

Clinard, H. (1985). Listen for the difference. *Training and Development Journal,* 39, 10, 39.

Cooper, P.J., Calloway-Thomas, C., and Simonds, C. J. (2007). *Intercultural communication: A text with readings.* Boston: Pearson Allyn and Bacon.

Gudykunst, W.B. (2005). *Theorizing about intercultural communication.* Thousand Oaks, CA: Sage Publications.

Hall, E.T. (1959). *The silent language.* Greenwich, CT: Fawcett.

Harris, J.A. (2000, March). *Listening across culture: From theory to practice.* Paper presented at the 2000 International Listening Association Convention, Virginia Beach, VA.

Imhof, M. (1998). What makes a good listener? Listening behavior in instructional settings. *International Journal of Listening,* 12, 81–105.

Imhof, M. (2001a). How to listen more efficiently. Self-monitoring strategies in listening. *International Journal of Listening,* 15, 2–19.

Imhof, M. (2001b, November). *The social construction of the listener: good and poor listening behavior across situations, perceived listener status, and cultures.* Paper presented at the National Communication Association convention, Atlanta, GA.

Imhof, M., and Janusik, L. (2006, July). Development and validation of the Imhof-Janusik listening concepts inventory to measure conceptualization differences between cultures. *Journal of Intercultural Communication Research,* 35, 2.

Imhof, M., and Weinhard, T. (2004, April). *What did you listen to in school today?* Paper presented at the 25th annual convention of the International Listening Association, Ft. Myers, FL.

International Listening Association Definition of Listening. (1995, July). Cited in A. Wolvin, On competent listening, *The Listening Post 54,*

Kroeber, A., and Kluckhorn, C. (1993). Cited in P.J. Cooper, C. Calloway-Thomas, and C.J. Simonds (2007). *Intercultural communication A text with readings,* Boston: Pearson Allyn and Bacon.

Neuliep, J. (2003). *Cultural communication: A contextual approach.* Boston: Houghton Mifflin.

Ostermeier, T. (1987, July). *Learning intercultural listening concepts through participating in intercultural communication exercises/simulations.* Paper presented at the International Listening Association Summer Conference, Toronto, Canada.

Ostermeier, T. (1989). Perceptions of cultural values and communicating inter-culturally: A simulation experience, *World Communication Journal*, 18, 1, 33–47.

Ostermeier, T. (1992, March). *The intercultural interview: An experience in intercul-tural listening*. Paper presented at the meeting of the International Listening Association, Seattle, WA.

Ostermeier, T. (1993). Perception of nonverbal cues in dialogic listening in an intercultural interview. *Journal of the International Listening Association*, Special Issue. 64–75.

Ostermeier, T. (Summer, 1995). Meaning differences for nonverbal cues: Easier or more difficult for the intercultural listener?" *Intercultural Communication Studies*, V, 1, 19–40.

Ostermeier, T. (1996, March). *Intercultural listening and facial/vocal cues: The gen-der factor*. Paper presented at the 1996 International Listening Association Convention, Sacramento, CA,

Ostermeier, T. (1997a, March). *Gender, nonverbal cues, and intercultural listening: Part II Conversational space and hand gestures*. Paper presented at the International Listening Association Convention, Mobile, AL.

Ostermeier, T. (1997b, July). *An intercultural student to student interview project: A descriptive study*. Paper presented at the 14th Biennial Conference of the World Communication Association, San Jose, Costa Rica.

Ostermeier, T. (1999). *Confronting the challenges of intercultural listening*. Paper presented at the 7th Annual International Conference on Cross Cultural Communication, Louisville, KY.

Purdy, M., and Newman, N. (1999, March). *Characteristics of Good and Poor Listeners (Listening and Gender Research, Stage 1)*. Paper presented at the International Listening Association Convention, Albuquerque, NM.

Samovar, L., and Porter, R. (1994). *Communication between cultures*, 2nd edn. Belmont, CA: Wadsworth Publishing.

Thomlison, T.D. (1997). Intercultural listening. In M. Purdy, and D. Borisoff (Eds.). *Listening in everyday life: A personal and professional approach* (2nd ed.), pp. 79–120. Lanham, MD: University Press of America.

Timm, S., and Schroeder, B.L. (2000). Listening nonverbal communication train-ing. *International Journal of Listening*, 14, 109–25.

Trenholm, S., and Jensen, A. (2000). *Interpersonal communication*, 4th edn. Belmont, CA: Wadsworth.

Wolvin, A.D. (1987, Summer). *Culture as a listening variable*. Paper presented at the International Listening Association Summer Conference, Toronto, Canada.

Wolvin, A.D., and Coakley, C. (1996). *Listening*, 5th edn. Madison, WI: Brown and Benchmark Publishers.

11

Listening in Spirituality and Religion

Diana Corley Schnapp

Listening has been an integral aspect of spirituality and religion through the ages, the assumption being that if one attempts to connect either internally or externally with a source that guides or controls one's life and self, some type of reception of message must occur. It is assumed that individuals listen to: a higher power; the universe; self; "inner voices;" other people; nature; sounds; spirit guides; and/or a combination of these. This chapter will examine listening in both spirituality and religion by reviewing current publications and the comments of qualified persons using the terms "listening" or "listen" in the context of spirituality and religion and how the context employs listening behaviors.

What is the Meaning of the Terms: Listening, Religion, and Spirituality?

The nature of this chapter demands definitions of some frequently-used terminology, the most fundamental of which is *listening*. One of the inherent problems in examining the role of listening in these contexts is that the definition of listening is still in development. Glenn (1989) identified 50 definitions of the concept. In an effort to arrive at some consistency for research and educational purposes, the International Listening Association agreed to accept the following definition of listening: "the process of receiving, constructing meaning from, and responding to spoken and/or nonverbal messages" (Bentley and Bacon, 1996, p. 1). While this broad definition has been accepted by the Association, many scholars continue to regard listening as a multidimensional process which involves the physical, mental, emotional, and social behaviors of individuals (Brownell, 2002; Purdy, 1991; Wolvin and Coakley, 1996). Various models of the listening process include "preparing to listen, attending, hearing, cognitive processing, responding, interpreting, evaluating, remembering, and listening filters" (Brownell, 2002; Thompson, 2005; Wolvin and Coakley, 1996). Janusik (2002) asserts that there is no single accepted definition or model of listening, which is a complex cognitive and behavioral process, and that scholars focus on different aspects of the process.

The treatment of listening in spiritual and religious literature supports Janusik's observation. Writers of religious and spiritual articles and books assume that listening does occur, but they focus primarily on practicing listening and on specific aspects of the listening process rather than on a scientific analysis of how listening is related to spirituality and religion. Certainly there is a need to clarify what is meant by "listening" in these contexts, and then the relationship of that concept to beliefs and practices.

Adding to the confusion is the fact that the terms *spirituality* and *religion* may frequently be used together, but they connote different meanings (Schneiders, 2003). *Spirituality* has been defined in a number of ways depending on the writer's perspective. Two definitions serve as effective summaries of the concept: (1) "The four (sic) domains for spirituality: relationships with other people, within self, within nature, within a religion, and within a relationship with God" (Kass and Kass, 2000, p. 58); and (2) "A working definition of spirituality suggests it is both embodied and transcendent, and involves notions of a holistic, not-strictly-rational connection within the self, and interconnectedness with others, including the environment" (National Communication Association, 2008). Lonsdale (1992) defines "Christian spirituality" as "life in the spirit as sons and daughters of the Father and brothers and sisters of Jesus Christ" (p. 19).

The Concise Oxford American Dictionary (2006) defines *religion* as: "(1) the belief in and worship of a superhuman controlling power, esp. a personal God or gods; (2) details of belief as taught or discussed: (3) a particular system of faith and worship; (4) a pursuit or interest to which someone ascribes supreme importance" (p. 753). Comparison of the definitions suggests that *religion* focuses on being a part of a community which adheres to a specific set of beliefs and practices, whether one is active in that faith community or not; whereas *spirituality* encompass those thoughts and actions whereby we as individuals seek the truth about ourselves and our lives in relation to self, others, and to a higher power. One may be spiritual without being religious and religious without being spiritual, or one may be both religious and spiritual at the same time.

This author contends that there are actually two contexts rather than one. At this point in time, however, the two are being examined as one context in the research goals of the International Listening Association.

Why is There a Need for Research Regarding the Relationship between Listening and Religion/Spirituality?

An extensive review of tables of contents and articles in religious and spirituality journals suggests that while there is a great deal of writing being published with respect to spirituality and religion that mentions listening, very little work has been done using empirical study. See, for example, tables of contents of journals indexed in the following resources: Hartford Seminary Library 2008; International Listening Association, 2008; National Communication Association, 2008; Questia, 2006; Religious Research Association, 2008; Yahoo Directory *Religious Journals*, 2008.

At the time of this writing, *The International Journal of Listening* has published only one spiritual/religious focused article during its 20 years of publication (International Listening Association, 2008; Corley Schnapp, 2008). The papers and programs presented at the annual meetings of the International Listening Association do include a much broader representation of interest in the contexts (International Listening Association, *Index to Convention Papers*, 2006). Beginning in the 1990s, programs focused on ways to practice listening skills in a variety of spiritual and religious applications. Among these are: Armstrong, Timm and Schroeder, 2002; Cordova, 20064; Gering, 1996; Glenn, 1999; Kearley, 2002; Kollar and Landes, 2008; Nixon, 2000; Paulin 2005; Shafir, 2001; Thompson, 2003; Warland and Fadden, 1990; and Watson, 1999).

The National Communication Association (2008) does have a Spiritual Communication Division "dedicated to the study, criticism, research, teaching, and application of communication phenomena in the context of spirituality," but this search found no studies related specifically to listening in the tables of contents of the numerous journals published by the Association.

Hedahl (2001) cites three reasons for the lack of research in the Christian tradition: listening skills have been defined as belonging to contemplative tradition and pastoral counseling; emphasis has been placed on doing whereas listening is perceived as passive; and the culture places emphasis on speaking rather than silence. She points out that while listening is advocated in most religions, the literature focuses more on a speaking–listening dyad, which omits a great deal of religious and spiritual interaction. She also concludes that a skill based listening approach is missing from the literature and the research.

In 2006, an international conference co-sponsored by the International Listening Association and Rockhurst University focused on research in listening using Progress Review Groups to identify areas of concern in listening and to propose research projects. The context group dealing with Religion and Spirituality identified as potential for research "recognizing and neutralizing our own emotionally-charged words and phrases in intrapersonal, interpersonal, and interfaith dialogue with the context of an interfaith listening study" (Janusik, 2007, p. 8). The group stated as a desired outcome of their research study to be completed in 2008: "to develop listening strategies to initiate and promote positive and productive interfaith dialogue" (p. 8).

In spite of the seeming lack of empirical research, there is information available related to listening in the contexts. Hart (1980), Hedahl (2001), and Savage (1996) offer specific guidelines for listening for ministry. Shafir (2000) examines the tenets of Zen Buddhism's relationship to effective listening. She advocates that individuals listen with the heart, body, and mind: "to focus on the process of listening in order to keep our everyday lives healthy, peaceful, and productive" (p. 23). Lindahl (2002, 2003, 2005), who focuses on interfaith spirituality, perhaps comes the closest to the research goals of the "Research in the Contexts" meeting of 2006.

Because of the current broad definitions of listening, there have been a number of other communication studies that either directly or indirectly concern the reception of messages in the contexts. Wright (1993) identified rhetorical practices in classical Ch'an Buddhism. If listening includes linguistics and cognitive processing, then additional broader communication studies, including a number of language-based studies, related not only Judeo-Christian study, but also to Eastern Philosophies as well have been published. Eilberg-Schwartz (1988), for example, proposes a Rabbinic theory of language, while Carpenter (1992) examines the language of the VEDA in India. Dalferth (1992) deals with God and the mystery of words. Erhling (1984) also focuses on language related to context of meaning. Shinn (1992) analyzed the use of language and symbols in relationship to the naming of the Divine. The use of ritual language in everyday life as used by the Christian Right was the subject of an article by Meigs (1995). Waltner (1991) reports an analysis of Koine Greek, the language of the first century Christians, as it relates to the faculty of hearing, attention to, and consideration of what is being said, and to understand and perceive the sense of what is being said. Thiselton (1980) relates the function of language to hermeneutics, the science of the interpretation of the scriptures, by examining the relationship among Being (Higher Power), language, and man, including concepts of the relationship of language and thought. Ladd and Spilka (2002) tested the idea that spiritual individuals practice focus of prayer by focusing upward (human with divine), inward (with oneself), and outward (human to human); but they did not find a dominating factor in the direction of prayer focus.

Despite the number of references that may be found, most of the writers focus primarily on practicing listening and on portions of the listening process rather than on a scientific analysis of how listening relates to spirituality and religion. Such focuses are of value, but they need to be supported by research rather than assumptions.

To Whom or To What do we Listen?

The articles published to date focus the listening behaviors in three different areas: listening to a higher power or spirits; listening to "inner voices"; and listening to other people.

A common theme in religious listening literature is that of listening to the higher power or spirits, which encompasses a number of identities for that power. In Judeo-Christian-Islamic literature, the listening is to God, *YHWH*, Allah, the prophets, scripture, the Holy Spirit, Jesus, saints, and angels. Those who consider listening to a higher power indicate that God may be heard in scripture, silence, community, other people, nature, literature, and other beings (Ackerman, 2001; Brueggemann, 2000; Childs, 2005; Honze, 2004; Lesnick, 1998; Lonsdale 1992; Meyer, 2003; Paulin, 1993, 2005; Stanley, 1995).

Both the Old and New Testaments are filled with references to the importance of hearing and listening. See Table 11.1 for a display of how many times words related to listening appear in scripture (WORDsearch 7.0, 2005).

Table 11.1   References to hearing and listening in two versions of *The Holy Bible*

	Translation	
	King James Version (KJV)	New International Version (NIV)
Hear	553	379
Heareth	52	0
Hearing	46	56
Hears	3	53
Heard	642	577
Listen	1	352

In addition to the examples presented in the table, the words listen, listening, listened, and other forms of the word occur an additional 88 times in the New International Version translation. *Cruden's Concordance* (1968) lists the word *harken,* a commandment meaning that one should listen, 160 times in the King James Version of the *Holy Bible.* As the translations shifted from the preferred translation of the King James Version language of the 1600s to the language of the twentieth century, the words listen, and listening became more prominent. The use of the word may be in reference both to man hearing God and to God hearing man.

Jesus and the writers of the New Testament books refer numerous times to hearing and listening, implying that listening is an important part of one's functioning as a Christian (See for example: Matthew 11:15; Luke 10:16; John 10:27; Acts 3:22; Romans 10:14, NIV). Watson (1999) offers an analysis of listening by Jesus as exemplified in scripture, indicating passages that show that Jesus listened to God, employed patience and empathy, asked effective questions, reinforced and summarized, and gave direct feedback. The latter behaviors are associated with interpersonal and empathic listening. Passages of the New Testament also state that hearing is considered the first step in believing that Jesus is the Christ (Romans 10:14, 17, NIV, 1991). The *Holy Bible* is read aloud during worship services, at weddings, at funerals, and on special occasions, which implies that listening to scripture is part of the practice of the ceremonial occasions.

In Christianity, New Age, Eastern Philosophies, Inter-faith, Native American, and Pagan, the source of the message is attributed to the "inner voice," nature, the Universe, spirit guides, and "life." The New Age writer Harra (2005) suggests methods of tuning in to "spirit guides." Schmidt (2002), in a historical examination of the importance to hearing in the theology of the eighteen and nineteenth centuries, examines the attitudes and practices of listening to spirits, including angels and the devil. Contemporary attention to listening to angels is the subject of Paulin (1996) as well as Daniel, Wyllie, and Ramer (1992). The latter authors include an expanded chapter on paying attention, focusing, and conversing with one's personal angel. Burnham (1990) drew wide attention to the subject of angels and their communication with man past and present in a best-selling book based on the stories told by people who claim to have not only seen angels, but also communicated with them. Fakhry (2004) interprets the *Qur'an* to say that angels do bring messages to individuals.

Hexham (1999) discusses listening to nature and the earth in contemporary Paganism. In addition, listening to nature, Mother Earth, Father Sun, and other external spirits permeates the religion of Native Americans. Similarly, listening to sounds in nature is part of the ongoing practice of spirituality of each of these groups. Not only are various tribes attentive to the presence of spirits all around in both the animate and inanimate, but in healing as well.

For those who believe that God speaks directly to them, it is difficult, if not impossible, to separate listening to a higher power from listening to the "inner voice." In fact, much of the literature referring to listening to God and/or spirits relates to listening inwardly. Harvey (1961) observes, "For much of Christian history, the ear was the way to God: 'hearing things' meant hearing God's voice directly without mediation" (p. 252). The problem with these conclusions is whether the source is actually a higher power or is merely a form of intrapersonal communication, which Roberts, Edwards, and Barker (1987) define as, "the physiological and psychological processing of messages that happens within individuals at conscious and non-conscious levels" (p. 2).

Among religious writers, the subject of listening to sermons and how listening functions in worship services is common. A review of the holdings of the Jewish Community Center, the Hebrew Academy, and libraries of Nazarene, Jesuit, Episcopal, Church of Christ, Baptist universities and Roman Catholic theology institute libraries resulted in a number of titles of articles and books that focus on listening to scripture (see for example Brayerton, 2006; Gering, 1996; Heer, 2006; Lyons, 2006;

Meyer, 2003; Moretz, 2005). McClure (2004) employed interviews and analysis to determine listener's perceptions of the preacher. He concluded that preachers should compare their own perception of their sermons to those of the parishioners. Howden (1989) studied the effects of age, sex, and education on hearer responses to sermons.

Baxter (1980) advocates the ear as the major doorway to the mind, and therefore, "Perhaps Christians should have their attention drawn to the responsibility of listening, for it plays a key role in God's plan" (p. 93). Glenn (1999) proposes a curriculum for teaching churches to listen in worship services. Her content focuses on identifying general and specific purposes for listening in worship as well as techniques for listening to music, prayer, scripture and sermons, and use of imagery.

Religious traditions also advocate "listening" to spiritual writings and theological traditions from the past (Holmes, 2002; Polter, 1997). The sounds of language in the form of poetry and storytelling are also present in most religions and spiritual practices. When searching for listening resources, it is not unusual to find many references to listening to literary forms as part of the spiritual (Eskenazi, 2003; Gallagher, Paulin and Grant, 2002; Redmond, 1992; Sanford, 2002). The sound of language is significant in the spiritual ways of the Native American, Celtic, Inter-faith groups, and Pagans (Newell, 1997; Brodeur, 1997).

A problem arises in writers' use of the word *listen* to mean *attention to and/or responding to* reading scripture or other religious writing in that if the written word is read, a different type of communication experience from listening occurs, and this calls for differing communication skills. The factors of reading were distinguished from factors related to listening by Spearritt (1962). Irvin (1952) also compares reading with listening to distinguish the characteristics of each. Unless the scripture or religious literature is presented orally, is it accurate to say that the receiver "*listens* to the Word?"

Meditation and Listening

A number of writers advocate listening to the "inner voice" for guidance and enlightenment (Burton, 2004; Carlson and Hawkins, 2003; Connor, 1992; Palmer, 1999; Willard, 1999). Fischetto (2000) uses biblical examples of people whose ability to listen brought them a closer relationship with God; and he discusses the value of listening and meditation to grow stronger physically, emotionally, and spiritually.

Among Eastern philosophies and traditions, listening inwardly is important as a practice. Wong (1997) describes the meditation form of internal observation as beginning with awareness of thoughts, emotions, or sensations. The focus of one's awareness is an aspect of listening.From the Hindu point of view, meditation begins with attention to mind, to what you are doing, and to others. Krishnamurti (1999) describes meditation as "absolute silence of the mind" (p. 43) during which the person meditating listens to his ideas. Passages of the *Tao Te Ching* describe the use of listening and hearing sound in order to achieve The Way (Mitchell, 2000, pp. 12, 14). Fadiman and Frager (1997) describe the third stage of Sufism as "the direct experience of the presence of God within" (p. 13). Gyatso Tenzen (2005), the fourteenth Dalai Lama of the State of Tibet, describes the stages of meditation including aspects of the nature of perception and cognition, both of which may or may not be aspects of the listening process. He does, however, believe that there are distinctions between the sensory process of hearing and mental experiences. Piver (2002) also describes the process of meditation as focus and being receptive to quietness and to what the peacefulness of emptying oneself brings. Buddhist author Thich Nhat Hanh (2001) advocates "the practice of compassionate listening and use of loving speech" for the purpose of understanding and transforming anger (p. 4). He observes that looking deeply into the nature of our perceptions and looking deeply into the other person with compassion come from Buddha. Zen Master Dae Gak (1997) advocates that listening is the fundamental practice of any spiritual path, "a practice that returns us to our true way-the way of human beings, the way of compassion" (p. 1). Chetwynde (2005) compares the meditations of Zen Buddhism and Christianity.

New Age writer Michael Brown (2005) describes practicing presence awareness as "tuning in to one's 'Inner Presence', a Being, and how to become one with this Being: to consciously activate the power of our Divine Presence" (p. 9). *Tuning in* involves learning and applying perceptual tools, intending to listen, and identifying the messenger. Another New Age writer, Carmen Harra, (2005) promises to instruct readers (hearers?) on how to *hear* the wisdom of the Invisible World through hypnosis, astrology, dreams, mediums, clairvoyance, and other mystic, spiritualist methods. Roman (1986) writes of receiving telepathic messages and being open to higher guidance. He says this is done through *tuning into* energies within and around us through auras, feelings, and thoughts.

Kaplan (1995) offers a practical guide to Jewish Meditation. Yahweh's admonition to his people to think on His word daily suggests meditation and listening to the message of the Lord (Plaut, 1981; NIV, 1991).

Prayer as Listening

The subjects of centering prayer and contemplative prayer also raise questions with regard to listening inwardly. Calhoun (2005) defines *centering prayer* as "a form of contemplative prayer where the pray-er (sic) seeks to quiet scattered thoughts and desires in the still center of Christ's presence" (p. 207). *Centering prayer* is waiting before the Lord in open attentiveness, attending to the presence of the Holy Spirit. The process allows for the recognition of thoughts then gently releases those thoughts to God. The goal, as is true in Eastern philosophies of meditation, is to become empty of one's self. In this type of prayer, the purpose is to spend time in the presence of God and to become one with God.

Contemplative prayer is defined by Calhoun (2005) as, "to develop an open restful receptivity to the Trinity that enables me to always be with God just as I am." ... Keeping our hearts alert and awake to the presence of God, we listen" (p. 211). Contemplative prayer has been brought to the attention of contemporary seekers by Thomas Keating (2006) and Brother Lawrence (1982) among others. Matthews (2004) examines a contemplative approach to communication based on the writings of Thomas Merton. Barry and Connolly's (1982) comments on contemplation include aspects of the listening process, particularly those of empathic listening. The vocabulary used by these authors sounds very much like the objective of empathic listening in interpersonal communication. However, even if one focuses on a metaphysical or abstract "presence," is the activity listening or another form of interaction? Keating (2006), a leading proponent of contemplative prayer, asserts that contemplative prayer is *not* the same as listening. If listening is defined as a multidimensional process, these practices fit with the definition. Perception and cognition are certainly viewed as aspects of the listening process, but the question remains: are these experiences listening or some other behavior?

Listening to Others: Pastoral Care and Interfaith Dialogue

Schultz and Ahrens (1996) define *pastoral care*, sometimes referred to as *caring ministry*, "to respond to fellow human beings in their time of physical, spiritual, and emotional need on behalf of one's faith community." *Times of need* include, but are not limited to, bereavement, birth, adoption, job loss, chronic illness, divorce, moving from one community to another, anger, youth in crisis, terminal illness and other life crises." *Faith community* is defined as "a group of people who hold in common a system of beliefs and practices relative to sacred things" (Corley Schnapp, 2003. pp. 4–5).

Hedahl (2001) asserts that "while ministers are expected to be listeners as a prior qualification for anything else they might do, (yet) ... listening instruction is lacking in most pastoral training (p. 95). Her table of the "Historical view of pastoral theology books on listening" provides some support for this view (p. 103). Pembroke (2002) concludes that "listening lies at the heart of pastoral ministry" (p. 1). In analyzing the types of attitudes and communication techniques used in pastoral ministry, he cites the behaviors of openness, availability, confirmation of the other, responding with and encouraging the use of feeling-language, and awareness, all of which are tools of compassionate, therapeutic and empathic listening (Wolvin and Coakley, 1996). Thompson (2003), identifies listening as an integral core of the methods of practicing pastoral care. A study examining women's silences in pastoral care was undertaken by Bons-Storm (1996), the results of which suggest that listening to the silences of women produces significant insight for pastoral caregivers.

In her survey of ministers, rabbis, priests, and other spiritual leaders to determine which specific listening behaviors they perceive that they employ in pastoral care, Corley Schnapp (2003) concluded that while respondents tended to rate themselves highly in each of the six types of listening skills, interpreting was used more frequently than the other skills; while understanding was used less frequently than the other types of listening skills surveyed. However, because of a small sample, the results were inconclusive. Non-Christian respondents indicated that they do not use the term "pastoral care" even though the concept was defined for them in the survey.

While the term "pastoral care" may not be used among Jews, there is still provision for listening to and caring for one another. An example is

Shiva, a gathering of friends and relatives who sit with a grieving person for a period of time following the burial of the relative. Although *Shiva* is a silent gathering, the presence of friends and relatives to the grieving person may be a type of listening. Slater (2004) writes of the Jewish compassionate practice of "mindful living," a concept that has already related to listening in other religious and spiritual traditions.

Ecumenical Dialogue and Interfaith Views

Ecumenical writers strongly address listening as part of the dialogic process (Barrigar, 1995; Berling, 1993; Friedman, 1983; Jones, 1999). Kasper (2000) states, "Today dialogue among cultures, religions, and churches is a presupposition for peace in the world" (p. 1). Both Brodeur (1997) and Hoffman (1997) are among the authors who consider listening as an essential aspect of interfaith dialogue. Brodeur (2005) describes the interfaith dialogue as being characterized by honesty, trust, and openness as being important for the quality of listening and understanding.

Lindahl's interfaith books focus on listening as sacred. Her books provide very basic, skills oriented techniques for practicing listening as spiritual awareness. Among the topics she includes are listening for soul, integration, holy connections, listening to God, the inner voice and others. (2002). She also explores contemplative listening as "exploring the quality of silence," (p. 13) and "listening to the True Self: the voice of the soul" (2003, p. 29). Her book for children encourages them to use their senses to explore ways that God listens and is present in everyday lives (2005).

Although his focus is evangelism, Johnson (1994) strongly encourages his reader to begin the efforts of converting another by listening to the beliefs and questions of those of other religions. He asserts that only by listening to and understanding the beliefs of others can one advocate a particular religious message.

Relationship between Culture and Listening Behavior

The cultural experiences of individuals contribute to the meaning of the messages they hear during the religious experience, so all may not listen in the same way. In Eastern cultures, the sounds may even be processed differently in the brain than in Western cultures. This view is supported by Samovar and Porter (1995), "we want to reemphasize that while perception takes place inside each individual, it is culture that primarily determines the meanings we apply to the stimuli that reach us" (p. 80).

In addition, listening to nature, Mother Earth, Father Sun, and other external spirits permeates the spirituality of Native Americans. Listening to sounds in nature is part of their ongoing practices. Tribes attend to the presence of spirits all around in both the animate and inanimate. Interaction with spirits may be achieved through singing, dancing, and drumming. Among the Navaho, "Sings" are central to healing. Navahos participate in a Sing performed by a shaman to heal and put their bodies, spirits, and minds on the right way. In the dance, the ear must be attentive because the dancer must be in harmony with the drum. Each step is with a beat, and the dancer must know exactly when to step. A change in beat signals a change in meaning of the dance. The Hopi cleanse the ceremonial space by burning small bundles of sage and wafting the smoke around the area to clear the way for spirits to come, another link to the use of the dance and music as spiritual.

In African American spirituality, prayer has been a stronghold of encouragement. Prayer collections reflect the history of the culture from its beginnings in Africa to the present time. (Schomburg Center for Research in Black Culture, 2003). Persons from other cultural or religious groups may observe African Americans in prayer and worship, but do not perceive the event in the same way as the African American worshipers. The origins of the prayers and music are related closely to the African American experience in a unique way. If the prayers have different meaning for the listeners, what is each hearing?

Hagedorn (2006) discusses the significance of drumming in African religious services. African slaves brought the forms of music from their homeland to the United States. Williams and Dixie (2003) assert that black people hear the lyrics and music of religious and spiritual songs differently from others because both the blues and the gospel were responses to the black experience and reflect not only the experiences of the people, but also the tone of their lives. While other cultural people might appreciate the rhythms and melodies of the music in African American churches, scholars of the black experience in America see the religious music as an inherent part of the culture, an outlet for emotions unexpressed in other channels and a method of expression of self and one's history. Lomax (1993) observed that the primary African ritual that came to the New World was the dance. He notes that the tradition of the symbolic dances that bring the gods to the services and honor them there "took many forms in the New World, including that of the present day Holy Rollers" (p. 71). In his attempts to record African American music through the Mississippi Delta in the 1940s, Lomax (1993) came to believe that the volume, emotion, dancing, and interactive communication between preacher and church participants was the expression of the people's existence. Listening would be a primary component of the communication in these settings.

Hawaiian chants, like those of many indigenous peoples, are used for protection or worship. The practitioners believe that spirits inhabit all aspects of nature. The ancient Hawaiian religions are closely bound with the land and with the sounds of nature. Clicking sticks, drums, and rattles accompany the dances and chants. Blowing on a conch shell is part of the beginning of ritualistic music. The rate, rhythm, and intensity of the drumming and accompaniment of any other instruments used tell the listener how to respond. Does listening to the drums and clicking sticks call for a different type of processing than listening to the chants?

Cultures whose spirituality is based in Shamanism practice ceremony, sacred dance, vision quest, and pilgrimages to places of power in nature. An example of a tribe that practices Shamanism is the Huichol Indians of central Mexico, who from their home near Ixtlan in the Sierra Madre Mountains practice Shamanism daily. In order to maintain their peaceful, agricultural life, they live in a continuous cycle of ritual and devotional exercises, all of which require various listening practices to songs and instruments.

How Does Listening to Sound and Music Relate to the Spiritual?

Music, both vocal and instrumental, is a universal in both religion and spirituality. Since music can be such an important aspect of worship, meditation, contemplation, education, and encouragement, an examination of how listening relates to music in these contexts is very appropriate. A review of books, journals, and interviews with qualified persons in music and religious contexts suggests that every religious and spiritual practice ranging from primitive to high church employs some kind of music, which raises the questions: Does listening to different styles of music and types of music call for differing types of listening skills? Is listening the primary communication employed during ritualistic use of sound and music in ritual and worship? Blacking (1995) points out that in societies where music is not written down, but rather is learned by repetition and hearing, informed and accurate listening is important and a matter of ensuring continuity of the musical tradition.

In a study of how sound may be used to focus the attention of worshippers in church buildings, Roth (2003) describes how church buildings have been constructed in such a way that the building reflects the focus of the attention of the congregation. Contemporary church buildings now employ "sound engineers" during construction to achieve a particular effect with the music. Many pages could be filled with comments on the responses to organs, pianos, and bands as part of the worship service. The question arises concerning the purpose of differing types of music: how much of the sound employed is for the entertainment of the attendee and how much is employing listening for the acts of worship, learning, and encouragement?

The sound of bells signals individual messages in Eastern religions, Catholic services, and Protestant calls to worship. Bells are present as "bell choirs" in Lutheran and Swedish churches. The ringing of the church bell, in American and European villages, can signal a gathering, a warning, or a wedding or funeral. The intensity of the sound, the frequency of the ringing, and the number of rings differ according to the message suggested by the sound of the bells. Thus, the listener is forced to attend and focus to interpret the meaning of the sound. Bells are also used in the Buddhist meditation steps to signal the approaching end of each meditation segment. Cordova (2006) describes the purpose of bells in Zen Buddhism as "mindfulness bells" used to call one's attention to the present moment.

Wong (2000) also describes the importance of music in Buddhism: "Buddhist music is traditional, religious chant and instrumental music performed in the context of a ritual…. the text of Buddha's teaching is intoned during the chant, (so) vocal music holds primary importance over instrumental music." The vocal music is not singing, but is reciting scriptures in a particular harmonic and rhythmic pattern, which can be accompanied by instruments. The sounds of instruments or bells affect the emotions and perceptions thereby altering the mind – an aspect of listening. Where chanting is incorporated into meditation, novice monks learn the music by hearing every day what is intoned by the monks in the religious service. The purposes served by the music include: teaching; attracting people to Buddhism; a reminder to come away from every activities and thoughts to a place reserved for the sacred; and as a framework by marking sections of the service.

In Jewish history, so significant was the trumpet as a means of communication that a Feast of Trumpets was celebrated (Numbers 29:1–6; Leviticus 16: 23:26–32 NIV, 1991), which later became *Rosh Hashanah*, the observance of the New Year (Plaut, 1981). Today the sound of the *Shofar* begins the observance of *Rosh Hashanah* and reminds the Jewish people of their history. In contemporary Judaism, music tradition and purpose differs from one ethnic division of Judaism to another. Eisenberg (2004) describes the variations in use of instruments and vocal music as part of the worship: Hassidism emphasizes wordless vocal melody; Ashkenzaic tradition recites in singsong fashion; while in Sephardic ritual the leader keeps up a steady chant while the congregation chants only in specific sections. The congregation certainly employs listening skills to varying degrees in following the service. Does each type of chant or melody call for a different type of listening?

According to Khan (2006), Sufism has a very different attitude from Islam about the role of music. "What is wonderful about music is that it helps us to concentrate or meditate independently of thought – and therefore music seems to be the bridge over the gulf between form and the formless "(p. 3). Kahn's comments suggest that in Sufism, music is of key importance. The "whirling dervishes" associated with Sufism are probably one of the best examples of listening to the sounds to the point of losing connection with the rest of the world around and concentrating on the spiritual. What kind of listening is going on during this type of ritual? Is the listening a conscious application of a set of behaviors with respect to the music? If so, how much listening must be conscious for the behavior to be considered listening? The sect of Judaism known as Kabbalah claims a close correlation between the spiritual practice and music. The Kabbalah writers (2006) claim that the receptors work within man because there is spiritual information in the musical sounds.

Finally, consider the role of music in the Christian tradition. *The Holy Bible* evidences that singing was certainly a part of early Christian practices. The early Christians sang when they gathered. The writers of the New Testament admonished Christians to "Speak to one another with psalms, hymns, and spiritual songs" (Ephesians 5:19). Diverse Christian groups have similar viewpoints about the meaning of music in the religion. Songs were and are meant to be heard: "Let the word of God dwell in you richly as you teach and admonish one another with all wisdom, and as you sing in psalms, hymns, and spiritual songs" (Colossians 3:16, 1985). Kleinig (2005) addresses the songs as not only to be heard by the worshippers, but also to be heard by God in communion with other spiritual voices. The Center for Church Music (2006) reminds readers that the purpose of singing is for instruction. Other Christian writers and musicians give numerous reasons to explain why worshipers listen to music: to hear what God says (by singing or hearing) scripture; for interpretation and understanding; for edification, for encouragement; for instructions; for entertainment; for appreciation. The Center asserts that songs sung by religious people "are about substance, that is, things that involve thinking" (p. 10598) and that the congregations should be fully involved in singing, listening, and learning." So this assumes that if we sing, we hear what we are singing and think about the meaning of what we sing before, during, and after we sing. How does "working at" music affect the way we listen? According to Choral director and Worship Leader Dr. Rodney Bell (July 12, 2006, pers. com.), Benjamin Britten suggested that we are "working for the chance to listen" by recognizing notes, hearing the sounds in your brain before sounding the note outwardly, and producing the sound. At least two of the components identified with the listening process are reflected in these ideas, those being hearing and understanding.

To what extent does the heritage of a particular church affect the musical listening ability or preferences? For example, Lutheran churches traditionally use highly classical music such as Bach, while Southern, fundamentalist churches incorporate gospel music. Does a change in the origins of the music change the listening behaviors? Musician and church Worship Leader Scott McDonald, (2006, pers. com.) says, "People connect with their memories through music. The way we listen is influenced by our experiences." How do events in our lives affect how we listen spiritually? Do we listen differently if we are in a painful time or joyful time in our lives outside the place of worship? For example, following the attack on the World Trade Center in New York in 2001, the attention of citizens in the United States focused sharply on spiritual matters. Was the listening to instrumental music or singing different at that time than if no threat had been directed at the country? If a person is in great joy, does the music have a different sound to the listener than if one is not particularly emotional?

How does a change in the characteristics of music affect listening behavior in worship settings? Contemporary church music is leaning more toward simple, short songs and melodies rather than employing complex four to eight part harmony. Many churches today are placing videos and simple music on large overhead screens, reflecting an American society that is more visually oriented than aurally trained and is unwilling to take the time and effort to deal with learning challenging music. Are the visual and the aural processes distinct from one another, and are churches sacrificing listening for visual stimulation or does the combination of visual and aural enhance the message?

How does the presentation ability of choirs or instrumental groups affect whether the listener grasps the meaning in a spiritual setting? While Bell (2006) stated that the quality of a presentation can affect the reception of the music in a spiritual sense, Davis 1996 puts responsibility for the spiritual significance of a musical experience on the listener as much as the performer: "Likewise in music, spiritual listening habits and responses are as important as well-rehearsed musical numbers. Good music must be received in the right way in order to be effective" (p. 1).

How does our purpose for being present to the music affect how we listen? If listening is just "faked attention" to pass the required ritual time, our listening will not be the same as if we are involved because we desire to be closer to God. If our motivation to listen is that we want God's favor, we may listen in church in a different way than we would listen in a different setting. Perhaps the extent of involvement in the message changes depending on the purpose of the listening. But do we have actual research to support the idea that in spiritual communication we use different listening skills for different purposes?

How do the characteristics of the audience including age, gender, socio-economic level, and education affect how they listen to music? A survey of teenagers by Resch (1996) characterized church music in today's contemporary setting: choral, not instrumental; sung by a group of singers rather than by a soloist; characterized by simple musical texture and understandable text. In order of most to least important functions of church music, they believe that church music is an expression of religious belief, part of the presentation of God's word, a way for people to use their talents to serve God, a way to establish or change people's moods, and a performance that entertains. The teens responding to the survey did not bring into the church service their own personal preferences in rock or pop music. There is much potential here to investigate how the music, both vocal and instrumental, that church groups employ influences attendance.

Summary

Religion is recognized throughout sociology and anthropology as one of the major institutions of a society. Spirituality permeates the lives of diverse people. It is obvious from the writing being published that listening as a communication construct is recognized among spiritual and religious people. However, the meaning of listening and how it is to be applied in the context still needs much investigation.

QUESTIONS FOR DISCUSSION

1 Why is the definition of listening problematic in the contexts of religion and spirituality?
2 How important is it to distinguish between religion and spirituality when considering the role of listening?
3 What evidence is there that research in listening, as related to the contexts, is lacking?
4 What is the relationship between listening and intrapersonal communication?
5 How do the following groups perceive listening as a construct: Roman Catholic; Judaism; Islam; Protestantism; African Americans; Native Americans; Sufi; Tao; Buddhist; New Age; Hindu?
6 What problem is inherent in using the terms "listen" or "hear" if the written word is the source of the message?
7 What is the relationship between prayer and listening?
8 What role does listening play in pastoral care?
9 How does listening function in ecumenical dialogue?
10 How does the construction or location of a place of worship or assembly affect the type of listening that takes place in that setting?
11 Is dancing a form of listening? Why or why not?
12 What factors in a religious/spiritual setting might serve as barriers to listening?
13 What unanswered questions about listening in religious and spiritual contexts need to be investigated?

References

Ackerman, J.W. (2001). *Listening to God: Spiritual formation in congregations.* Bethesda, MD: The Alban Institute.

Armstrong, K.B., Timm, S.A., and Schroeder, B.L. (2000, March). *Listening as a mechanism for spiritual understand*. Symposium at the meeting of the International Listening Association, Virginia Beach, VA.

Barrigar, C.J. (1995). Linguistic theory and ecumenical convergence. *Journal of Ecumenical Studies*, 32, 1, 1–12.

Barry, W.A., and Connolly, W. J. (1982). *The practice of spiritual direction*. New York: Seabury.

Baxter, B.B. (1980). *Family of God: A study of the New Testament church*. Nashville: Gospel Advocate.

Bentley, S.B., and Bacon, S. (1996, Spring). The all new, state of the art ILA definition of listening: now that we have it, what shall we do with it? *Listening Post*, 5, 1.

Berling, J.A. (1993). Is conversation about religion possible? *Journal of the American Academy of Religion*. LXI, 2, 1–22.

Blacking, J. (1995). *How musical is man?* Seattle: University of Washington Press.

Bnei Baruch The World Center for Kabbalah Studies (2006). *The wisdom of Kabbalah: Music of Kabbalah*. Retrieved on July 9, 2006 from: http://www.kabbalah.info/music

Bons-Storm, R. (1996). *The incredible woman: listening to woman's silences in pastoral care and counseling*. Nashville, TN: Abingdon Press.

Brayerton, D. (2006). *Listening for God through 1 and 2 Timothy and Titus*. Kansas City, MO: Beacon Hill Press.

Brodeur. P. (1997). Description of the guidelines for Inter-faith celebrations. *Journal of Ecumenical Studies*, 34, 4, 551–72.

Brodeur, P. (2005). From the margins to the centers of power: the increasing relevance of the global interfaith movement. *Cross Currents*, 55, 1, 1.

Brueggemann, W. (2000). *Texts that linger, words that explode: Listening to prophetic voices*. Minneapolis, MN: Fortress Press.

Brown, M. (2005). *The presence process: A healing journey toward present moment awareness*. Vancouver: Namaste Publishing.

Brownell, J. (2002). *Listening attitudes, principles, and skills*. Boston, MA: Allyn and Bacon

Burnham, S. (1990). *A book of angels: Reflections on angels past and present and true stories of how they touch our lives*. New York: Ballentine.

Burton, V. (2004). *Listen to your life: following your unique path to extraordinary success*. Colorado Springs, CO: Waterbrook Press.

Calhoun, A.A. (2005). *Spiritual disciplines handbook: practices that transform us*. Downers Grove, IL: Intervarsity Press.

Carlson, P.J., and Hawkins, P.S. (2003). *Listening for God: Contemporary literature and the life of faith*. Minneapolis, MN: Augsburg Fortress.

Carpenter, D. (1992). Language, ritual, and society: reflections on the authority of the VEDA in India. *Journal of the American Academy of Religion*, LX, 1, 57–77.

Center for Church Music (2006). *Songs of pilgrimage*. Grand Haven, MI: Center for Church Music.

Chetwynde, T. (2005). *Zen and the kingdom of heaven: reflections on the tradition of meditation in Christianity and Zen Buddhism*. Boston, MA: Wisdom Publications.

Childs, B.S. (2005). Speech-act theory and Biblical interpretations. *Scottish Journal of Theology*, 58, 4, 375–92.

Colossians 3:16. (1985). *The NIV Study Bible New International Version*. Grand Rapids, MI: Zondervan.

Concise Oxford American Dictionary. (2006). New York: Oxford University Press, Inc., p. 753.

Connor, G. (Ed.). (1992). *Listening to your life: Daily meditations with Frederick Beuchner*. San Francisco, CA: Harper.

Cordova, N. (2006, April,). *Wise speech and deep listening in mindfulness practice.* Paper presented to the annual meeting of the International Listening Association, Salem, OR.

Corley Schnapp, D. (2008). Listening in context: Religion and spirituality. *The International Journal of Listening*, 22, 2, 133–40.

Corley Schnapp, D. (2003, July). *Listening in pastoral care*. Paper presented to the meeting of the International Listening Association, Haninge, Sweden.

Dalferth, I.U. (1992). God and the mystery of words. *Journal of the American Academy of Religion*, LX, 1, 79–104.

Daniel, A., Wyllie, T., and Ramer, A. (1992) *Ask your angels*. New York: Wellspring/Ballatine.

Davis, P. (March/April 1996). The lost art of listening: scriptural thoughts on church music. *Frontline*, 6, 2.

Eilberg-Schwartz, H. (1988). A Rabbinic theory of language? *Journal of the American Academy of Religion*, LVI, 4, 763.

Eisenberg, R.L. (2004). *The JPS Guide to Jewish Tradition*. Philadelphia: The Jewish Publication Society.

Ephesians 5:19, (1985). *The NIV Study Bible New International Version*. Grand Rapids, MI: Zondervan.

Erling, B. (1984). Language, games and context of meaning: Wittgenstein and Anders Nygren. *Journal of the American Academy of Religion*, 52, 4, 691–708.

Eskenazi, T.C. (2003).. Listening to our mothers: Women of Reform Judaism: women's commentary to Torah. *The Chronicle Hebrew Union College Jewish Institute of religion*, 62, 13.

Fadiman, J., and Frager, R. (1997). *Essential Sufism*. San Francisco, CA: HarperSanFrancisco.

Fakhry, M. (Trans.) (2004). An interpretation of the *Quar'an*. English translation from the meanings: A bilingual edition. New York: NYU Press.

Fischetto, A.J. (2000). *Transformed: intimacy with God: Learn how to be still and know God personally, passionately, and powerfully.* Shellington, PA: Alpha Omega Counseling Center.

Friedman, M. (1983). The human way: A dialogical approach to religion and human experience. *Journal of the American Academy of Religion, 52*, 3, 67–77.

Gak, D. (1997). *Going beyond Buddha: The awakening practice of listening.* Boston, MA: Charles E. Tuttle.

Gallagher, J., Paulin, K. and Grant, F. (2002, March). *Listening and laughter are good for the body and soul.* Symposium conducted at meeting of the International Listening Association. Virginia Beach, VA.

Gering W.M. (1996, March). *Listening to a sermon.* Presentation at the meeting of the International Listening Association. Sacramento, CA.

Glenn, E.C. (1989). A content analysis of fifty definitions of listening. *Journal of the International Listening Association, 3*, 21-31.

Glenn, E.C. (1999, March). *Listening in worship services: A curriculum for increasing effectiveness.* Paper presented to the meeting of the International Listening Association, Albuquerque, NM.

Hagedorn, K.J. (2006). Toward a theology of sound: drum talk, *oricha* worship, and other ecstatic phenomena. *Harvard Divinity Bulletin, 34*, 2. Retrieved on June 20, 2006 from: http://www.hds.harvard.edu/news/bulletin_mag/articles/34-2_hagedorn.html

Hanh, T.N. (2001). *Anger: Wisdom for cooling the flames.* New York: The Berkeley Publishing Company.

Harra, C. (2005). *Everyday karma.* New York: Ballentine Books.

Hart, T.N. (1980). *The art of Christian listening.* New York: Paulist Press.

Hartford Seminary Library (2008). *Religion articles from journals and periodicals.* Retrieved on July 20, 2006 from: http://www.library.hartsem.edu/religionarticles.htm

Harvey P. (1961). Hearing things: Religion, illusion, and the American Enlightenment (review). *Spiritus: A Journal of Christian Spirituality, 2*, 2, 252–4.

Hedahl, S.K. (2001). *Listening ministry: Rethinking pastoral leadership.* Minneapolis, MN: Fortress Press.

Heer, K. (2006). *Listening to God through Ephesians.* Kansas City, MO: Beacon Hill Press.

Hexham, I. (1999). Contemporary paganism: Listening people, speaking earth. *The Canadian Review of Sociology and Anthropology, 36.* Retrieved on May 15, 2006 from: http://questia.com

Hoffman, G.K. (1997). *Listening to obtain peace and reconciliation by understanding both sides of international and intercultural conflicts.* Santa Barbara, CA: University of Santa Barbara, Project Crossroads.

Holmes, S.R. (2002). *Listening to the past: The place of tradition in theology*. Boston, MA: Pater Noster Press.

Honze, M. (2004). *Listening for God*. Wheaton, IL: Tynsdale.

Howden, W.D. (1989). Good sermon, Preacher: the effects of age, sex, and education on hearer responses to preaching. *Review of Religious Research*, 31, 2, 196.

International Listening Association. *Index to Convention Papers Resource Center* (1980–2005). Retrieved on August 25, 2008 from: http://www.listen.org/Templates/resourcecenter.htm

International Listening Association. *Index to the International Journal of Listening/ Journal of the International Listening Association*. (1987–2006). Retrieved on August 28, 2008 from: http://www.cios.org/www.ijlmain/htm

Irvin, C.E. (1952). An analysis of certain aspects of a listening training program conducted among college freshmen at Michigan State College. Doctoral Dissertation. Michigan State University. *Dissertation Abstracts International*, 19, 4039-A.

Janusik, L.A. (2002). Teaching listening: What do we do? What should we do? *International Journal of Listening*, 16, 5–39.

Janusik, L.A. (2007 Fall/Winter). "Fall listening forum update." *Listening Post*, 94, 8.

Johnson, R.W. (1994). *How will they hear if we don't listen?* Nashville, TN: Broadman and Holman.

Jones, M.S. (1999). Evangelical Christianity and the philosophy of interreligious dialogue. *Journal of Ecumenical Studies*, 36, 378–96.

Kahn, H.I. (2006). *The Sufi message of Hazrat Inayat Khan, Vol.II*. Geneva, Switzerland; Wassenaar Publications.

Kaplan, A. (1995). *Jewish meditation: A practical guide*. New York: Pantheon Books.

Kasper, W. (2000). The nature and purpose of ecumenical dialogue. *The Ecumenical Review*, 52, Retrieved on June 22, 2006 from: http://www.find-articles.com/p/articles/m1-m2065/is_3_52

Kass, J.S., and Kass, L. (2000). *Manual/Resources for resilience: Building a resilient world through spirituality*. Cambridge, MA: Behavioral Health, Education Initiative, Greenhouse, Inc.

Kearley, M.A. (2002). *Mindfulness beach walk as meditation*. A presentation to the meeting of the International Listening Association. Virginia Beach, VA.

Keating, T. (2006). *Open mind open heart*. New York: Continuum.

Kleinig, J.W. (2005, July 26). *Worship and the way of holiness*. Plenary address for the Communion on Worship of the Lutheran Church-Missouri Synod. Kenosha, WI.

Kollar, N., and Landes, J. (2008, March). *Listening to religious talk, spiritual reflections, and theological discussions*. Paper presented to the annual meeting of the International Listening Association, Portland, ME.

Krishnamurti, J. (1999). *This light in oneself: True meditation*. Boston: Shambhala.

Ladd, K.L., and Spilka, B. (2002). Inward, outward, upward: cognitive aspects of prayer. *Journal for the Scientific Study of Religion*, 41, 3, 475-484.

Lawrence, Brother (1982). *The practice of the presence of God*. New Kensington, PA: Whitaker House.

Lesnick, L.A. (1998). *Listening for God, religion, and moral discernment*. New York: University Press.

Lindahl, K. (2002). *The sacred art of listening*. Woodstock, VT: Skylight Paths Publishing.

Lindahl, K. (2003). *Practicing the sacred art of listening*. Woodstock, VT: Skylight Paths Publishing.

Lindahl, K. (2005). *How does God listen?* Woodstock, VT: Skylight Paths Publishing

Lomax. A. (1993). *The land where the blues began*. New York: The New York Press.

Lonsdale, D. (1992). *Listening to the music of the spirit: The art of discernment*. London: Longman and Todd, Ltd.

Lyons, G. (2006). *Listening to God through Revelation*. Kansas City: Beacon Hill.

Matthews, G. (2004, March). *Thomas Merton and a contemplative foundation for the practice of communication*. Paper presented at the annual meeting of the International Listening Association. Ft. Meyers, FL.

McClure, J.S. (2004). *Homiletical case studies*. St. Louis, MO: Chalice Press.

Meigs, A. (1995). Ritual language in everyday life: the Christian right. *Journal of the American Academy of Religion*, LXIII, 1, 85–104.

Meyer, J. (2003). *How to hear from God: Learn to know his voice and make the right decisions*. New York: Time Warner Faith.

Mitchell, S. (2000). *Tao Te Ching: A new English version with forward and notes*. New York: Perennial Press.

Moretz, J. (2005). *Listening to God through Mark*. Indianapolis, IN: Wesleyan Publishing Company.

National Communication Association. *Spiritual studies*. Retrieved on August 30, 2008 from: http://www.natcom.org/nca/Template2.asp?bid=5067

Newell, J.P. (1997). *Listening for the heartbeat of God: A Celtic spirituality*. London: SPCK, Holy Trinity Church.

NIV (1991). *The NIV Study Bible New International Version*. Grand Rapids, MI: Zondervan.

Nixon, B. (2000). *Have faith in listening*. Presentation to the meeting of the International Listening Association. Virginia Beach, VA.

Palmer, P.J. (1999). *Let your life speak: Listening for the voice of vocation*. San Francisco, CA: Jossey-Bass.

Paulin, K. (1993, March). *Listening to God: Making contact with our own spirituality*. Presentation to the meeting of the International Listening Association, Boston, MA.

Paulin, K. (1996, March). *Angels and listening: Co-creating celestial foundations.* Presentation to the meeting of the International Listening Association, Sonoma, CA.

Paulin, K. (2005, April). *Listening to God for empowerment.* Presentation to the meeting of the International Listening Association. Minneapolis, MN.

Pembroke, N. (2002). *The art of listening dialogues, shame, and pastoral care.* London: T&T Clark/Handsel Press.

Piver, S. (2002). Joyful mind: A practical guide to Buddhist meditation. China (Distributed by St. Martin Press): Rodale.

Plaut, W.G. (Ed.). (1981). *The Torah: A modern commentary.* New York: Union of American Hebrew Congregations.

Polter, D.S. (Ed.). (1997). *Listening to life's messages: Adapted from the works of The Lulavitcher Rebbe.* Brooklyn, NY: SIE.

Purdy, M. (1991). Intrapersonal and Interpersonal Listening. In Borisoff, D. and Purdy, M. (Eds.). *Listening in Everyday Life,* pp. 21–58. Lanham: University Press of America.

Questia. (2006). *List of religious journals.* Retrieved on May 10, 2006 from: http://www.questia.com

Redmond, B. (1992, March). *As the spirit soars, so does the heart.* Symposium presented to the meeting of the International Listening Association.

Religious Research Association. *Review of religious research* Retrieved on June 12, 2006 from: http://rra.hartsem.edu

Resch, B. (1996). *Adolescents' attitudes toward the appropriateness of religious music.* Unpublished dissertation. Indiana University. UMI 9704828.

Roberts, C, Edwards, R. and Barker, L. (1987). *Intrapersonal communication processes.* Scottsdale, AZ: Gorshuk Scarisbrick.

Roman, S. (1986). *Personal power through awareness.* Tiburton, CA: H.J. Kramer, Inc.

Roth, R.C. (2003). *How early American sounded.* Ithaca, NY: Cornell University Press.

Samovar, L.A. and Porter, R.E. (1995). *Communication between cultures.* Belmont CA: Wadsworth.

Sanford, A.W. (2002). Painting words, testing sound: visions of the Krishna in Paramanhd's sixteenth century devotional poetry. *Journal of the American Academy of Religion,* 70, 1, 55–81.

Savage, J. (1996). *Listening and caring skills in ministry.* Nashville, TN: Abingdon Press.

Schmidt, L.E. (2002). *Hearing things, religion, illusion, and the American Enlightenment.* Cambridge, MA: Harvard University Press.

Schneiders, S. M. (2003). Religion vs. spirituality: A contemporary conundrum. *Journal of Christian Spirituality,* 3, 2, 163–85.

Schomburg Center for Research in Black Culture. (2003). *Standing in the need of prayer.* New York: Schomburg Center for Research in Black Culture.

Schultz, G., and Ahrens, J. (1996). *Befriender training*. Milwaukee, WI: Ministry Development Partners.

Shafir, R.Z. (2000). *The Zen of listening: Mindful communication in the age of distractions*. Wheaton, IL: Quest Books.

Shafir, R.Z. (2001, March). *Mindfulness and the movie*. Presentation to the International Listening Association. Chicago.

Shinn, L.D. (1992). Words, symbols, experiences, and the naming of the Devine. *Journal of Ecumenical Studies*, XXIX, 3-4, 418–31.

Slater, J.P. (2004). *Mindful Jewish living: Compassionate practice*. New York: Arviv Press.

Spearritt, D. (1962). *Listening comprehension – A factorial analysis*. Melbourne, Australia: G.W. Green and Sons.

Stanley, C. (1995). *Thoughts on listening to God*. Nashville, TN: Thomas Nelson.

Tenzen, G. (Dalai Lama). (2005). *The Universe in a single atom: The convergence of science and spirituality*. New York: Morgan Road Books.

The Holy Bible (n.d.) The authorized King James Version. Cleveland and New York: The World Publishing Company.

Thiselton, A.C. (1980). *The two horizons: New Testament hermeneutics and philosophical description with special reference to Heidigger, Bultman, Gadamer, and Wittgenstein*. Grand RapidsMI: William B. Eerdmans Publishing Company.

Thompson, K. (2003, July). *Touching the world one person at a time*. Presentation to the meeting of the International Listening Association. Heninge, Sweden.

Thompson, K., Leintz, P., Nevers, B., and Witkowski, B. (2005, April). *Teaching and assessing listening across the curriculum*. Paper presented to the International Listening Association. Minneapolis, MN.

Waltner, E. (1991, March). *An analysis of Koine' Greek: Emphasis on hearing and listening*. Presentation to the meeting of the International Listening Association. Jacksonville, FL.

Warland, S.G, and Fadden, S. (1990, March). *You are what you hear: Cultural myths, stories, and ontology*. A seminar presented to the meeting of the International Listening Association, Indianapolis, IN.

Watson, K.W. (1999). *Listening miracles: What would Jesus do?* Paper presented to the meeting of the International Listening Association, Albuquerque, NM.

Willard, D. (1999). *Hearing God: Developing a conversational relationship with God*. Downers Grove, IL: Intervarsity.

Williams, J., and Dixie, Q. (2003). *This far by faith*. New York: Amistad Harper Collins.

Wolvin, A.D., and Coakley, C.G. (1996). *Listening*, 5th edn. Boston, MA: McGraw-Hill.

Wong, B. (2000). *A survey of Buddist music*. Retrieved on July 19, 2006 from: http://sophia.smith.edu/`jhubbard/budmusic.htm

WORDsearch 7.0, (2005). Available at: www.wordsearchbible.com

Wong, E. (1997). *The Shambhala guide to Toaism*. Boston, MA: Shambhala.

Wright, D.S. (1993). The discourse of awakening: rhetorical practice in classical Ch'an Buddhism. *Journal of the American Academy of Religion*, LXI, 1, 23–40.

Yahoo Directory. *Religious journals*. Retrieved on August 28, 2008 from: http://www.dir.yahoo.com/Society_and_Culture/Religion_and_Spirituality/Faith_and_Practices

12

The Integrative Listening Model: An Approach to Teaching and Learning Listening

Kathleen Thompson, Pamela Leintz, Barbara Nevers and Susan Witkowski

This chapter presents an integrative listening model designed by a collaborative team of educators at Alverno College. The authors introduce a unique and practical framework for listening across the curriculum. They explain the components of the Integrative Listening Model (ILM), illustrate the stages in the listening process itself, and provide samples of how listening can be incorporated into classroom activities, assignments and assessments in various disciplines. In a systematic and comprehensive way, the ILM framework presents concrete strategies for developing one's own listening ability. It also stresses contextual and personal filters that impact listening behaviors, as well as self assessment and goal-setting, to promote ongoing listening development.

The ILM reflects the authors' beliefs that listening is far more than just hearing and that genuinely *effective* listening requires commitment, understanding, and practice. It addresses psychological, emotional and cognitive factors that influence human communication and offers a promise of life-long benefits.

> Educated people know how to pay attention – to others and to the world around them. They work hard to hear what other people say. They can follow an argument, trace logical reasoning, detect illogic, hear the emotions that lie behind both the logic and the illogic, and ultimately empathize with the person who is feeling those emotions. (Cronon, 1998–9)

The listening qualities mentioned by Professor Cronon do indeed represent significant communication objectives for educated adults. How well do we listen? And how do educated adults learn to listen effectively? Communication scholars remind us that students spend more time listening as a way to learn than they do using any of the other communication abilities (Barker, Edwards, Gaines, Gladney, and Holley, 1980; Davis, 2001), yet few of them have opportunities at the undergraduate level to develop their listening as a fundamental ability for learning. Most students do not receive comprehensive instruction in listening because few colleges and universities require such courses; and communication courses that do include units on listening generally focus on skill development, and at that, only briefly (Janusik and Wolvin, 1999). So there seems to be a discrepancy. Listening scholars agree that listening is a separate and distinct communication ability, but there are few listening courses available to assist students to become more effective listeners.

At Alverno College, however, listening has been part of communication coursework since 1973 when the institution introduced its ability-based curriculum. At that time, all students registered for a series of listening labs that emphasized analytical listening, the type of listening traditionally expected of students when they were in lecture settings or when they needed to analyze oral presentations. In retrospect, we now realize that we were preparing students for and giving them practice in listening to formal, usually well-prepared podium speeches, and, by default, not acknowledging and working with other types of listening interactions that people have every day in their professional, social, and interpersonal lives. So even though we were doing something on a sustained basis to teach listening, our scope was somewhat narrow, perhaps because there had been no agreement among communication scholars on a single definition of listening (Glenn, 1989) or on an effective approach to teaching it.

However, in 1994, a group of scholars in the International Listening Association (ILA) did reach consensus on a definition of listening: "Listening is the process of receiving, constructing meaning from, and responding to spoken and/or nonverbal messages" (Emmert, 1994, p. 6). Simple yet comprehensive, that milestone definition clearly acknowledged cognitive and behavioral dimensions of listening.

Early in 2002, using the ILA definition as a working platform, a group of four faculty and academic staff representing various areas within the college formed a listening task force and began looking at listening instruction to make it more comprehensive, developmental, discipline-specific, and, like all learning, a lifelong ability. In other words, our goal was to fully integrate listening into our curriculum, giving it a status as prominent as reading, writing, and speaking. Moreover, we realized that our students and graduates will face significant challenges posed by the globalization of economies, by personal and professional interactions, and by sweeping technological advances. As Bentley proclaims, "[N]ew technology has changed whom we are listening to, what we are listening for, when … and how we listen" (1999, p. 3). She further states:

> [B]ecause of our new listening environments, our use of … context to determine meaning may be changing. Also because we cannot give feedback, ask questions, or paraphrase in an asynchronous conversation, the behaviors we use to indicate listening may also be changing. Add to this the complications of listening to knowledge, which is often abstract, and the fact that we are listening to people from a variety of cultures, and the stage may be set for more changes in our listening behaviors. These changes are far reaching, and have significant implications for how we will study and teach listening skills in the future. (Bentley, 2000, p. 130)

Addressing the foregoing implications, we developed a comprehensive definition of effective listening and used it as a basis to construct a unique framework for teaching and learning listening across the curriculum. That framework, the Integrative Listening Model (ILM), reflects our belief that building listening competence requires a systematic, developmental approach; opportunities for listening practice in varied contexts and for different purposes; multiple opportunities for self assessment and feedback; and goal setting.

The Integrative Listening Model (ILM)

The Integrative Listening Model is based on our definition of effective listening:

the dynamic, interactive process of integrating appropriate listening attitudes, knowledge, and behaviors to achieve the selected goal(s) of a listening event.

A framework specifically designed to assist individuals in developing their listening abilities systematically and developmentally, the ILM (see Figure 12.1) includes four stages: prepare to listen; apply the listening process model; assess listening effectiveness; and establish goals for future listening events. Each stage addresses the attitudes, knowledge and behaviors appropriate to successful completion of that stage. Although the ILM appears to be cyclical in nature, it is helpful to think of it as interrelated, discrete components, each uniquely important to the listening process,

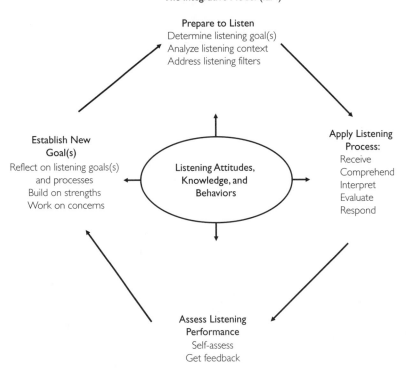

Figure 12.1 The Integrative Listening Model

yet individually accessible to the learner for instructional purposes. Initially, students develop proficiency with the entire process by focusing on those discrete components; eventually, with practice, they can access any one or any combination of its components as they internalize the ILM.

Hence, to achieve listening proficiency, a student moves through four developmental levels (see Figure 12.2). Each level requires

	Level 1 Self-assesses strengths and weaknesses, identifying the attitudes, knowledge, and behaviors that helped or hindered her listening process	Level 2 Shows understanding of listening as a dynamic, mindful process and identifies strategies to increase listening effectiveness	Level 3 Applies the Integrative Listening Model and uses listening strategies appropriate to specific academic settings	Level 4 Applies effective listening attitudes, knowledge, and behaviors consistently in personal, academic, and professional settings
PREPARES TO LISTEN	Listens to a given stimulus as directed	Addresses the physical, mental, and emotional factors that influence the listening process	Determines goal(s), analyzes context, and addresses listening filters	Considers carefully listening goals, context, and filters and anticipates adjustments that may be required by a situation
APPLIES THE LISTENING PROCESS	Receives, comprehends, and responds appropriately to at least some part of a message	Receives, comprehends, interprets, and responds appropriately to the essence of messages	Receives, comprehends, interprets, evaluates, and responds to both verbal and nonverbal components of messages	Adapts the integrative listening process, as necessary, to attend to multiple layers of a message
ASSESSES EFFECTIVENESS OF LISTENING PERFORMANCE	Identifies some strengths and weaknesses regarding attitudes, knowledge, and behavior in a listening performance	Identifies and analyzes strengths and weaknesses regarding attitudes, knowledge, and behaviors in listening performances	Analyzes and judges specific strengths and weaknesses regarding attitudes, knowledge, and behaviors in academic listening	Shows refined analysis and judgment of own listening ability as an integral aspect of life long learning
ESTABLISHES NEW GOALS	Determines area(s) to develop based on a discrete listening performance	Reflects on self-assessment to determine patterns in listening performances and sets goals for ongoing development	Reflects on self-assessment to refine listening performances in academic disciplines	Reflects on self-assessment to continue growth as a listener in all settings

Figure 12.2 Listening criteria matrix

increasingly more complex understanding of the listening process and factors that influence listening, more skillful application of the listening process in varied contexts, and more sophisticated assessment of listening performances.

Stages of the Integrative Listening Model

Listening involves more than the physical process of hearing and observing the verbal and nonverbal communication of self and others. It requires the listener to adopt appropriate attitudes and behaviors, as well as to consciously bring prior and developing knowledge to a listening event.

Stage 1: Prepare to listen

Listening preparation is key to achieving the desired outcomes of any communication event. By determining the listening goal(s) beforehand (whenever possible), analyzing the listening context, and addressing the influence of various listening filters, a student can effectively participate in the listening encounter itself with thoughtfulness and self-assurance.

Determine listening goal(s) Listening goals involve people, settings, and tasks/purposes. Because goals are varied and incorporate both verbal and non-verbal components, an effective listener must determine if the immediate goal is solely or a combination of, for example:

- *Discriminative*: recognizing stimuli and their nuances (for example, a knock at the door, a sigh, a raised eyebrow in the course of conversation, an instructor's vocal emphasis);
- *Comprehensive*: understanding/analyzing/making meaning (for example, getting directions, receiving answers to questions, participating in a task-driven social interaction event, connecting new information with prior knowledge);
- *Evaluative*: judging the merits of a message (for example, responding to a TV commercial, seeking a second opinion for a medical problem, deciding which candidate to vote for, re-thinking a previously held stance);
- *Appreciative*: responding aesthetically to sounds and sights (for example, enjoying a symphony, a poetry reading, nighttime sounds around a campfire, the laughter of children);

- *Empathic/therapeutic*: perceiving and responding non-judgmentally to the emotional needs of others (for example, consoling a friend who has suffered a loss, understanding the subtext in a teenager's angst, sharing the joy of a recently promoted colleague);
- *Interpersonal*: interacting with another to develop, sustain, or enrich a relationship (for example, chatting over coffee, exchanging views on a best-selling book, getting to know a new neighbor, working with a peer on a class project).

Analyze listening context   Context might be described as the circumstances and elements surrounding a listening event. Without an understanding of that context, the listener cannot effectively comprehend and respond to the message. In order to appropriately analyze the context, she must determine answers to the questions Who? What? Why? and For whom?
That is:

- *Who* is presenting the message? (for example, an office manager? a friend? a historian? a candidate for office?);
- *What* is the occasion for delivery of the message? (for example, a goal-setting session? a concert? a community town meeting? a classroom presentation of a discipline framework?);
- *Why* is this presentation being made? (for example, to push a political agenda? to stimulate fresh thinking on a stubborn problem? to reach a business goal? to share a personal concern?);
- *For whom* is the message being presented? (for example, a class? an activist group? angry citizens? a frightened child?).

Address the influence of listening filters   Listening filters are internal and external factors that influence all aspects of the listening situation. They either positively or negatively affect the listening process; thus, it is imperative that the effective listener take inventory of them and, before the listening event begins, find ways to address them. Some of the many listening filters are:

- *Culture*: Ethnic background, religious belief, dominant first language may affect the processing of information.
- *Listening style*: Some listeners focus on "the bottom line"; others savor every detail; still others concentrate on the speaker-listener relationship.

- *Age*: Length of attention span, hearing acuity, and entrenched stances are frequently age-related.
- *Brain dominance*: Creative individuals may perceive and process messages differently than analytical individuals.
- *Physical condition*: A listener who is not feeling well, who is hungry or tired, or whose adrenalin is running high may have trouble concentrating on a message.
- *Atmosphere*: A room's temperature, acoustics, and sight lines can affect listening, as can a balmy breeze beckoning through an open window.
- *Psychological states*: A listener who is reluctant, stressed, over-tired, or preoccupied may face significant listening barriers, as may one who is looking forward to a weekend event or is excited about having landed a coveted new job.
- *Attitudes and assumptions*: Preconceived ideas about the speaker, the message, or the event may influence listening.
- *Prior knowledge*: As one takes in new or conflicting information, prior knowledge can have a positive or negative influence on message reception.
- *Time*: A listener who feels rushed might have trouble giving attention to a message or lack the necessary motivation to sustain focus.

The effective listener will recognize, analyze, and address the influences of various listening filters in advance of or as they occur during the listening event. While some adaptive strategies may depend very much on the listener's awareness of her own capabilities, other strategies might be as simple and practical as sitting in the front of the room, taking brief notes, maintaining eye contact, enthusiastically determining to benefit from the listening experience, or overtly trying to empathize with the speaker's perspective and stance.

Stage 2: Apply the listening process model

The Integrative Listening Process Model is designed to show the components of the listening process itself (see Figure 12.3). The five distinct components – *receive, comprehend, interpret, evaluate,* and *respond* – work together to some degree in every listening encounter, although emphasis at any given moment may be primarily on one or two of the components, depending on the listening context and purpose. For example, in

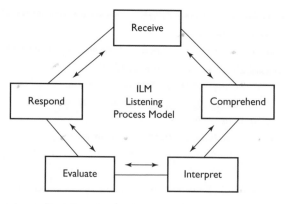

Figure 12.3   ILM Listening Process Model

a classroom situation, listeners must rely heavily on the ability to comprehend information well in order to learn new ideas and compare and contrast them with their previously held knowledge and opinions. In a political debate, listeners also must carefully interpret and evaluate what they hear to determine the credibility of the speaker and the logic and value of the message. In conversations with friends, however, listeners may be called upon to suspend judgment altogether in order to provide an empathic ear (see Table 12.1).

Stage 3: Assess effectiveness of listening performance

Key to ongoing development of effective listening is the listener's ability to reflect on her performance to determine what she is doing and whether or not her behaviors are effective. During and after the listening event, she needs to self assess. Others, such as instructors or peers, will also assess her performance and provide feedback.

As she self assesses *during* the event, the listener recognizes the special circumstances of the context, as well as her own attitudes and behaviors (both identified in Stage 1). She adjusts accordingly. For instance, if the student recognizes that she is losing concentration during a class presentation, she can adjust her posture and start taking notes. If she has a negative attitude toward the topic or the speaker, she can make a conscious effort to temporarily set aside her bias in order to concentrate on fully absorbing the message. If she recognizes that the message challenges her previous understanding of the topic, she can commit herself

Table 12.1 Listening process components

Process Components	Description	Listening Behaviors
Receive	Consciously attend to, collect, and accurately distinguish verbal and nonverbal components of messages, using all the senses	• Decide to listen with focused concentration • Optimize existing physical conditions for hearing • Minimize or eliminate potential psychological and intellectual listening barriers • Perceive and identify all verbal and nonverbal data • Address technology appropriately as a mediating/influencing factor
Comprehend	Decode and understand verbal and nonverbal components of messages	• Listen to understand rather than to evaluate or to respond • Recognize patterns; label and organize information into schema • Understand vocabulary and infer meanings of unfamiliar words using context clues • Compare and contrast new information with prior knowledge • Take notes • Ask clarifying questions, when appropriate, to check for meaning • Paraphrase, summarize, synthesize either silently or verbally
Interpret	Construct meaning about and draw inferences from messages within a specific context	• Be willing to suspend personal bias temporarily • Consider context of communication (who, what, why, and for whom) • Factor in goals of communicator(s) • Recognize uniqueness of own listening style
Evaluate	Make informed judgments about relative merit of messages	• Identify preconceived notions about sender and message • Judge credibility of sender • Analyze logic of message • Evaluate quality of content • Re-evaluate prior knowledge in light of new information
Respond	React appropriately to message/sender	• Consider options for responding (mode, timeliness, style, etc.) • Show empathy and respect • Choose appropriate verbal and nonverbal responses • Check to assure accurate perception of response • Integrate or reject new information

Note: Listeners rely on the cognitive skill of memory to store and recall information at every phase of the process. Although memory is not included as a separate component in this listening process model, learning some techniques to increase short- and long-term memory is strongly recommended as part of the approach for developing effective listening.

to listening for points of similarity and possible compromise. When she self assesses *after* the event, the listener reviews her own response in relation to explicitly stated criteria (see Figure 12.2).

Stage 4: Establish new goal(s)

Once they are learned, some activities like bike riding are never forgotten. But listening is different. Because it is dynamic and complex, it requires ongoing development. Using peer and instructor feedback and her own self assessment, the student establishes new goals to keep growing as a listener and to refine her listening process.

Reflect on listening goal(s)

- Conscientiously consider how well one has achieved the goal(s) of specific listening performances.
- Use feedback from others and self assessment to set, modify, or reevaluate goal(s) when planning for future performances.

Build on strengths

- Identify the specific attitudes, knowledge, and behaviors to maintain because, during this experience, they were conducive to an effective listening performance.
- Strive to activate the attitudes, knowledge, and behaviors that will result in more effective listening performances.

Work on concerns

- Identify those aspects within one's repertoire of attitudes, knowledge, and behaviors that did not serve one well in a particular listening performance.
- Strive to conscientiously minimize or avoid in the future those aspects that could reduce the overall effectiveness of the listening process.

The Integrative Listening Model in Practice

Even before they begin their first semester of classes, Alverno students are introduced to listening as an ability they will learn about and develop as they progress through their courses. During a communication placement assessment designed to elicit baseline performances in listening, reading, writing, computer literacy, and quantitative literacy, participants listen to a videotaped presentation. The assessment facilitator encourages them to take a few minutes to prepare to listen by thinking about, then writing down, something that could affect their listening (for example, their physical or emotional state, possible environmental distractions, their attitude toward the topic), as well as something they could do to address that filter (for example, take deep breaths, put on – or take off – a sweater, resolve to listen with an open mind). Following the presentation, students prepare written responses to a few questions about their listening performance and complete a written self assessment which asks them to identify a listening strength and an area to work on.

Then, within the first several weeks of the semester, they meet one-on-one with an experienced assessor to compare their self assessment with that of the assessor. By the end of the appointment, they come away with the understanding that, as Alverno students, they not only listen to learn, but also learn to listen; with the help of their instructors, they will increase their listening competence and apply their skill in multiple learning contexts.

In the required communication seminars that follow, instructors introduce and students apply the ILM in various ways. One instructor purposely introduces the ILM inductively and subtly even before the students are aware of the course's emphasis on developing listening abilities. In the first class, each student interviews another, then introduces that classmate to the whole group. Afterwards, students self assess their listening during the interview and respond in writing to two questions: (1) What did you do that helped you to listen effectively? and (2) What would you do differently to help you listen more effectively if you were to do this activity again?

Compiling their input, the instructor categorizes the responses under two headings (Listening strategies and Listening filters), and returns the lists to the class in the next session (see Appendix12.1). During a brief discussion, the students begin to discover for themselves that listening is a process involving attitudes, knowledge, and behaviors.

Subsequently, each student then gets a chance to practice her listening by becoming the "primary listener" for one other student while that student is giving her first formal podium speech. The listener again self assesses her listening performance by answering questions related to preparing to listen, applying the listening process, and setting goals for working on her listening. In addition, the listener gets immediate feedback from the speaker regarding her accuracy with comprehending the speaker's message. The cycle is repeated two more times during the semester. What began as a subtle focus on listening gradually becomes an obvious and intense emphasis on developing one's own listening effectiveness by going through all the stages in the ILM.

The instructor notes that, because some student speakers are just learning to prepare and effectively deliver an oral presentation, some listeners may face a challenging listening task. But, the random pairing of speaker and listener mirrors real-life listening events. Not every listening event is well organized and occurs under ideal conditions, and yet there is usually the need (the expectation, even the demand) to listen effectively in spite of speaker, listener, or environmental contingencies. Since listening is not just an academic ability and since the ILM is a framework for lifelong listening, this type of listening practice is a productive and insightful experience for the students. They discover that listening doesn't just happen, nor is it a passive activity. Good listeners *plan* to listen, deal with filters, and methodically apply the listening process.

Continuing Development in Integrative Listening

As students become more familiar with the discrete elements of the ILM and more aware of its efficacy as a vehicle of learning, they have opportunities to reveal their listening skills within academic experiences that incorporate all aspects of the listening process. While these experiences appear in a variety of configurations, the format seen in Appendix 12.2 is typical.

Moving into more advanced – evaluative – listening events, specifically those based on disciplinary concepts, students expand their listening proficiency, especially in showing their growing ability to:

- identify their goal(s) in a listening situation;
- determine a speaker's perspective and recognize how that perspective informs the speaker's stance;
- assess the credibility and logic of a message;
- assess the credibility of a speaker's sources;
- assess their own attitudes and knowledge regarding a topic and their possible responses to a discipline-based message; and

- consider how they might continue to refine their listening performance in academic contexts.

In the 2005–2006 academic year, in response to a request from the listening task force, Alverno faculty and academic staff submitted numerous samples of listening activities, assignments and assessments being effectively implemented across the curriculum. Following are selected examples from Alverno colleagues in art, nursing, biology, and education.

In a studio art course, the instructor realized that the students were not putting much weight on recognizing verbal feedback as "real" feedback, so she designed a listening assessment to be used after a critique that asked students (1) what they heard about their work in terms of its strengths and weaknesses, (2) when during the critique they realized that their brains "clicked off", and (3) what they heard that kept their interest. If a student did not seem to be particularly engaged in the discussion, the instructor caringly asked a question like, "What's going on in your head now?" to get at listening filters, individual attention span, or receptivity or degree of open-mindedness to feedback. In addition to helping the students internalize the ILM and learn by listening, the answers to all of these questions identified teachable moments for the course instructor.

To emphasize the importance of comprehensive, interpersonal, and empathic/therapeutic listening when interacting with clients, an instructor in an intermediate nursing course, *Health Assessment: Individual, Family, and Community*, designed an assignment that gives the students practice with those types of listening while simultaneously applying the family nursing theories they are learning in class. The students are asked to interview a family in order to assess the family's structure, function, development, and system/interaction patterns. Both the form and the content of this assignment reflect in a very obvious way the four components of the ILM.

Each section of the assignment begins with a heading that restates exactly the ILM components (Prepare to listen, Apply the listening process, etc.). In the section *Prepare to listen*, the instructions direct the students to set a goal, to observe the context of the family's environment, and to be ready to address their listening filters. The instructor suggests that a primary filter might be their adjustment to their relatively new role of "nurse" as opposed to that of "student." In the section *Apply the listening process*, the instructor provides additional helpful information by recommending that the students "ask questions for clarification" to aid them in their comprehension of the oral input they are receiving and warns them about the need to carefully interpret that input because sometimes there is a "significant difference between what is said and what the student nurse actually sees." In the section *Assess listening performance*, the students are told to self assess their work using the criteria that are distributed at the same time as the assignment. Here again, they are given advice to help them become better listeners. They are informed that the students who have previously completed this assignment often comment on their nervousness or their lack of adequate questions or appropriate follow-up questions. In other words, the more students know about the experience they are about to undergo, the better they can prepare to listen to the family members. Finally, in the section, *Establish new goals*, the students reflect on their ability to accomplish their listening goal and ways to build on strengths and work on weaknesses. The students will have many more opportunities to interview clients, to work on the goals they set, and to keep practicing the ILM in their academic and professional work.

In an upper level biology course, *Examining Evolution: Biology and the History of an Idea*, students are challenged to comprehend a wide range of concepts relating to evolution. So interactive listening becomes a crucial element of this course. However, the instructor does not explicitly teach the model; he assumes that, at this level, students have internalized the ILM and are able to apply it with understanding. Indeed, there is a need for them to do so because of the additional social and political emphasis on controversial aspects of evolution: frequently, students are unable to discern the scientific concepts from broader issues.

Each week, students enter into small group discussions after reading a variety of articles, submitting written responses to what they have read, and receiving in-class clarification of any particularly difficult passages. They expect one another to further illuminate ideas that appear in the articles.

The course design reflects application of the ILM in several ways. The initial goal of their listening is clear. Students need to comprehend one another's understanding of the readings in order to prepare for additional discussions and assessments of their knowledge. Because of their careful preparation, they are able to proceed through the listening process together, *receiving, comprehending, interpreting, evaluating,* and *responding* directly to the information the others are sharing. As the course progresses and the discussions become more complex, students are accountable at increasingly more challenging levels of listening. They engage in more sophisticated comparison of the various authors' views, using discussion prompts that emphasize their need for careful listening. Such prompts ask them to: (1) comprehend the views represented by each of the participants; (2) analyze the similarities and differences among the multiple views; and (3) evaluate their author's stance in light of the new information.

Throughout the course, the instructor maintains a commitment to the ILM because of the controversial nature of some views expressed by students over the subject of evolution. Whatever their extra-scientific commitments to origin stories from other frameworks, the instructor hopes the students engage with one another and the material in ways that reflect the best of civil discourse and openness in liberal learning. By employing the ILM consistently, students become especially aware of how their listening context can be analyzed, how listening filters can influence their learning, and how they can effectively address listening filters that may impede understanding of course content. This awareness also allows them to establish *new listening goals* for subsequent discussions.

In a senior capstone course, *Philosophy of Education*, students explore universal questions in the field of education. The course is designed as a listening seminar in which it is just as important to listen carefully to one's own concerns and questions about the field of education and to pose those questions to the class for their consideration, as it is to explore possible answers through additional reading, lecture, and class discussion.

To prepare for this listening and learning experience, students must have completed all of their major education courses and several, if not all, of their teaching field experiences. In the first class of the semester, the instructor reviews the ILM framework and models the type of listening and discussion she wants students to emulate in future classes. Subsequently, a primary student facilitator is selected each week to listen to and record peer questions on the board and organize the discussion that follows. In the first half of the class, students are invited to enter into a thoughtful, silent reflection about the universal questions in education. Only those who raise their hands, posing questions to be recorded by the student facilitator, may speak. This process is purposely not rushed, and all students are urged to carefully consider each question, silently, as a means of going deeper into their own thinking and perhaps triggering their own related questions. It means that for some of the time, they are learning to listen to silence. They are learning to be fully focused on their own and their peers' thinking for an extended period of time.

Once the facilitator decides that there are enough questions on the board for that particular class session, she finds commonalties among the individual questions, groups them logically, and decides where to start the discussion. Every other week, the instructor assesses students' listening and learning by requiring each one to write a 2–3 page paper reflecting her mental journey on the path of discovering some of the answers to the universal questions that were posed. Students receive written feedback on their papers, and as a follow-up assignment, respond to others' papers in one-on-one discussions.

In exploring the bigger picture of education in this manner and identifying key issues, education students not only learn to think critically about their chosen profession, but they also learn to value listening deeply to self, comprehending and appreciating the complexities of the issues they will face in the field of education and valuing the element of reflective silence in the process. This listening is clearly sophisticated as it integrates all elements of the listening process with the universal concepts of education.

Eventually, as they equip themselves to apply their listening abilities to professional and other life-long situations, students are able appropriately to adapt their listening styles to both predictable and unpredictable goals and contexts. They have acquired sophisticated versatility and competence in the listening process. To provide evidence of their proficiency, they may be asked to present, in oral or written form, a report reflecting that proficiency in, for example, a career interview in which they have participated. Or they might complete a peer listening response to a classmate's sales presentation for a business setting or an education major's lesson plan. The possibilities for assessment at this advanced level are limited only by the student's or instructor's imagination.

Conclusion

Learning to listen effectively is a complex, challenging, and lifelong undertaking, a dynamic process that requires skillful integration of appropriate listening attitudes, knowledge, and behaviors. The Integrative Listening Model provides a unique and practical framework to address this process.

It is valuable to both teachers and students because it addresses the factors that influence human communication such as the contextual and personal filters we need to consider as we prepare to listen effectively. Simply put, it enables students to become keenly aware of why and how they listen, as well as the influences that affect their listening, and it provides them with the tools for improvement. More importantly, students who apply the model take an active role in their own listening development through self assessment and goal setting. They begin at stage one and progress systematically, as reflected in the Listening Criteria Matrix (see Figure 12.2), until they have achieved the ability to apply the model independently and creatively in all listening contexts. As the students at Alverno College respond to and work with this model, they learn that listening is indeed more than hearing and that effective listening requires commitment, understanding, and practice. They discover that applying the Integrative Listening Model is a wise investment, offering immediate payback in terms of increased understanding of others and the world around them. Additionally, application of the model provides insights into and tools for the ongoing development of their own listening abilities. Like any good investment, effective listening provides the students with valuable long-term benefits: competence; confidence; and productivity in their academic, personal, and professional lives.

QUESTIONS FOR DISCUSSION

1 Explain why effective listening involves attitudes, behaviors and knowledge.

2 Compare/contrast the Integrative Listening Model (ILM) with other listening models you've learned. What distinctive features does the ILM have?

3 Describe a listening situation you were in. Using the ILM, analyze what you did to listen effectively and what you could have done to be a better listener. Set a goal you can work on the next time you are in a similar listening situation.

4 Describe another listening situation you were in. What kinds of internal and external listening filters affected *your* listening process in that situation? Why are some of these filters more difficult to address than other?

5 When people think of listening filters, they usually think of factors that interfere with their listening. What are some filters that had a beneficial or positive effect on your listening? Explain why these filters were effective.

6 Identify a pattern you recognize in your listening (for example, "bottom line" listening, attentive observation of the speaker's body language, a tendency to "drift," careful note-taking). Discuss at least two non-academic situations in which you are aware of these patterns in practice. Explain how effectively they do or do not work for you.

7   What are some unique ways that you, as a student in your discipline/major, listen to learn?
8   Many of our jobs require us to multi-task. How well do you do this and how does multi-tasking affect your listening?
9   What are the listening demands that you will encounter in your professional life? How can you use the ILM to meet those demands?
10   Most people will say that they are good listeners. In your opinion, are some people naturally born good listeners?
11   How can the ILM help you to become an effective life-long listener?
12   How would you adapt the ILM for someone who has a visual or aural disability?

Appendix 12.1: Working Toward an Integrative Listening Model

Listening strategies

Based on the interview activity during Class 1, these are strategies that you already know and use:

1   Be genuinely interested in what the speaker has to say, OR create an interest.
2   Maintain focus and concentration on the speaker.
3   Ask the speaker questions (if the situation permits); ask questions that you are interested in knowing the answers to.
4   Ask questions in some kind of order; ask appropriate follow up questions.
5   Keep the task in mind; relate what you have heard to what the task required.
6   Maintain eye contact with the speaker.
7   Watch the speaker's body language and facial expressions.
8   Become fascinated with the speaker's voice.
9   Paraphrase or repeat back to the speaker what she said to verify the correctness of the information being received.
10   Take some notes to assist with concentration and memory, OR postpone taking notes in order to give full concentration to the speaker.

Listening filters

Internal and external factors that affect the listening process and that the listener can address:

1   "Didn't know the person I was interviewing so I felt uncomfortable asking her questions."
2   "Bothered by the noise in the room from the other students doing their interviews."
3   "Fumbled around trying to come up with the 'right' words when taking notes."
4   "Asked too many questions; didn't pre-plan my questions."

5 "Started planning my own presentation before I finished the interview."
6 "Worried about own presentation while listening to the other students give theirs and began to think that I had too much information compared to theirs."
7 "Needed more time; felt rushed."
8 "Didn't follow the plan suggested by the instructor."
9 "Noticed that my student stopped talking when I started jotting down notes."

Appendix 12.2: Integrative Listening

Theory of Multiple Intelligences – videotaped interview with Howard Gardner

Respond to the following to show your understanding of listening as "a dynamic, mindful process."

Preparing to listen

- Identify at least one physical/mental/emotional filter that might have influenced your listening effectiveness in this listening experience.
- Explain how you addressed the filter(s) in order to enhance your listening effectiveness.

Applying the listening process
Receiving

- Express the speaker's main point in the form of a thesis statement.
- Identify at least two nonverbal aspects involved in the interview and explain how they affected your reception of the message.
- Explain how at least one element of technology in the recorded presentation affected your reception of the message.

Comprehending

- Explain how new information in this presentation has stimulated/challenged/reinforced your prior knowledge of the topic. Be specific about your prior knowledge and connect it with specific references to information from the presentation.

Note: If the information was entirely new to you, explain in a comprehensive paragraph or two what you believe to be your dominant intelligence and, based on the information presented, explain why you think so. Describe at least one learning experience you've had in the past to validate your response.

Interpreting

- Describe what you did to suspend any biases you might have regarding the presenter or the message itself.
- Explain what you recognize about your own listening style. How well did that listening style work for you in this experience?

Responding

- Briefly describe what information from the presentation you accept and what you reject. In each case, explain why.
- What strategies did you use to remember the major elements of the message?

Self assessing

- Based on your responses above, assess your overall effectiveness as a listener for this experience. Focus on a couple of things you know you did well.
- Identify a challenge you faced in this listening process. Be specific.

Establishing new goals

- Describe at least one area you will focus on – and what you will do in that area – to continue to develop your listening effectiveness.

References

Barker, L., Edwards, R., Gaines, C., Gladney, K., and Holley, F. (1980). An investigation of proportional time spent in various communication activities by college students. *Journal of Applied Communication Research, 8*, 101–9.

Bentley, S. (1999, November). *Listening in the 21st Century.* Paper presented at the National Communication Association Convention, Chicago, IL.

Bentley, S. (2000). Listening in the 21st Century. *Journal of the International Listening Association, 14*, 130.

Cronon, W. (1998–9 Winter). 'Only Connect': The Goals of a Liberal Education. *Phi Beta Kappa, The Key Reporter, 64*, 2, 2–4.

Davis, D. (2001, Summer). Two ears and one mouth: Two eyes and one hand. *ILA Listening Post, 77*, 10–13.

Emmert, P. (1994). A definition of listening. *Listening Post, 51*, 6.

Glenn, E. (1989). A content analysis of fifty definitions of listening. *International Journal of Listening, 3*, 21–31.

Janusik, L.A., and Wolvin, A.D. (1999). *Listening treatment in the basic communication course text.* Paper presented at the meeting of the International Listening Association, Albuquerque, NM.

Index